LD SERIES

RED SOX

Y PARK

s. NATIONAL LEAGUE

NE

NDITIONS

K HEREOF.

ERVISION OF

sioner of Baseball

GAME 7

RAIN CHECK

BOSTON RED SOX

SEC. BOX

SEAT

BOX SEAT $12.00

19 128 K 4

SEC. BOX

SEAT

BOSTON RED SOX
FENWAY PARK
1946 WORLD SERIES
AMERICAN LEAGUE VS. NATIONAL LEAGUE

BOX SEAT

$7.20

Est. Price $6.00 - Tax $1.20 - TOTAL

★ ★

GAME 3

Right hereby reserved to refund said price and revoke license granted by this ticket.

Thomas A. Yawkey
PRES.

REMEMBERING FENWAY PARK

AN ORAL AND NARRATIVE HISTORY OF THE
HOME OF THE BOSTON RED SOX

HARVEY FROMMER

STEWART, TABORI & CHANG | NEW YORK

DESIGNED BY THINK STUDIO, NYC

Published in 2011 by Stewart, Tabori & Chang
An imprint of ABRAMS

Cataloging-in-Publication Data has been applied for and may be obtained from the Library of Congress.
ISBN 978-1-58479-852-1

Editor: Jennifer Levesque
Designer: Think Studio, NYC
Production Manager: Tina Cameron

The text of this book was composed in Helvetica Neue, Serifa, Clarendon, Franklin Gothic, and
Hoefler Text.

Printed and bound in China
10 9 8 7 6 5 4 3 2 1

Stewart, Tabori & Chang books are available at special discounts when purchased in quantity for pre-
miums and promotions as well as fundraising or educational use. Special editions can also be created
to specification. For details, contact specialsales@abramsbooks.com or the address below.

115 West 18th Street
New York, NY 10011
www.abramsbooks.com

CONTENTS

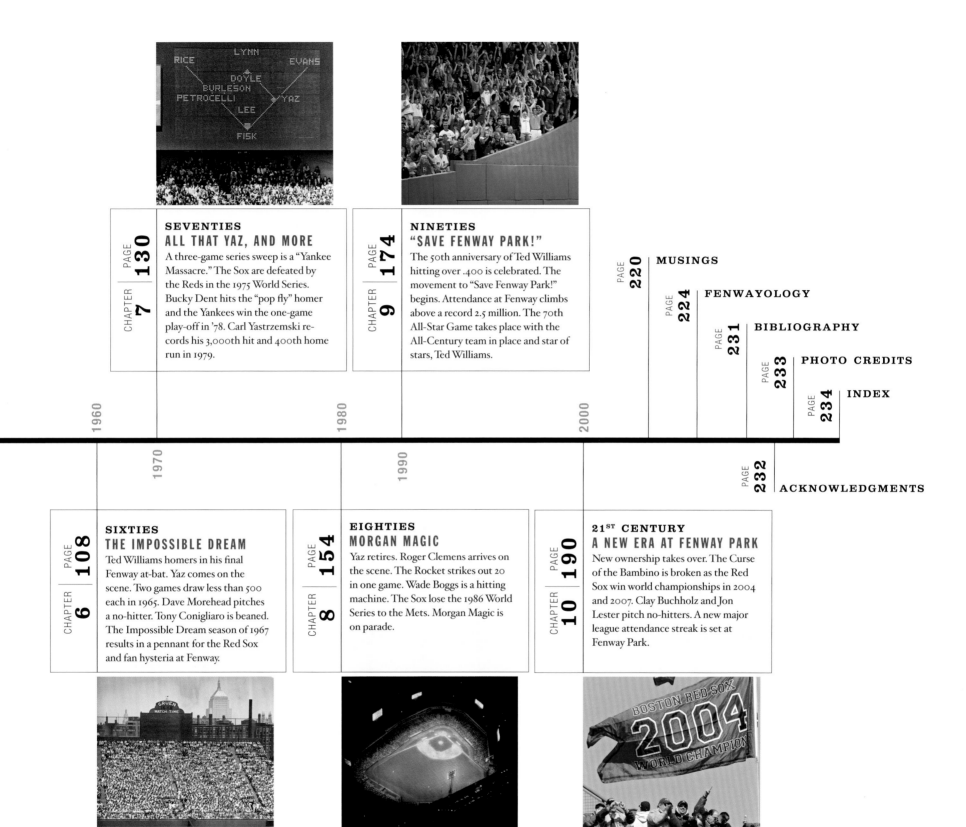

1960 1970 1980 1990 2000

They call me "Mr. Red Sox." And that is a special honor considering all the great stars and personalities who have been with the franchise through all the years.

It's been a wonderful ride for the kid out of Portland, Oregon, who signed for a $500 bonus. I first showed up at Fenway Park in 1942 and never believed that when 2011 rolled around, I would still be on the scene, still be coming to the ballpark, still be putting on the Red Sox uniform, still having my own locker in the clubhouse.

The organization has honored me by naming the right-field foul pole after me, putting me in the Red Sox Hall of Fame, retiring my number.

As author Harvey Frommer, in this book, brings the great story of Fenway Park to all of us in tremendous detail, I think back to all the greats I have known, those I played with or saw play at Fenway Park, a kind of Who's Who in Sox history—Mr. Tom Yawkey, Joe Cronin, Ted Williams, Dom DiMaggio, Bobby Doerr, Tex Hughson, Mel Parnell, Boo Ferriss, Dick Radatz, Reggie Smith, Carlton Fisk, Fred Lynn, Tony Conigliaro, Jimmy Rice, Jim Lonborg, Carl Yastrzemski, Luis Tiant, Dwight Evans, Dennis Eckersley, Roger Clemens, Wade Boggs, Mo Vaughn, Nomar Garciaparra, Dustin Pedroia, Curt Schilling, Jacoby Ellsbury . . .

I think back to so many moments at Fenway, good and bad—our winning the 1946 pennant, Ted Williams hitting a home run in his final at-bat, the Impossible Dream season, the Carlton Fisk home run, that 1975 team that battled the Reds in the World Series, the Bucky Dent homer, the heartbreak loss of the 1986 World Series to the Mets, the great changes in the old ballpark and the exciting work done by the new ownership, the thrill of breaking the "Curse of the Bambino" and winning world championships in 2004 and 2007.

I have played for, coached, managed the Sox. I have been in the front office, a television and radio announcer, even an ad salesman. I have probably seen more Red Sox games, hit more fungoes, put in more time at Fenway Park than anyone else in Red Sox history.

As I said, it has been some ride. Seven decades' worth and counting, and I have enjoyed every moment of it. Many of these moments are captured in this book through Harvey Frommer's riveting narrative, through great photos, and most importantly through the words of those who lived it.

Fenway has an aura in Boston like the ruins in Rome. The place has a mystery. It has ghosts. It has an interesting set of shadows. The tragedy of the Red Sox constantly failing in the fall gave it a sensibility that attracted an underworld, underground people.

There's something about the relationship between a game that attracts the joy of summer and a team that always seemed to be correlated with the tragic dimension of fall. The Red Sox were not the summer team, the boys of summer. They were the fallen boys, the lost boys of autumn. And that had its own attraction.

Victory produces forgetfulness. But loss on the brink of victory produces memory. And it sustains because along with the players who participated in almost getting there, you had a sense of almost getting there. You tended to identify with those underdogs because it simultaneously brings you to the edge of something you thought you had.

The fact that right field in Fenway enables so many otherwise limited talents to succeed is balanced by that center field and that huge fence in left field. A number of hits that would otherwise be home runs become singles in Fenway Park.

There's something about that park that affects the whole sensibility of the batter, and yet it produced the greatest hitter of all time. They called him the Kid but they also called him the Splendid Splinter because of the way he would demonstrate his ability. He wouldn't compromise, and yet he was a flashy player. He was a player who even though he seemed so ungenerous in his relations with the fans, gave all through the generosity of his playing. Ted Williams was in a sense an embodiment of Fenway Park because of his mood swings.

There are a number of academics outside Boston who have loved the Red Sox because the team appealed to their melancholia. Fenway as a space appeals to their melancholia, too. It elicits thinking and poetry.

THE

VOICES

GRAY & DAVIS
Train Load Shippers
SOLD EVERYWHERE
Ky. Taylor Whiskey.
R. H. HIRSHFIELD Co. N.E. AGTS.
ALL HILTON'S
Spring & Summer Suits
ARE NOW SELLING
AT HALF PRICE
THE HILTON CO.
WASHINGTON ST & TEMPLE PLACE
LOWNEY'S
P C INNINGS 12345
17 9 BOSTON 3
15 8 NEW YORK 0
THOMAS W LAWSON
OFFERS $250 TO ANY BATTER WHO HITS THIS SIGN
$1000 TO THE FIRST WHO SMASHES
THE SYSTEM
DELANO
HAT

BOB ALLGAIER is a retired CIA administrative officer. He was a vendor at Fenway Park in the late 1940s and 1950.

SPARKY ANDERSON, Baseball Hall of Famer, is the only manager to lead a team from each league (the Cincinnati Reds and the Detroit Tigers) to a world championship. He played for the Philadelphia Phillies in 1959.

MIKE ANDREWS played for the Red Sox from 1966 to 1970. He was chairman of the Jimmy Fund.

MATT BATTS was mainly a backup catcher for the Red Sox from 1947 through 1951.

HARRY BAULD is an English teacher and writer who taught at the Putney School in Vermont and Horace Mann in New York.

CARL BEANE is the public address announcer and the "Voice of the Red Sox."

RON BLOMBERG was the former Yankee who appeared at Fenway as the first designated hitter in American League history, on April 6, 1973.

DENNIS RAY "OIL CAN" BOYD pitched for the Red Sox from 1982 to 1989. His best years for Boston were 1985–1986.

BOB BRADY, a longtime Red Sox rooter, is a member of the executive committee of the Boston Braves Historical Association and editor of its newsletter.

DICK BRESCIANI is Red Sox vice president/historian. He joined the organization in 1972 as assistant public relations director, founded the Red Sox Hall of Fame in 1995, and was inducted into their Hall in 2006.

TOM BRUNANSKY is a former Red Sox outfielder known best for "the catch" in 1990.

GENE BRUNDAGE has been a Fenway Park usher since 1994 and is an ardent Sox fan.

ALAN CAMASSAR is an auto group director in southeastern Connecticut and a longtime Red Sox fan.

LARRY CANCRO has been senior vice president of Fenway Affairs since 2003. He created "Wally the Green Monster" and is responsible for the "Friendly Fenway" program, which has brought concerts to the ballpark and introduced the playing of "Sweet Caroline" and "Dirty Water" during games.

BERNIE CARBO was a journeyman major league outfielder who is immortalized in Red Sox history for his pinch-hit three-run homer in game six of the 1975 World Series.

TOM CARON has been a member of NESN's Red Sox broadcast team since 2002, first as a sideline reporter and since 2004 as the network's baseball studio host. He grew up cheering for the team in Lewiston, Maine.

ED CARPENTER is a lifelong Red Sox fan. He has been a Fenway Park tour guide since 2006.

JERRY CASALE pitched the majority of his major league games in a Boston Red Sox uniform (1958–1960).

JOE CASTIGLIONE has been a radio broadcaster for the Red Sox since 1983, the second-longest tenure of any Boston broadcaster. He is the author of *Broadcast Rites and Sites: I Saw It on the Radio with the Boston Red Sox.*

TINA CERVASIO was a NESN Red Sox field reporter, 2006–2008. She is currently the courtside reporter for the New York Knicks and host on MSG Network in New York.

TONY CLONINGER is a former pitching coach for the Red Sox and Yankees.

RUSS COHEN is part owner and director of communications for www.sportsology.net, a rabid fan of the New York Mets, and a sometime Red Sox rooter.

GENE CONLEY pitched for the Red Sox from 1961 to 1963 as part of an 11-year big-league career.

JOE COSGRIFF is assistant to the assistant vice president/winemaker of the BLOHARDS and a rabid rooter for the Red Sox.

THOMAS J. DALY worked at Fenway Park from 1941 to 1945 as a stile and office boy. Ordained to the priesthood in 1952 and rising to be a monsignor, he has remained a loyal Red Sox fan through the years.

ANNE D'ARCY, associate director of the Office of Worship and Spiritual Life for the Archdiocese of Boston, is a longtime Red Sox fan.

JOHN D'ARCY, Bishop of Fort Wayne–South Bend, Indiana, is a lifelong and ardent Red Sox fan.

ART DAVIDSON is sports editor of the *Metro West Daily News* and former chairman of the Boston chapter of the Baseball Writers Association of America.

IKE DELOCK, as both a reliever and a starter, pitched for the Red Sox from 1952 to 1963.

DOM DIMAGGIO was a seven-time All-Star and classic Red Sox leadoff hitter and center fielder for his entire 11-year career. He was nicknamed the "Little Professor" because he wore glasses.

BOBBY DOERR, a former Red Sox star second baseman, was elected to the National Baseball Hall of Fame in 1986 and is the oldest living player enshrined. He also is a member of the Red Sox Hall of Fame.

TOM DONAHUE is the manager of Don Shula's Steakhouse at the Hilton Hotel in Naples, Florida. A native New Englander, he has remained a genuine Red Sox fan.

MICHAEL DUKAKIS is a former governor of Massachusetts and was the Democratic presidential nominee in 1988. He is a professor of political science at Northeastern University, a visiting professor of public policy at UCLA, and a lifelong Red Sox fan.

DENNIS ECKERSLEY pitched for the Red Sox from 1978 to 1984 and in 2004 became a member of the National Baseball Hall of Fame and the Red Sox Hall of Fame. Currently he is a baseball studio analyst for TBS and NESN.

CHRISTIAN ELIAS is the operator of the historic manually operated scoreboard at Fenway Park and also serves as the director of premium seat sales for Live Nation Boston.

DWIGHT EVANS was an 8-time Gold Glove outfielder who played 19 of his 20 major league seasons with the Boston Red Sox. He is a member of the Red Sox Hall of Fame.

DAVE MEADOWS "BOO" FERRISS pitched for the Red Sox from 1945 to 1950. A member of the Red Sox Hall of Fame and the Mississippi Hall of Fame, he served five years as a pitching coach for Boston in the 1950s and 26 years as a baseball coach at Mississippi State University.

DICK FLAVIN is a longtime Red Sox fan and an acclaimed satirist. The winner of seven Emmy Awards for television writing and commentary, he has performed his "Teddy at the Bat" tribute across the USA.

STEVE FOLVEN is a diehard Red Sox fan and Babe Ruth impersonator.

WHITEY FORD, a Hall of Famer, Yankee pitcher for 16 seasons, coach, and broadcaster, enjoyed pitching in Fenway Park.

TERRY FRANCONA has been Red Sox manager since 2004, when he led the team to its first World Series title since 1918.

FREDERIC J. FROMMER is a Washington-based reporter for the Associated Press and the author of four books on baseball.

A. ARTHUR GIDDON was a batboy for the Boston Braves from 1922 to 1923. A longtime Red Sox fan and a retired lawyer, he celebrated his 100th birthday at Fenway Park on April 25, 2009.

DON GILE was a utility man for the Boston Red Sox from 1959 to 1962. Gile hit a home run in his final major league at-bat.

LOU GORMAN is a lifelong Red Sox fan who was the general manager of the club from 1984 to 1993 and is now the team's executive consultant for public affairs. He is a member of the Red Sox Hall of Fame.

PUMPSIE GREEN, the first African-American player on the Red Sox, was on the team from 1959 to 1962.

SCOTT GREENBERG is associate academic vice president at Framingham State College.

JAMES "JIMMIE" GREENE is an actor who lives in Los Angeles. In his growing-up years he lived in New England and rooted for the Red Sox.

TERRY GUINEY is managing partner of the Hotel Commonwealth in Boston. A longtime Bostonian, he is an avid Red Sox fan and Dartmouth alum.

JOHN HARRELSON was a graduate student in the Master of Arts in Liberal Studies program at Dartmouth College. He is a native of Longmeadow, Massachusetts, and a Red Sox zealot.

BUTCH HOBSON was primarily a third baseman for the Red Sox from 1975 to 1980. He managed the team from 1992 to 1994.

JOHN HOLWAY is the author of six books on the Negro Leagues. His *Red Tails Black Wings,* about the Tuskegee airmen, will be made into a motion picture by George Lucas.

PEARL HOUGHTELING is a vendor at Fenway Park and a premed student from Harvard. She has been a fervent Red Sox fan since she was five years old.

RALPH HOUK was a former Yankee catcher and manager. He piloted the Red Sox 1981 to 1984, when he oversaw the development of a talented core of young players led by Roger Clemens.

BRUCE HURST was a standout southpaw for the Red Sox from 1980 to 1988. He is a member of their Hall of Fame.

DAVE HUTCHINSON is a longtime radio show host and broadcaster.

JEFF IDELSON, president of the National Baseball Hall of Fame and Museum, began his career as an intern in the Red Sox public relations department in 1986.

ROGER KAHN is a veteran and astute observer of the sporting scene. He has written many books on baseball, including the classic *The Boys of Summer.*

EDDIE KASKO is a 10-year major league veteran who managed the Red Sox in the early seventies.

BOB KEANEY is the historian for the North Shore Spirit team of Lynn, Massachusetts, and a genuine Red Sox fan.

GEORGE KELL, a member of the National Baseball Hall of Fame, was a star major league third baseman for 15 years and a member of the Red Sox from 1952 to 1954.

JOHN KENNEDY played for the Red Sox from 1970 to 1974. He shared a May 29 birthday with President John F. Kennedy.

JONAH KERI is a writer for ESPN.com, the *New York Times,* and other publications, covering both baseball and college basketball.

DON KOSAKOWSKI is a retired high school teacher and coach. He is also a Red Sox zealot.

BILL LEE was one of the most electric Red Sox hurlers from 1969 to 1978. The author of *The Wrong Stuff* and *Have Glove, Will Travel,* he is a member of the Red Sox Hall of Fame.

DON LENHARDT was a utility man who had two stints with the Red Sox in the 1950s.

JIM LONBORG won the Cy Young award as the ace of the Red Sox staff during their 1967 "Impossible Dream" season. He is a member of the Red Sox Hall of Fame.

CARL LOVEJOY is director of development at Kimball Union Academy and a genuine Red Sox fan.

MIKE LOWELL led Boston in RBIs in 2007, powering the team to its second world championship in four years. He was the World Series MVP.

FRED LYNN starred for the Red Sox for seven seasons in the 1970s. In 1975 he became the first player to win the Rookie of the Year award and league MVP in the same season. He is a member of the Red Sox Hall of Fame.

FRANK MALZONE was one of the top third basemen in Red Sox history, a three time Gold Glove winner. He played from 1955 to 1965 and was an eight-time All-Star. He is a member of the Red Sox Hall of Fame.

RICH MARAZZI is a rules consultant for the Yankees, Red Sox, Indians, and Astros, and the author of several baseball books.

ED MARKEY is a longtime Democratic congressman from suburban Boston. He has followed the Red Sox for a long time.

JARED MAX is the sports director of WCBS Radio in New York City and a devoted observer of the baseball scene.

DANIEL MCGINLEY-SMITH is a longtime Red Sox fan and a dermatologist in Vermont.

WALTER MEARS is a Pulitzer Prize–winning journalist who was a reporter, Washington bureau chief, columnist, and vice president for the Associated Press for nearly 46 years. He is a devoted fan of the Red Sox.

LENNY MEGLIOLA is a veteran *MetroWest Daily News* reporter, sports editor, and senior sports writer who has covered the Celtics and Red Sox.

SAM MELE is a former major league player and manager who had two stints as a Boston Red Sox outfielder, in the late 1940s and mid-1950s.

DAVID R. MELLOR, director of grounds for the Boston Red Sox, has many years of caring for baseball fields. He is a sports turf consultant.

LOU MERLONI, "Framingham Lou," is a former Red Sox infielder and fan favorite, a hometown hero. He is a NESN analyst.

LOU MERLONI SR. is the father of Lou Merloni and a devoted Red Sox fan.

JON MILLER is an acclaimed baseball announcer. He was with the Red Sox in the early 1980s and currently does radio/TV for the San Francisco Giants as well as ESPN Sunday Night Baseball.

RICK MILLER played for the Red Sox from 1971 to 1977. A superb defensive outfielder, he was named "Unsung Hero of 1972" by the Boston Baseball Writers Association.

GEORGE MITROVICH is president of the City Club of San Diego, the Denver Forum, and chair of the Great Fenway Park Writers Series.

BILL MONBOUQUETTE is a member of the Red Sox Hall of Fame. He was a star hurler for Boston from 1958 to 1965.

LEIGH MONTVILLE was a columnist for the *Boston Globe*. He is the author of *Ted Williams* and *The Big Bam*.

JOE MOONEY began as the Red Sox head groundskeeper at Fenway Park in 1971. He is director of grounds, emeritus.

DAVE MOREHEAD, a Red Sox pitcher from 1963 to 1968, tossed a no-hitter for the team in 1965.

JOE MORGAN was born just 17 miles from Fenway Park. The Red Sox manager from 1988 to 1991, he presided over "Morgan Magic" and is a member of the Red Sox Hall of Fame.

JOHN MORTON grew up in a small town in southwestern New Hampshire where he watched the Red Sox in black and white on TV. He participated in Nordic skiing in two Winter Olympic Games.

MIKE NARRACCI is the senior coordinating director for Red Sox games on NESN.

TRACY NIEPORENT is director of marketing/partner of the Myriad Restaurant Group, a diehard fan of the New York Mets, and an avid follower of the sports scene.

BILL NOWLIN is one of the founders of Rounder Records. Author and editor of more than 20 books on the Red Sox, including *Red Sox Threads,* he has been to about 1,000 games at Fenway Park.

MEL PARNELL was a star hurler for the Red Sox in the 1940s and 1950s, and later a broadcaster for the team. He is in the Red Sox Hall of Fame.

CHARLIE PATTERSON has been a Red Sox fan since the 1946 World Series. He had been a college fundraising administrator and associate athletic director at Wake Forest University.

DONALD E. PEASE is professor of English, Avalon Foundation chair of the humanities, and director of the Master of Arts in Liberal Studies Program at Dartmouth College.

JOHNNY PESKY is Mr. Red Sox. A member of the Red Sox Hall of Fame whose number has been retired by the team, he has been a player, manager, coach, and goodwill ambassador for the Red Sox since the 1940s.

JIMMY PIERSALL is one of the greatest center fielders in Fenway Park history, a two-time Gold Glove winner and two-time All-Star.

BUCKY PIZZARELLI, the most-recorded jazz guitarist of all time, has collaborated with a long list of jazz greats and has performed at Fenway Park.

JOHN PIZZARELLI is the son of Bucky and a well-known singer/guitarist and longtime Red Sox rooter. He is familiar to Boston fans as the voice of the Foxwoods commercial "The Wonder of It All."

ERIC PORTNOY is a designer based in Boston and a longtime Red Sox fan.

JOHN QUINN is the lieutenant governor of Red Sox Nation–New York. He has been featured in four films about the team, including the 2004 MLB World Series film, and is the Tuesday night trivia host at Professor Thom's, the leading Red Sox bar in New York City.

JOANNA RAPF is a professor in the film studies department at Dartmouth College and Professor of English and film and video studies at the University of Oklahoma.

JEAN RHODES is a psychology professor at the University of Massachusetts, and the author of *Becoming Manny*.

BROOKS ROBINSON is a baseball Hall of Famer and former star third baseman for the Baltimore Orioles. He has fond memories of playing at Fenway Park.

HERB ROGOFF is an illustrator and editor and publisher of the monthly baseball magazine *One More Inning*.

STEVE RYDER is a retired educator and businessman and a lifelong Red Sox zealot. He was witness to the mythic and last Ted Williams home run and the agony of the Bucky Dent home run.

BOB SANNICANDRO is a high school baseball coach and a former Red Sox clubhouse attendant.

MIKE SCHAFER is head of school at Kimball Union Academy in New Hampshire. He is an involved Red Sox rooter.

MELISSA "MEL" SCHMITTROTH is a theatrical audio engineer. She is an ardent baseball fan.

DON SCHWALL was the 1961 Rookie of the Year. He pitched for the Red Sox from 1961 to 1962 and appeared in the 1961 All-Star Game at Fenway Park.

JAMES SHANNAHAN worked for the Red Sox from 1990 to 2002 in the Facilities, Marketing, and Broadcasting departments.

JOHN SHANNAHAN is the brother of James and is captain of the Mudville Base Ball Club, a vintage baseball team based in Holliston, Massachusetts. He has been a devout Red Sox fan since 1964.

DAN SHAUGHNESSY has been a sportswriter for the *Boston Globe* for more than two decades. Author of or contributor to such books as *Curse of the Bambino*, and *At Fenway: Dispatches from Red Sox Nation,* he has covered the Red Sox for more than 30 years.

HOWIE SINGER is a television director for Madison Square Garden Network on their New York Knicks telecasts. He has been a Red Sox fan since the "Impossible Dream" season of 1967.

SAM SKOLER lived in Quincy, Massachusetts, and was a businessman in the New England area. One of his great passions was going to games at Fenway Park.

JANET MARIE SMITH was senior vice president/planning and development for the Red Sox. She directed the renovation and area planning for Fenway Park.

TED SPENCER is the former chief curator of the National Baseball Hall of Fame and Museum and a lifelong Red Sox fan.

DAVE STANLEY, a supervisor at Trumbull-Nelson in Hanover, New Hampshire, is a dedicated Red Sox fan who saw his first game at Fenway Park in the ALCS 2008.

JOHN "NICK" STEENSTRA is a technical analyst in the Judiciary Administrative Office of the Courts in New Jersey. He has been a fan of the Red Sox since 1967.

BOB SULLIVAN is a lifelong Red Sox fan and a graduate of Dartmouth College. He is the editorial director of *Life* Books and the author of *Our Red Sox: A Story of Family, Friends, and Fenway,* among other books.

FRANK SULLIVAN was a top starting pitcher for Boston in the fifties, winning 13 or more games for 5 straight years. He is in the Red Sox Hall of Fame.

BILL SUMMERS JR. is a former National Football League referee. His father was a longtime American League umpire who worked a great many games at Fenway Park.

ERICA TARLIN is a librarian, a loyal Red Sox fan, and a member of the board of directors of Save Fenway Park!

LUIS TIANT is a member of the Red Sox Hall of Fame. He threw four straight shutouts in 1966 and excelled as the Red Sox ace in the seventies, becoming a fan favorite known as "El Tiante."

GARY TITUS is webmaster for shermfeller.com and a rabid Red Sox fan.

JERRY TRUPIANO is a radio sportscaster and a former play-by-play voice of the Boston Red Sox from 1993 to 2006.

BRUCE TUCKER, born and raised in Lynn, Massachusetts, is a businessman in Wakefield, New Hampshire, and a Red Sox zealot.

CHARLIE WAGNER pitched for the Red Sox from 1938 to 1942 and in 1946. He went on to be a scout and minor league instructor for the organization.

BILL WERBER passed away at age 100 in 2008. He pitched for the Red Sox from 1933 to 1936 and was the author of *Memories of a Ballplayer: Bill Werber and Baseball in the 1930s.*

CHRIS WERTZ grew up within earshot of Fenway Park. Moving to New York, he opened Professor Thom's, the biggest Red Sox bar outside of Boston. He also is the first New York governor of Red Sox Nation.

DAN WILSON lives and practices law in Boston. He is a past president (2000–2006) of Save Fenway Park!

RICK WISE pitched for the Red Sox from 1974 to 1977, one of five major league teams he played for in an 18-year career.

EDDIE YOST never played for the Red Sox, despite Senator John Kerry's claim that Yost was his favorite Red Sox player. Yost was a coach for Boston from 1977 to 1984.

DON ZIMMER was the Red Sox manager from 1976 to 1980 and was a coach with the team from 1974 to 1976 and again in 1992. He has had a very long career working for several different teams in various capacities.

—TEENS—

A NEW BALLPARK FOR BOSTON

It was damp and chilly throughout New England for most of the spring of 1912, and in Boston, it took a few tries before baseball at a brand-new ballpark could be played in decent weather.

On April 9, the Red Sox and Harvard's baseball team met in an exhibition game in football weather, and as one who was there observed, "with a little snow on the side." About 3,000 braved the elements. Boston won the game, 2-0, with both runs driven in by their pitcher, Casey Hageman.

RED SOX YEAR BY YEAR 1912 – 1919

YEAR	WON	LOST	PCT.	GB	ATTENDANCE
1919	66	71	.482	20.5	417,291
1918	75	51	.595	—	249,513
1917*	90	62	.592	9.0	387,856
1916*	91	63	.591	—	496,397
1915*	101	50	.669	—	539,885
1914	91	62	.595	8.5	481,359
1913	79	71	.527	15.5	437,194
1912*	105	47	.691	—	597,096

*WORLD CHAMPIONS

The scheduled official Opening Day match on April 12, however, was rained out. Finally on April 20, the weather improved a bit, and Fenway's first major league game—the Sox versus the Yankees (then known as the Highlanders)—was set to be played before a crowd of 27,000 on soggy, lumpy grounds and infield grass transplanted from the Huntington Avenue Baseball Grounds, the team's former home.

Boston mayor John "Honey Fitz" Fitzgerald threw out the ceremonial first ball. The man, whose grandson would become the thirty-fifth president of the United States, was an ardent member of the "Royal Rooters"—a group of Red Sox fans who staged pregame parades accompanied by the singing of "Tessie" and "Sweet Adeline."

Ordinarily the game would have been the stuff of front-page headlines in New England dailies. Six days earlier, however, the largest passenger ship in the world had struck an iceberg and gone down in the icy waters of the Atlantic. The news of the sinking of the *Titanic* on its maiden voyage and the accompanying loss of 1,517 lives would eclipse all other stories.

Nevertheless, it was good news in Boston that the Red Sox finally had a modern ballpark. The original field that the team—then known as the Boston Somersets—played on was a former circus lot where sand covered much of the outfield and a tool shed sat in the middle of center field.

Owner General Charles Henry Taylor, a Civil War veteran and owner of the *Boston Globe,* had decided back in 1910 to build a new ballpark in the Fenway section bordering Brookline Avenue, Jersey Street, Van Ness Street, and Lansdowne Street. It would cost $650,000 (approximately $14 million today) and seat 35,000. Ground was broken September 25, 1911.

An attractive red brick facade, the first electric baseball scoreboard, and 18 turnstiles, the most in the majors, were all features being talked about. Concrete stands went from behind first base around to third while wooden bleachers were in parts of left, right, and center field. Seats lined the field, allowing for excellent views of the game but limiting the size of foul territory.

Elevation was 20 feet above sea level. Barriers and walls broke off at different angles. Center

ment making viewing of games easier for overflow gatherings. A 10-foot-high slope in left field posed challenges for an outfielder who had to run uphill for balls hit over his head.

This was the Opening Day lineup for the 1912 Boston Red Sox:

Harry Hooper	RF
Steve Yerkes	2B
Tris Speaker	CF
Jake Stahl	1B
Larry Gardner	3B
Duffy Lewis	LF
Heinie Wagner	SS
Les Nunamaker	C
Smokey Joe Wood	P

The Sox, with player-manager first baseman Jake Stahl calling the shots, nipped the Highlanders, 7–6, in eleven innings. Tris Speaker—who would bat .383, steal 52 bases, and 8 inside-the-park home runs that year at Fenway—drove in the winning run. Spitball pitcher Bucky O'Brien got the win in relief of Charles "Sea Lion" Hall. The first hit in the park belonged to New York's Harry Wolter.

Umpire Tommy Connolly kept the ball used in that historic game, writing "Opening of Fenway Park" and brief details of the game on it.

PAGE 22: The crowd gets into it at the start of the 1912 World Series
OPPOSITE: (starting top left) The great Tris Speaker follows through on his swing; Ernie Shore pitching; Tris Speaker getting ready to hit; Harry Hooper swinging bat
ABOVE: A very young Babe Ruth pitching

field was 488 feet from home plate; right field was 314 feet away. The 10-foot wooden fence in left field ran straight along Lansdowne Street and was but 320½ feet down the line from home plate, with a high wall behind it. There was a 10-foot embank-

Hugh Bradley hit the first home run in Red Sox history over the wall on April 26 in the sixth game played at Fenway Park. "Few of the fans who have been out to Fenway Park believed it was possible," the *Boston Herald* noted. That would be Bradley's only dinger in 1912.

As a youth Joe Cashman spent a lot of time at Fenway Park and went on to become a longtime sportswriter in Boston. He especially studied the "Golden Outfield" of Tris Speaker, Harry Hooper, and Duffy Lewis. Hooper wore the first sunglasses used in baseball; they were purchased from Lloyds of Boston.

"Outfielders never played near the wall in those days," Cashman explained. "Few balls were hit out there. There was no one Tris Speaker's equal going back for a ball. He was like a fifth infielder. A base runner on second base would check the shortstop and second baseman. Next thing he knew, Tris Speaker would sneak in from center field and pick him off.

S is for Speaker,
Swift center-field tender,
When the ball saw him coming,
It yelled, "I surrender."

Ogden Nash, *Sport Magazine,* January 1949

"Harry Hooper," Cashman continued," played in a tough right field, worst in the majors. Duffy Lewis in left never bounced the ball. It was in the air all the way in. The sun would come in over the top of the single-decked stands—Lewis had to play the sun field."

Boston's first star left fielder, George Edward "Duffy" Lewis, out of San Francisco, played for the Bosox from 1910 to 1917. Duffy mastered the art of handling the incline named for him—"Duffy's Cliff." "At the crack of the bat," he explained, "you'd turn and run up it. You had to pick up the ball [with your vision] and decide whether to jump, go right or left, or rush down again. It took plenty of practice. They made a mountain goat out of me."

Before an overflow crowd on May 17, 1912, the park was formally dedicated, but the hometown fans had their day spoiled as the White Sox trimmed the Red Sox, 5–2.

Hall of Fame-hurler-to-be Walter Johnson, on a 16-game winning streak and en route to a 33-win season, was in Boston with his Washington teammates on September 6, 1912. Clark Griffith, the Washington manager, said that Red Sox ace Smokey Joe Wood would be a coward if he did not face Johnson. No coward was Wood—he was ready on short rest. A 22-year-old from the Kansas plains and the mining towns of Colorado, Wood—it was said—could throw a baseball through a two-by-four.

When Walter Johnson was asked if he could throw harder than Smokey Joe, his reply was, "Can I throw harder than Joe Wood? Listen, my friends, there's no man alive can throw harder than Smokey Joe Wood."

The Wood-Johnson matchup was one of the most dramatic of all time by two top-of-the-tier hurlers. Built up like a championship boxing match in the newspapers, hype and hullabaloo preceded it.

"They gave our weight, biceps," Wood said. The idea was to build up the challenger versus the champion in order to build up the house.

BELOW: 1912 Opening Day, Red Sox vs. Yankees lined up
OPPOSITE: Construction of Fenway Park in 1911; fans all dressed up and going to a game

An estimated 30,000 showed for the battle of the superstar pitchers. It was the first and only time fans were allowed to ring Fenway's outfield walls.

"The playing field," wrote sportswriter Melville E. Webb Jr., "was surrounded by a triple, even quadruple, rank of humanity, at least 3,000 on the embankment. So thickly were the spectators massed, and so impossible was it for the squadron of police to keep them back, that the players' pits [dugouts] were abandoned, the contestants bringing their war clubs out almost to the baselines."

Possessor of a 13-game winning streak, Wood gave up six hits. Johnson allowed five. But the "Big Train," as he was called, yielded a sixth-inning, two-out ground-rule double to Tris Speaker. Duffy Lewis flared a ball to right that skipped off the glove of the Senators' right fielder. Speaker scored. Wood concluded the dramatic 1-hour, 46-minute contest with his ninth strikeout for his 14th straight win. The 1–0 triumph was 1 of 10 shutouts he hurled that season. Wood would win 34 games, strike out 258, post an earned-run average of 1.91, and be the horse of the Red Sox staff—the favorite of fans at Fenway.

Business in Boston virtually shut down on September 23 as 100,000 cheered the Red Sox returning from a western trip by train into South Station. So popular and so successful were the Sox that on the Boston Common, Mayor "Honey Fitz" Fitzgerald gave the team the keys to the city.

That 1912 team was loaded with talent, especially in pitching. In addition to Joe Wood, Buck O'Brien and Hugh Bedient were 20-game winners.

Boston posted its second-best home record in history, 57–20, a .740 winning percentage. Winning a record 105 games, losing just 47, the Red Sox glided to the American League pennant. Their competition in the World Series was the Giants of New York.

Additional wooden bleachers were in place in center and right-center. Seats on the slope cost $1, the same as for the left-field bleachers.

The Boston Royal Rooters, Red Sox fanatics to the core, traditionally paraded on the field before games in step with the rhythms of a big brass band. Now, on the eve of game one of the World Series, having traveled down to New York City, hundreds of them, accompanied by two brass bands and led by Mayor Fitzgerald and by "leading man" "Nuff Ced" McGreevey, marched around Times Square in Manhattan, singing to the tune of "Tammany":

Carrigan, Carrigan,
Speaker, Lewis, Wood, and Stahl,
Bradley, English, Pape, and Hall,
Wagner, Gardner, Hooper, too;
Hit them! Hit them! Hit them! Hit them!
Do boys, do.

The word in the street was that if John J. McGraw's Giants could beat Joe Wood, they could win the Series. Before the opening game, Wood received death threats in letters postmarked New York. One, written in red ink and adorned with a drawing of a knife and a gun, proclaimed, "You will never live to pitch a game against the Giants in the

World Series. We are waiting to get you as soon as you arrive in town."

But the 22-year-old right-hander who threw "smoke" was not the type to be intimidated. Pitching and prevailing, 4–3, in game one at the Polo Grounds, going the distance and striking out 11 Giants, Wood stood up to all challenges. After the game he said, "I threw so hard I thought my arm would fly right off my body."

The Royal Rooters followed the team to the Polo Grounds and back to Fenway Park as the Series alternated between the two venues, singing such songs as "Tessie" and "When I Get You Alone Tonight," angering Giant fans and charming Red Sox partisans.

But on October 15, as the Royal Rooters prepared to take their seats at Fenway for the seventh game of the World Series, they discovered that their usual accommodations had been sold out from under them, a consequence of some box office confusion. The Rooters made up their

mind that without them, there would be no game. Ignoring pleas that they leave the ballpark, their bands blaring "Tessie," they remained in place until their "stay-in" was resolved by ranks of mounted police who swept across the field, nudging them out of the park. One Royal Rooter, as disoriented as he was disenchanted, tumbled over the right-field fence on his way out and bellowed, "To hell with Queen Victoria!"

The Royal Rooters fumed and postured outside the park until they were presented with a compromise: They would be allowed to view the game from along the left-field foul line.

Winner of games one and four, Wood was on the mound for game seven. But it was not his day. Seven of the first nine Giants in the first inning reached base, and six of them scored. The Giants romped, 11–4, knotting the series at three games each, with one tie.

Game seven saw Tris Speaker pull off one of baseball's rarities—an unassisted double play by an outfielder. Known for playing an exceptionally shallow center field, Speaker snared a Fletcher line drive in the top of the ninth. Racing in, "Spoke" stepped on second base, doubling Wilson.

Game eight was for the world championship—October 16 at Fenway Park. The Red Sox won the coin flip and were awarded the home-field advantage. The riveting finale of the 1912 World Series would be played before a half-capacity crowd as a result of it being scheduled at the last minute as a makeup due to the game two tie, as well as the game-fixing rumors that swirled about and the Royal Rooters' rhubarb.

Ace Christy Mathewson of the Giants, winless in this Series, after going the distance in the tie game and dropping game five, matched up against Boston's 22-year-old Hugh Bedient. The game was 1–1 after nine tense innings. Mathewson was still out there. Wood took over in the eighth for Bedient.

In the top of the tenth, New York scored a run. Boston pinch hitter Clyde Engle started the home

10th by hitting a routine fly ball to center field.

"And now the ball settles," the *New York Times* reported. "It is full and fair in the pouch of the padded glove of [Fred] Snodgrass. But he is too eager to toss it to Murray and it dribbles to the ground."

Engle reached second base. Harry Hooper was robbed of a hit when Snodgrass made a nifty grab of his long drive. Engle moved to third base. Next up was Yerkes. He walked. Speaker singled. Engle scored. The game was tied. Duffy Lewis was walked intentionally, loading the bases. Third baseman Larry Gardner belted a deep fly ball to Josh Devore in right field. Yerkes tagged up and scored.

And the Red Sox had their second world championship. Fred Snodgrass's error would go down in history as "the $30,000 muff," the difference between the winning and losing shares for the two teams in the Series. And Fenway Park was off to a glorious start.

On opening day in 1913, the second season at Fenway, the Red Sox lineup looked like this:

Harry Hooper	RF
Steve Yerkes	2B
Tris Speaker	CF
Duffy Lewis	LF
Larry Gardner	3B
Hal Janvrin	1B
Heinie Wagner	SS
Hick Cady	C
Charley Hall	P

PAGE 28–29: The crowd waiting to get into Fenway
OPPOSITE: A classic 1917 shot: All-Star Team at Fenway

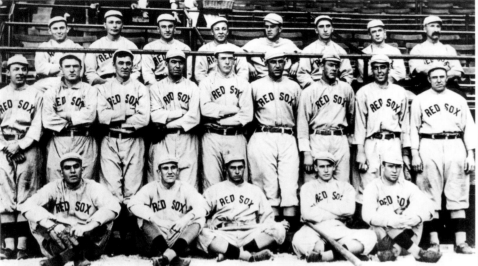

THE BOSTON RED SOX 1912

LEWIS, THOMAS, GARDNER, HENDRICKSON, BEDIENT, KRUG, WAGNER, KRIKE. TRAINER.
YERKES, CARRIGAN, O'BREIN, HALL, NUNAMAKER, STAHL, CADY, PAPE, ENGEL.
COLLINS, HOOPER, WOOD, SPEAKER.

QUIRK RED SOX   SPEAKER   WOOD   CADY   THOMAS   O'BRIEN   BRADLEY   LEWIS
HOOPER   CARRIGAN   YERKES   HENRIKSEN   ENGLE   NUNAMAKER   HALL   GARDNER   COLLINS   STAHL
MASCOT
WAGNER   BEDIENT   PAPE   KRUGG

▲ SEASON 1912 ▲
CHAMPIONS OF THE AMERICAN LEAGUE
▲ BOSTON RED SOX ▲

BOSTON RED SOX
1915
SPEAKER HOOPER CADY MAYS GREGG COLLINS HALEY COOPER LEONARD LEWIS
GARDNER JANVRIN FOSTER CORRIGAN HOBLITZEL GAINER BARRY
THOMAS McNALLY SCOTT HENRIKSEN WAGNER

The average age of the 1913 Red Sox was 24 years and 6 months. It seemed they had a good chance to repeat as world champions.

But that was not to be. Smokey Joe Wood, who lost the Opening Day game, was reduced to part-time employment by a broken hand and his rugged work schedule the previous season. The outfield continued to play well (Speaker hit .363), but without Wood as an anchor, the pitching staff was just average. The team hit only 17 home runs. Finishing the season at 79–71, the Sox sank to fourth place, 15½ games out.

On December 21, 1913, the Bosox were sold to an investment group headed by Joe Lannin, who had started his working career as a bellhop. By the start of the new season, Lannin would be sole owner of the Red Sox. Stalwart Jake Stahl had retired in the middle of the 1912 season and was replaced by catcher Bill Carrigan as player-manager. With a new owner and Carrigan managing from the start, things were looking up.

On April 14, 1914, 24,741 showed as Fenway hosted Walter Johnson and the Senators. The "Big Train" had a no-hitter through the sixth inning and wound up with a 3–0 shutout.

On July 9, Boston added two young pitchers capable of hurling shutouts. The heralded hurlers were Babe Ruth and Ernie Shore of the Baltimore Orioles of the International League. On July 11, the Bambino made his Red Sox debut against Cleveland and was tagged for 3 runs on 8 hits and did not get the decision, although Boston defeated Cleveland, 4–3. Ernie Shore was more impressive three days later, pitching a two-hitter in the second game of a doubleheader, winning, 2–1.

With these two powerful pitchers in the house, the Bosox future seemed bright. On August 19, 1914, the Sox swept a doubleheader from Chicago,

pushing their record to 61–47, the second best in the big leagues at that time.

A team picture taken that day showcased 25 Bosox in front of their dugout, the nucleus of a dynasty that would exist from 1915 to 1918. The photo included Tris Speaker, Harry Hooper, Ernie Shore, Smokey Joe Wood, player/manager Bill Carrigan, Dutch Leonard, Rube Foster, and Duffy Lewis. Babe Ruth was missing in action, having been sent down to the minors for more seasoning.

But before long, the Babe was back in action. The six-foot-two Baltimore-born burly, brassy pitcher who supposedly had hit a baseball 400 feet when he was only 13 years old (something no major leaguer of that time had accomplished), was pitching against the Yankees on October 2. Their five errors helped the young pitcher's cause. He wound up with his first major league hit, too, a double off King Cole, and a victory in the 11–5 game.

World Series games were played at Fenway in 1914, but it was the Boston Braves, not the Red Sox, who played there. The National Leaguers rented the park for the fall classic because their playing field was still under construction. In 1915 and 1916 the Sox would play in the World Series using the 42,000-seat Braves Field as their home field.

Sox prowess and popularity, especially with the "Big Bam" Babe Ruth on the scene, was on the rise in a big way. Fenway Park led the league in attendance in 1914 with 481,359, an average of 6,093 a game.

In 1915 the Sox posted their fourth-best home record ever: 55–20, for a .733 percentage. Their overall record was 101 wins and just 50 losses. Total attendance was 539,885, an average of 7,104 a game.

In 1915, after dropping game one, the Sox won the next four to defeat the Philadelphia Phillies in the World Series. The "Golden Outfielders"—Duffy Lewis, Tris Speaker, and Harry Hooper—supplied a lot of the muscle for the triumph.

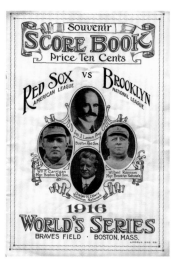

Oddities, marker moments, another world championship and ownership change were part of the scene at Fenway in 1916. Babe Ruth continued to amaze everyone with his all-around talent on the baseball field.

What was so rare at Fenway Park as a day in June was on parade June 20, 21, and 23, 1916. On the 20th, Tilly Walker walloped Boston's only homer at Fenway that season. Shortstop Everett Scott, who entered the game as a defensive replacement, played in the first of 1,307 straight games. Scott's streak ended in 1925, when he became a member of the Yankees.

On June 21, the Yankees were no-hit by George "Rube" Foster, 2–0, the first no-hitter pitched at Fenway. Sox owner Lannin lauded Foster's accomplishment and presented him with a $100 bonus, and the entire team with gold-handled pocket-knives engraved with the no-hitter date.

And on June 23, Ernie Shore added a jubilant coda to the loveliest of months, shutting out the Philadelphia A's, 1–0.

The magical moments at Fenway Park continued into August. On the 15th, Babe Ruth matched up again against Walter Johnson. A leaning-into-the-bleachers great catch by Washington center fielder Clyde Milan took away the big slugger's bid for a homer. Nevertheless, Boston eked out a 1–0 win in 13 innings.

On August 30, Dutch Leonard spun a no-hitter against St. Louis in a 4–0 win for Boston, even though the previous day, Leonard was hit very hard and unable to survive the first inning in the first game of a doubleheader.

Boston brought a stacked team (91–63, .591 in the regular season) into the World Series of

1916 against the Brooklyn Robins, where a young Casey Stengel was in top form offensively. Braves Field was once again the Series home field. It paid dividends especially in the final game, when the Sox drew a record 42,620.

That Series showcased the many Bosox weapons, especially Duffy Lewis, who batted .353, and Babe Ruth, who hurled 14 shutout innings in game two, part of a streak that would reach 29⅔ in the 1918 fall classic. Ruth's pitching as well as that of the other hurlers on the Sox did the Robins in, four games to one. Once again, the Boston Red Sox were world champions.

A sad footnote to that world championship was the disbanding of the Royal Rooters. Age and alcohol, it was claimed, had taken their toll. Other fans and fan clubs would grace Fenway Park, but none would ever match the verve of the Rooters and their leader, McGreevy, owner of a Boston saloon named 3rd Base.

Enter Harry H. Frazee.

A bill poster from Peoria, Illinois, a former bellhop like Lannin, a show business wheeler-dealer who owned a theater on 42nd Street in midtown Manhattan not far from the New York Yankees offices, Frazee was a gambler, always hustling, always scuffling for a buck, always over-extended in one theatrical deal or another.

On November 1, 1916, Frazee and two associates became the new owners of the Red Sox. Seller Joe Lannin said the price was $675,000; another report claimed it was $500,000. Whatever it was, things would never be the same at Fenway Park and with the Red Sox of Boston. Manager Bill Carrigan, in all likelihood, knew what was coming; he stepped down, claiming he needed to take care of other interests back home in Lewiston, Maine.

"Nothing is too good for the wonderful fans of the Boston team," declared Frazee before he even paid Lannin. Zealots should have taken Frazee at his word. For as the future was to show time and time again, he meant exactly what he said. Nothing—was too good.

Although he had a home in Boston, Frazee's main residence was in Manhattan, an apartment on Park Avenue. He was fond of saying, "The best thing about Boston was the train ride back to New York."

"I'm in the game to make money," Frazee remarked, "and a man is entitled to 20 percent annually on his investment. If I can't make that, I don't intend to spend my time in baseball and will be perfectly willing to hand the club over to some philanthropist who is willing to work his head off for the purpose of handing the ball players' large salaries."

Curiously enough, ownership of Fenway Park was not part of the Frazee deal for the Red Sox. The new owner paid an annual rental fee of $30,000 to the Fenway Realty Trust (read: former Red Sox owners the Taylor family and Lannin).

The Frazee Red Sox era began with high hopes for Fenway's faithful fans. Jack Barry was put in as player-manager on a team stacked with much talent.

On April 24, 1917, Yankee lefty George Mogridge pitched the first opposition no-hitter as well as the first no-hitter in Yankee history. It was said that the lean and long hurler had a lot under his cap, including resin.

Pitching masterpieces seemed to be part of the ethos at Fenway that season. Starting a game on June 23 against Washington, Babe Ruth walked the leadoff hitter, Ray Morgan. The Babe fumed as each ball was, he thought, mistakenly called by umpire Brick Owen. So enraged was Ruth at the bases on balls that he punched Owen. The Big Bam was ejected and later suspended for ten days. Ernie Shore replaced him on the mound. The player the Babe put on base was caught stealing, and Shore retired the next 26 batters in a row and posted a 4–0 win. That was the only "perfect game" (unofficial as it was, since Shore did not start the game) ever pitched at Fenway Park.

Not to be outdone, Babe Ruth was on his game even more than usual on August 10; he nipped the Tigers, 5–4, giving up just four hits. The margin of difference was a shot the Sultan of Swat swatted into the center-field bleachers, the longest homer at Fenway to that point in time. Twenty-one days later Ruth won his 20th game, beating the A's, 5–3.

The Babe's pitching stats over 1916–1917 were astounding: 47 wins, 15 shutouts. Over his career, he had a .671 winning percentage, the 10th best in history, and the 15th-best lifetime earned-run average.

And Babe Ruth was always there to lend a helping hand for a good cause. A benefit game was staged at Fenway on September 27 for the family of sportswriter Tim Murnane, who had died in February.

It was the Red Sox against an American League all-star team that featured an outfield of Ty Cobb; Tris Speaker, now with Cleveland; and Shoeless Joe Jackson. More than $14,000 was raised. Actress Fanny Brice helped sell programs. Former heavyweight champ John L. Sullivan coached at third base for the Sox. Ruth won the fungo-hitting contest. Joe Jackson had the longest throw. And behind the pitching of Babe Ruth and Rube Foster, the Red Sox won, 2–0. Everyone left Fenway feeling good.

However, there were not so many Sox fans feeling good at season's end. The White Sox won 100 games in 1917 and finished in first place. Frazee's Red Sox finished second, nine games out, with a 90–62 record. Attendance was down almost

ABOVE: Babe Ruth taking pictures of teammates

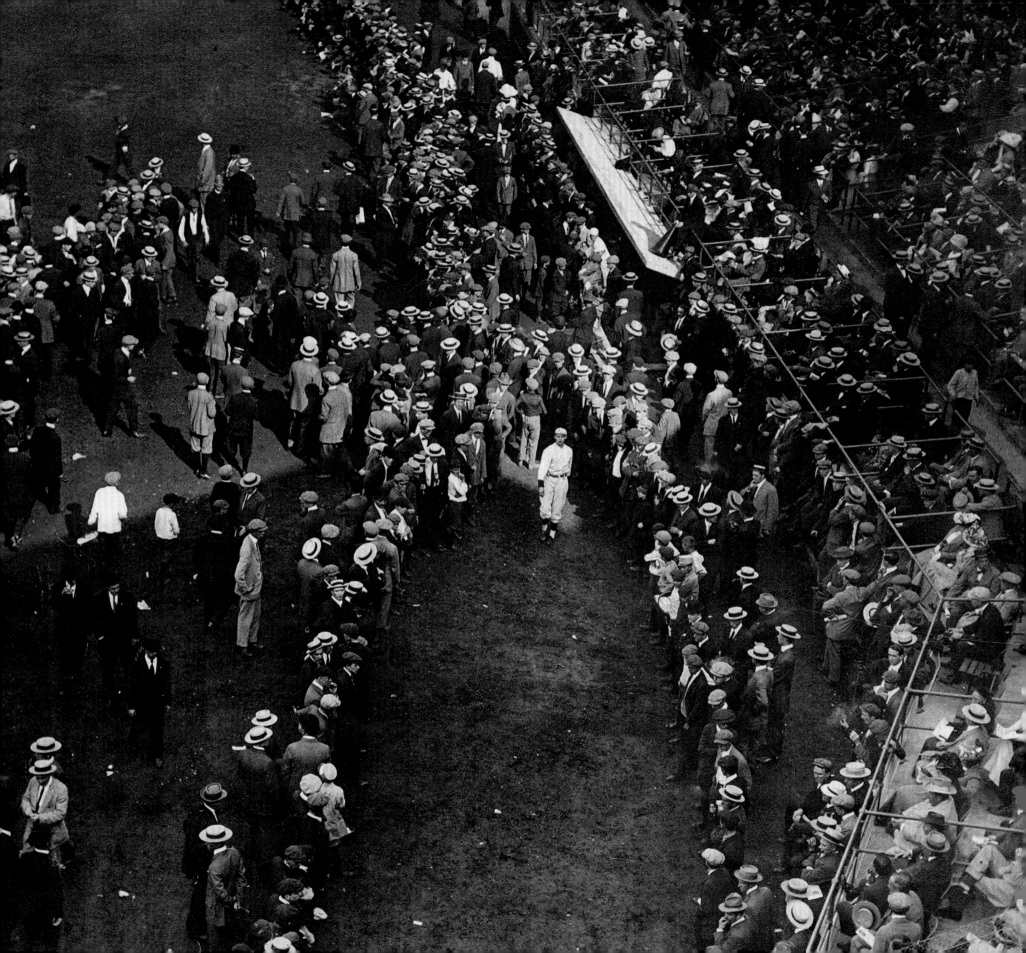

100,000 from the 1916 championship season.

World War I was impacting on happenings all over the world. Baseball was no exception. In 1918, Ed Barrow was the Bosox manager, replacing pilot Jack Barry, who had enlisted. Duffy Lewis, Ernie Shore, Herb Pennock, and other Red Sox players enlisted as well. Dutch Leonard would pitch half the season and then leave to build ships.

A planned World War I tax—3 cents on bleacher seats and 10 cents on other seats—was proposed but never enacted. For the first time newspaper ads attempted to push ticket sales. which were lagging because of the war.

Exigencies of the war reduced the number of games played in a season that now ended on Labor Day; the Red Sox played only 126 games, about 30 fewer than in the previous season.

On May 6, Babe Ruth played his first game as an outfielder. He smashed a tenth-inning shot over the fence to give Boston a 1–0 win over Cleveland. Prevailing rules, however, took the home run credit away from him because the winning run scored ahead of the shot. Ruth's circuit clout was reduced to a triple. As a result, record

books document the Babe bashing 11 home runs is 1918, none of them at Fenway Park. Nevertheless, winning 13 games, batting .300, and leading the league in home runs, he powered the Red Sox to the pennant. At the end of the shortened season, the Sox had finished 75–51, 2½ games ahead of Cleveland.

The 1918 Series was held early in September due to the World War I "Work or Fight" order mandating the premature ending of the regular season on September 1. The only World Series played entirely in September was between the Red Sox and the Chicago Cubs, with the Red Sox choosing to play at the smaller Fenway Park rather than Braves Field as they had in a couple of World Series past, and the Cubs deciding to play at the larger Comiskey Park rather than Wrigley Field, then known as Weeghman Park. Wartime travel restrictions created a 3–4 format for the "late summer classic"—the first three games in Chicago and the remainder in Boston.

In 1918, Fenway Park had notoriety because of dozens of gamblers who regularly hung out in the first-base pavilion. Their pervasiveness resulted in World Series teams being forbidden to announce the starting pitchers before games under penalty of a $25 fine.

"They had their same seats every day," Thomas Foley, a vendor at the time, recalled. "The ushers kept their seats for them. Half of them were businessmen—undertakers, doctors, lawyers, butchers—and betting was their recreation. Others did it for a living. They'd bet on everything."

Harry Frazee, ever the showman and because it was a time of war, decided to hire a band to play "The Star-Spangled Banner" (not the national anthem at the time) during the seventh-inning stretch. The band played. Standing at attention, players turned to face the flag. Those in the armed

forces saluted, and the crowd sang along. Loud applause punctuated the end of the singing.

All three games in Chicago featured Frazee's "The Star-Spangled Banner" ceremony. The Red Sox won two of the three games in Chicago where small crowds attended, providing slim gate receipts. Then both teams left the Windy City on the Michigan Central train headed to Boston.

At Fenway, Frazee directed things so that "The Star-Spangled Banner" was played just before the first pitch. That set a pattern in Boston for the song to be played on special occasions. Later when electric public address systems were in use, every game's start, all across the country, was preceded by the song. In this way, Harry Frazee became a historical footnote.

On Monday, September 9, back in Boston for game four, the Red Sox owner had a world championship on his mind. The Babe, batting sixth in the order, the only time a starting pitcher did that

OPPOSITE: Smokey Joe Wood warms up prior to his face-off with the legendary Walter Johnson
LEFT: John I. Taylor, owner of the Boston American League Team, watches the game
ABOVE: 1917 view of the field from behind home plate with buildings visible

matter of custom awarded to the victorious team.

The emblems were a prestige problem. The World Series shares were a money problem. Each victorious Red Sox player received a mere $1,108.45; each Cub, a measly $671.

Another world championship notwithstanding, Harry Frazee was hurting financially. Regular-season attendance at Fenway Park was nothing to write home about, and the gate for the World Series was slim. A few of his theatrical productions had bombed. Frazee had now gone from flush to flushed.

Ernie Shore and Duffy Lewis had been away in the service for the season, and, Frazee reasoned, the Sox had been able to win the championship without them. So he packed them off to the New York Yankees along with Dutch Leonard for four mediocre players and $15,000. Cash was the key to the deal. Once started, he knew he could get more cash the same way.

The big story of the 1919 season was George Herman Ruth, now an outfielder and a pitcher. On the mound for a weak Red Sox team as the fourth starter, he won 9 of 14 decisions with a 2.97 earned-run average. He was even better with the bat. Bashing 29 home runs, a new big-league record, the Caliph of Clout also paced the American League in runs scored and RBIs.

And even when he was not at his best, the Babe somehow found a way to prevail. On July 25, the Yankees touched up Ruth for 13 hits. The final score: Red Sox 8, Yankees 6.

More than 31,000 were at Fenway Park on Saturday, September 20, 1919, for the Red Sox versus the White Sox. Babe Ruth pitched in the first game of a doubleheader into the sixth inning. Then he moved to left field. The score was tied in the ninth when he slammed a shot over the left-field wall off Claude Williams. That was his 27th home run that season, tying the single-season record for home runs and making the Babe the hero of the 4–3 Red Sox win.

Boston would win the second game as well.

in World Series history, matched off against Lefty Tyler. The Cubs scored in the eighth inning, tying the game and stopping Ruth's scoreless streak of 29⅔ innings. But the Sox won the game, 3–2.

Amid rumors of a "fix," lackluster attendance contributed to making the 1918 World Series shares the lowest ever. Both teams threatened to strike and not finish the Series unless concessions were offered. The start of game five was delayed for an hour as discussions continued until players, at last, agreed to go on with the game.

"The death knell of World Series for all time was

sounded today, when the fifth game of the contest between the Cubs and Red Sox for the coin contributed by the fans was held up for an hour while players, club owners and members of the National Commission (the ruling body of baseball) haggled over the division," the *Chicago Tribune* reported.

Game five, before 24,694, saw Hippo Vaughn pitted against Sad Sam Jones. Chicago won, 3–0. For game six, only 15,238 showed. Carl Mays of Boston was more than up to the task. Allowing just three hits, he won, 2–1, and the Sox had their fourth title in seven years.

"[T]he 1918 triumph," the *New York Times* observed, "marks the fifth World Series that the Red Sox have brought to the high brow domicile of the baked bean. Boston is the luckiest baseball spot on earth, for it has never lost a World Series."

Because of the delay of game five, the National Commission withheld the championship emblems (there were no World Series rings at the time) as a

Between games, "Babe Ruth Day" ceremonies were staged. The Knights of Columbus of South Boston honored one of their own. No one knew it then, but it would be the last time that the great George Herman Ruth would appear at Fenway Park in a Red Sox uniform.

The 1919 Sox finished up 66–71, in sixth place, drawing 417,291. It was not a great ending for what had been a very good decade at Fenway. But worse news lay ahead.

On December 26, 1919, Harry Frazee announced that Babe Ruth had been sold to the New York Yankees for $125,000, double the price that had ever been paid for a player. "Frantic" Frazee, as they were calling him, also collected a $300,000 loan from the Yankees. Fenway Park was collateral.

Boston was aghast. "For Sale" signs sprouted across Boston Common and in front of the Boston Public Library, the message being if "Hairbreadth Harry," as he also was being called, had sold one Boston institution, he might just as well have sold a couple more.

The decade ended.
The "Curse of the Bambino" began.

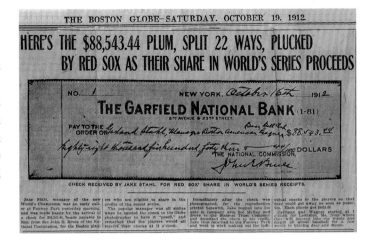

ABOVE: *Boston Globe* story about Red Sox World Series shares
OPPOSITE: 1912 World Series crowd
BELOW: Mascot Jerry McCarthy with Sox rooters, 1912 World Series

–TWENTIES–

FIRE SALE TIME

The Roaring Twenties would prove to be a dismal decade at Fenway Park. Wooden bleachers along the left-field foul line would burn down and not be rebuilt. There would be seven last-place finishes, and attendance would be at or near the bottom of the league. Talented men would take turns managing the flawed franchise: Ed Barrow, Lee Fohl, Frank Chance, Bill Carrigan, Hugh Duffy. All would feel the sting of failure. And Babe Ruth was gone.

	YEAR	WON	LOST	PCT.	GB	ATTENDANCE
	1929	58	96	.377	48.0	394,620
	1928	57	96	.373	43.5	396,920
	1927	51	103	.331	59.0	305,275
RED SOX YEAR BY YEAR	**1926**	46	107	.301	44.5	285,155
1920 – 1929	**1925**	47	105	.309	49.5	267,782
	1924	67	87	.435	25.0	448,556
	1923	61	91	.401	37.0	229,688
	1922	61	93	.396	33.0	259,184
	1921	75	79	.487	23.5	279,273
	1920	72	81	.471	25.5	402,445

But it was not only the Babe who was sold to the Yankees. Harry Frazee sent a steady stream of talent their way: catcher Wally Schang, premier pitcher Waite Hoyt, shortstop Everett Scott, pitchers "Bullet" Joe Bush and "Sad Sam" Jones, third baseman Joe Dugan, pitchers Herb Pennock and George Pipgras, and more.

"All Frazee wanted was the money," Harry Hooper said. "He was short on cash and he sold the whole team down the river to keep his dirty nose above water. What a way to end a wonderful ball club. I got sick to my stomach of the whole business. After the 1920 season I held out for $15,000. And Frazee did me a favor by selling me to the Chicago White Sox. I was glad to get away from that graveyard."

On Patriots' Day, 1920, George Herman Ruth was back in town. "In all the years the writer has witnessed baseball in Boston," the *Globe's* Melville E. Webb Jr. wrote, "he never has seen a former home team player so 'ridden' by the normally friendly fans."

But it was not the Babe who was booed. It was his Yankee teammate righthander Carl Mays. Both

players had led the Red Sox to victory in the 1918 World Series. Both Ruth and Mays became disenchanted with playing for the Sox. Both wound up as employees of Yankee owner Jake Ruppert.

Babe Ruth's first Fenway at-bat as a Yankee was just a bit after 10:00 A.M. before what the *New York Times* called "a crowd of 6,000 early risers." There was a competing draw: the Boston Marathon. Native Greek Peter Trivoulidas supposedly had trained on the course that had given the Marathon its name, and was the victor in what the *Globe* called "the greatest Marathon run ever staged in any land."

The Bambino got two hits in four at-bats in a losing cause as the Red Sox won the first game that day, 6–0.

Mays was the Yankee starter in the post-Marathon game. "With a real holiday setting," Webb observed, Ruth and Mays drew a crowd that rivaled a World Series turnout.

Relentlessly chided and booed, Mays responded, according to Webb, by "working every nerve and sinew . . . to rub it into the fans who were so keenly showing their disapproval."

The Red Sox led, 4–2, in the seventh. Mays heard loud catcalls as he left the field.

"Carl, standing the gaff, stopped near the Red Sox dugout and tipped his cap," Webb reported.

A four-run eighth inning locked the game up for Boston. Ruth's single in the ninth led to a meaningless Yankee run. "The crowd was strong for Babe... but they had the satisfaction of seeing the big fellow win no hero stripes on the occasion of his home coming," wrote Webb.

Another who would go down as a baseball immortal showed up on July 1 at Fenway. Surprisingly, only 3,000 fans were in the stands despite Walter Johnson's being on the mound for the Washington Senators. Those who were there were treated to a masterpiece: Johnson spun the only no-hitter of his 21-year career. After his 1–0 victory over the Sox, some teammates in the soggy clubhouse slapped the broad back of Johnson and others yelled, "Speech!"

"Goodness gracious sakes alive, wasn't I lucky?" was Johnson's reply.

New York versus first-place Boston, four-game series. Game one was May 27. Yankee Bob Shawkey walked in a run in the fourth inning and became so irritated that he began yelling at home-plate umpire George Hildebrand. The agitated Shawkey then took five minutes to tie his shoe on the mound. He resumed pitching and was credited with a called third strike on Harry Hooper. That prompted him to sarcastically tip his cap and bow low to Hildebrand, who ejected him from the game. Shawkey's parting shot was a swing at the ump, who banged him with his mask. The crowd loved it. Shawkey did not. A one week suspension and a $200 fine were the prices the Yankee hurler paid for his temper tantrum.

Fenway Park, Boston, Mass.

PAGE 40: Ferocious fire being fought at Fenway
OPPOSITE: Boston mayor James Michael Curley throws out the first ball

In the sixth inning of that game, Babe Ruth smacked his first Fenway homer as a Yankee—a mighty blast to right-center. Then he launched another, making it four homers in three days. The Sultan of Swat was the first twentieth-century player to accomplish that feat. A Yankee series sweep dropped the Sox out of first place, sending them into a downward spiral.

The bitter rivals met again in a September 4, 1920, twin bill. A record 33,027 fans crammed into Fenway. Another 10,000 were turned away.

"That was a once-in-a-lifetime day," former Fenway vendor Tom Foley recalled. "Two weeks before, at the Polo Grounds, he [Carl Mays] threw a ball at Ray Chapman's head and killed him. It was unintentional, but people were riled. This was his first appearance back in Boston, and everybody went to heckle him. I made $16 that day, all nickels and dimes."

Under Ed Barrow and then Hugh Duffy, the Red Sox finished in fifth place during the 1920 and 1921 seasons. Games at Fenway were not hot tickets. In 1920 the team had the sixth-worst attendance in the American League. In 1921 they would draw 279,273, the lowest in the league.

Arthur Giddon, who lived in Brookline, was a batboy in 1922 and 1923 for the Boston Braves. He also kept an eye on the Red Sox.

ARTHUR GIDDON: I went to Fenway from time to time. Living right in Brookline, I'd take the subway and was down at Kenmore Square in ten minutes. You didn't need to buy tickets in advance; you could get all the tickets you wanted.

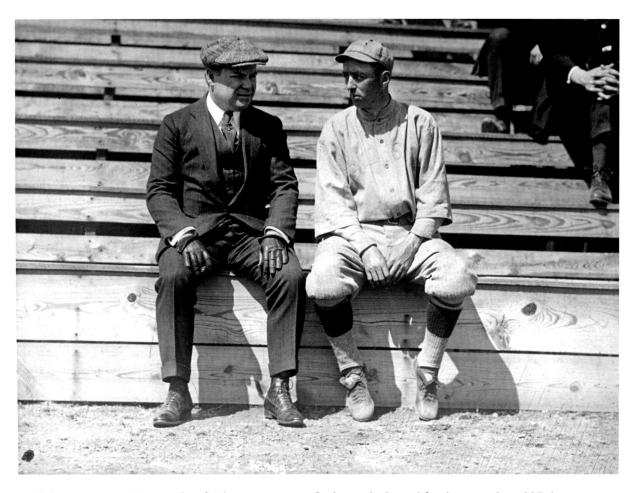

ABOVE: Owner Harry Frazee and star Jack Barry, deep in conversation
OPPOSITE: A hatted throng jammed in tight, 1924

Tickets were easy. Long pokes for home runs were harder to come by at Fenway in 1922. Center field was 488 feet and the deepest corner, just right of center, was 550 feet.

The 12th season of Fenway Park began in 1923, the year Yankee Stadium opened for the first time. Bob Quinn headed a Midwestern group that bought the Red Sox from Harry Frazee for $1.2 million, double what the not-well-liked owner had shelled out for the team in 1916. Quinn was actually asked by American League president Ban Johnson to purchase the team so it would be taken out of Frazee's hands.

A former general manager of the St. Louis Browns, Quinn knew baseball. But he inherited a team given severe body blows by Frazee, and a ballpark in need of many improvements.

Such was the hatred for the man who sold Babe Ruth to the Yankees that the cheering in some sections of New England for the new ownership was as if the Sox had won the World Series. The franchise, however, had been so depleted by Harry Frazee that any change seemed to be for the better.

Frank Chance was the new manager. Neither Chance nor change was on parade for the '23 Sox. The same old stuff was. The Bosox finished in last place—37 games out—with a record of 61–91 and a .401 winning percentage. At Fenway they were 37–40. On the road they were 24–51.

The Fenway faithful, what remained of them, saw players plying their trade in 1923 such as shortstop Chick Fewster, right fielder Shano Collins, center fielder Camp Skinner, left fielder Joe Harris, first baseman George Burns, second baseman Norm McMillan, third baseman Howard Shanks, catcher Al DeVormer, and pitchers Howard Ehmke and Bill Piercy.

As if to rub salt into the festering sore, on September 8, 1925, in the second game of a doubleheader, the Babe unloaded on southpaw Buster Ross. The Yanks beat up on the Red Sox, 7–4, and the Big Bam had his 300th career home run.

A highlight of the season was the unassisted triple play pulled off by Sox first baseman George Burns against the Indians on September 14. In the second inning, with Riggs Stephenson on second base and Rube Lutzke on first base, Burns snared a liner from Frank Brower, tagged Lutzke, and raced to second, sliding into the bag ahead of Stephenson. It was the third unassisted triple play in baseball's modern era.

A highlight of the season and of his career was a home run by a youngster signed in June by the Yankees. It was the first of 493 career home runs by Lou Gehrig. He hit it at Fenway on September 27, 1923, off Bill Piercy in an 8–3 New York win.

"I didn't get a bonus to sign," recalled Bill Rogell, who joined the Red Sox in 1925. I got three hundred bucks a month my first year. The club was all young guys. The owner of the club, Bob Quinn, tried to get by. And we didn't have the experience. In 1925, we lost 105 games."

The lower depths the Red Sox had sunk to were underscored by commentary in *Reach's Baseball Guide:* "Boston's last season reaped the fruits of four years' despoliation by the New York club, and for the second time in American League history, this once great Boston team, now utterly discredited, fell into last place—with

every prospect of remaining in that undesirable position indefinitely."

As the 1926 season began at Fenway Park on April 13, fans huddled together to keep warm in the frigid environment. But Yankee and Red Sox bats were hot, combining for 29 hits. New York scored four times in the first inning off Howard Ehmke, the first of six Boston hurlers. A five-run Boston sixth knocked Yankee starter Bob Shawkey out of the game. But when all was said and done, the Bronx Bombers walked off with a 12–11 victory.

Boston fans had come to expect losses like that. But they really were not prepared for what happened on the eighth of May, when the fourth fire in the same location in two days destroyed a great deal of the left-field bleachers and grandstand roof.

The other fires had been extinguished by fans who poured water from buckets. This time efforts to control the fire failed. Manager Lee Fohl and a few park workers tried their best with groundskeepers' hoses. The fire, however, spread to the grass, a billboard, and the wooden bleachers.

The cash-poor owner, John Quinn, used insurance money to cover payroll; he could not or would not rebuild the bleachers. A space strewn with cinders resembling a vacant lot remained for seven years as part of the ballpark environment. For eight seasons the ground behind the grandstand was the largest foul territory in the big leagues. Left fielders didn't complain, though, since they were able to catch foul balls for outs behind the stands.

"We didn't play Sunday ball in Boston at that time," Walter Shaner, an outfielder on the 1926 and 1927 Sox, said. "And we used to get on the train right after the ball game on Saturday and go to Detroit and play a Sunday game. And then we'd catch the train right after that and come back to Boston for the Monday game.

LEFT: Raising the flag in 1924
OPPOSITE: Babe Ruth bats against the Red Sox in 1926

"The first time I did it," Shaner continued, "I noticed Fred Haney, our third baseman, and two or three of the other boys taking suitcases—just to go over for the day and go back. And I couldn't figure out why until we got to Detroit. I found out that they had a friend who used to get Black Label beer in sacks from Canada and each sack of 24 bottles fit right into the suitcases."

In 1927, 34 homers would be hit at Fenway. The Red Sox as a team would hit only five, while Babe Ruth (eight) and Lou Gehrig (six) would outhomer the whole Boston team at Fenway that season.

The Yankees, especially Ruth and Gehrig, made June 21 the longest day of the year, even longer on the Sox and their generally upbeat manager, William Cardigan. They won a doubleheader, 7–3 and 7–1. Between games, Yankee second baseman Tony Lazzeri was honored by Boston's Italian-American community and presented with a specially designed ring.

On June 22, George Herman Ruth homered twice off Sox southpaw Hal Wiltse. The second shot, it was reported, exited Fenway, winding up in a vacant lot, then banging against a garage wall, where two boys and six men battled for the souvenir.

The next day the other half of the "home run twins," Lou Gehrig, pounded three home runs, a first at Fenway Park. It was the ninth straight Yankee victory, an 11–4 romp over the Red Sox.

Mostly throughout the '20s Fenway Park was a dreary, decaying, and despondent place, with empty seats a painful part of the daily atmosphere. That was not the case on a humid September 5, 1927, a doubleheader day between the downtrodden, last-place Sox and the upbeat, high-flying, first-place Yankees.

Fans flocked to Fenway drawn by Babe Ruth, Lou Gehrig, and company. More than 70,000 struggled to get into Fenway, and half of them were turned away.

"Ruth used to fill up all the ballparks," Walter Shaner mused. "When he'd come to Boston we couldn't get them all in. They would put the fans in the outfield. There was a bank in left field, Duffy's Cliff, and they had people all over the bank. If they hit a ball over my head, it was a two-base hit. The crowd was about ten feet behind me. So everyone made money off of Ruth."

"The weak spots in the wooden barricade on the Ipswich Street side of the park were rushed and several holes made through which the human flood poured in a merry torrent," observed Burt Whitman in the *Boston Herald*. The Associated Press reported that "hundreds stormed the gates after ticket sales were stopped."

Fans were pressed 15 to 20 feet against the outfield wall by police on horseback and then roped off. Umpires ruled that any ball hit into the mass would be a ground-rule double. Atop of fences, alongside outfield foul lines, from underneath the grandstand and nearby rooftops, fans seized whatever space for viewing they were able to squeeze into.

There were 26 games in 1927 where the Yanks lit up the opposition for 10 or more runs and posted a 25–1 mark. The lone defeat came in the first game of that Fenway doubleheader, an 18-inning, 12–11 heartbreaker loss. It also was the longest game of the season for the Yankees, 4 hours and 20 minutes. The second game was "speed" baseball, 55 minutes, called because of darkness, the Yanks 5–0 winners. Incredibly, 23-year-old Hal Wiltse, who had pitched three innings for Boston and was the victor in the first game, was the losing pitcher in the second game.

The next day the rivals were at it again—another doubleheader. Ruth blasted three home runs. His first one got everyone's attention.

"This long one yesterday was the daddy of all others," the *Boston Globe's* hero-worshipping prose expounded. "The ball was still climbing when it went high over the highest part of the high fence in center field, just to the left of the flagpole. Nobody at the park could tell where it

landed, but when it disappeared it was headed for the Charles River basin."

Talk about disappearing. The 1927 Red Sox posted a 51–103 record and finished in last place, 59 games behind the pennant-winning Yankees.

It was last place again in 1928—43½ games behind the pennant-winning Yankees. The "Curse of the Bambino" was working at fever pitch. The Sox could hardly win; the Yankees could hardly lose. Bill "Rough" Carrigan, winner of two world championships as manager in 1915 and 1916, had come back to failure with the not-quite-prime-time and downtrodden Red Sox roster—three last-place finishes—59, 43½, and 48 games, respectively, out of first place.

The Great Depression was just around the corner, and the economy would be in shambles across the nation and take a long time to recover.

At Fenway Park the decade of the '20s foreshadowed that downtime.

A poignant postscript to the 1920s took place on September 25, 1929. The Yankees were playing in Boston. News of the death in a New York City hospital of Bronx Bomber manager Miller Huggins came over the wires in the fifth inning. He had died from poison spreading through his body from a skin disease commonly known as St. Anthony's fire.

At inning's end, the game stopped. Men with megaphones moved about Fenway giving out the sad news to the small crowd of 7,000 fans. The center-field flag was lowered to half mast. Bareheaded, heads bowed, the Yankees and Red Sox and the umpires gathered around the home plate area for one minute of silence. In the stands, the fans rose in respect, many deeply touched by the moment despite the fact that Miller Huggins had been the manager of the hated Yankees.

The game resumed. In eleven innings, the Yanks nipped the Sox, 11–10.

SAM SKOLER: The team was not too good, but sitting in the bleachers in Fenway was still a thrilling experience for me. I came to America in the 1920s and almost immediately I became interested in baseball and a fan of the Boston Red Sox. I started in the bleachers, but as the years moved on, I moved closer and closer to home plate. It became a generational event for me—going with my friends, then my sons, later on my grandsons, an American thing to do.

OPPOSITE: Lou Gehrig shows off his power swing
ABOVE: Harry Frazee in suit—always plotting

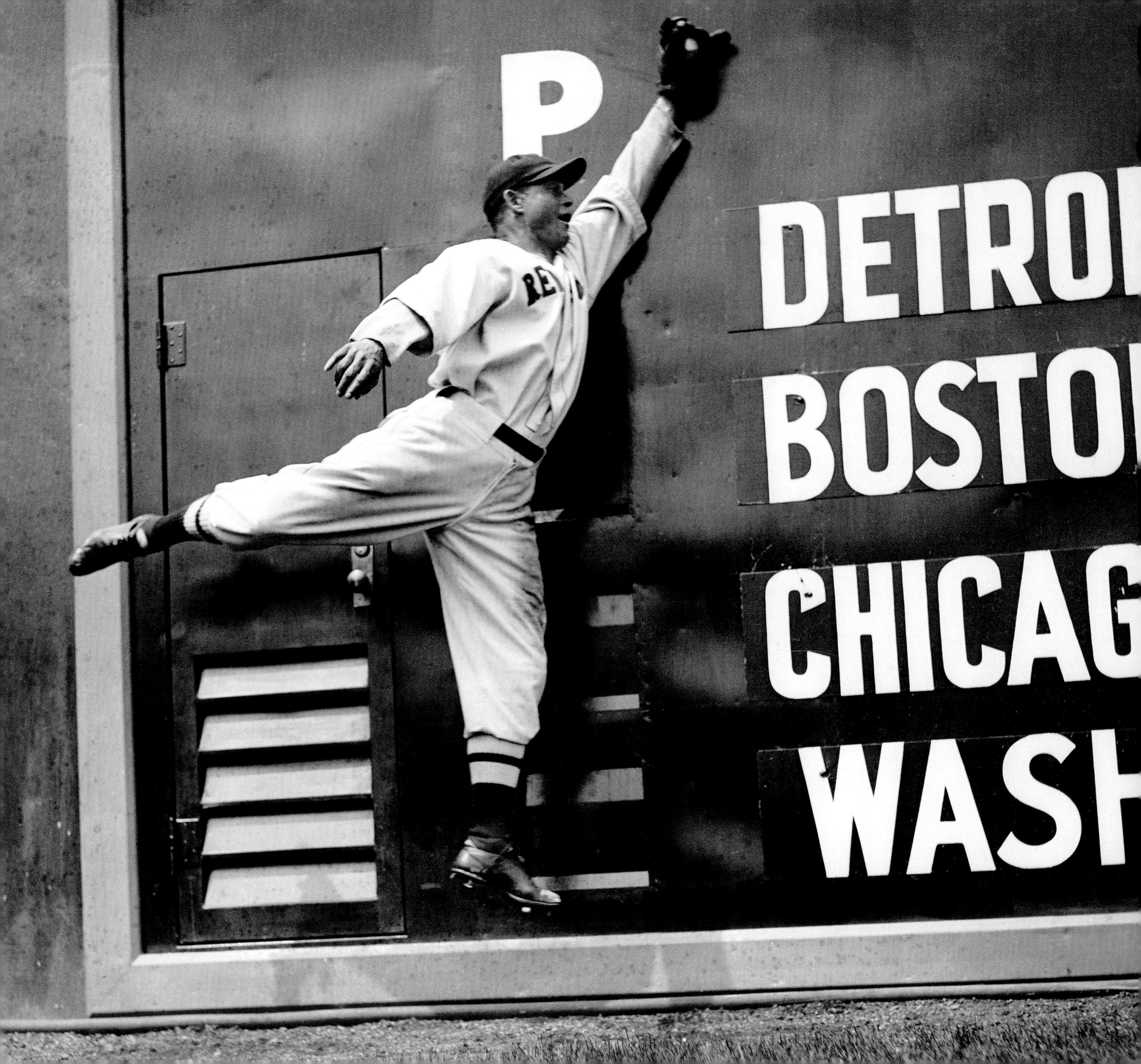
P
DETRO
BOSTO
CHICAG
WASH

—THIRTIES—

ENTER TOM YAWKEY

Momentous events for Fenway Park and the Red Sox were on the horizon as the new decade dawned: new ownership, a major fire, significant renovations, and the arrival of the greatest star in the history of the Boston Red Sox.

	YEAR	WON	LOST	PCT.	GB	ATTENDANCE
RED SOX YEAR BY YEAR 1930 – 1939	**1939**	89	62	.589	17.0	573,070
	1938	88	61	.591	9.5	646,459
	1937	80	72	.526	21.0	559,659
	1936	74	80	.481	28.5	626,895
	1935	78	75	.510	16.0	558,568
	1934	76	76	.500	24.0	610,640
	1933	63	86	.423	34.5	268,715
	1932	43	111	.279	64.0	182,150
	1931	62	90	.408	45.0	350,975
	1930	52	102	.338	50.0	444,045

An interesting coda to baseball history took place on the 28th of September 1930: George Herman Ruth returned to Fenway Park, this time as a pitcher, the role that had earned him much early fame and glory at Fenway. He walked away with a 9–3 complete-game triumph over his former team. But Lou Gehrig, positioned in the Sultan of Swat's normal position in left field, saw his streak of playing first base in 885 consecutive games end.

Under manager Heinie Wagner, the 1930 Bosox were one of the worst teams in franchise history, finishing dead last in the American League, with a record of 52 wins and 102 losses. Just 444,045 fans came to their home games, an average of 5,767 a contest.

The 1931 season saw Red Sox players sporting uniforms with numbers on them. "The easier to find them and boo them," a sarcastic fan noted. But Babe Ruth didn't need a number to be identified. His return to Fenway in a Yankee uniform always elicited cheers as well as jeers. On April 22, attempting to score from third base on a sacrifice fly, the Babe collided with Boston catcher Charlie Berry, an ex-professional football player. Ruth got the worse of it. Carried off the field, the hurting Big Bam was rushed to a hospital.

Earlier in that 1931 season, when the Shortwave and Television Corporation offered to televise games from Fenway Park, owner Bob Quinn complained, "It has rained every Sunday and our team is in last place. And you want me to let the fans see the games at home? How do you suppose we are going to pay for our players?"

The request was premature. It would take another 17 years before baseball from Fenway would be on TV. But Sunday baseball did debut that year on July 3 (the Yankees ripped Boston, 13–2). Actually, the Sox had received approval for Sunday games three years earlier, but since a church was close by the ballpark, Sunday games were played at Braves Field until conditions were right.

No matter the day, game attendance languished in the doldrums for the 1932 season, with only 182,150 passing through the Fenway turnstiles, an average of 2,366 per game, a home low for the decade. John Francis Collins, better known as "Shano," presided over the sorry mess, but only until June 18, 1932.

Collins sent a telegram from Cleveland to owner Bob Quinn announcing that after 55 games as manager he could not go on. At that point the Sox had won only 11 games, for a .200 percentage.

"It was all out of a clear sky to me," said Quinn. In came third baseman Marty McManus to fill the breach. The new skipper had a modest goal: a seventh-place finish. He had modest demands for his team: "There won't be any strict discipline. I'll try to enforce the rule that requires all the players to be in bed before midnight, but otherwise they'll have a lot of leeway."

McManus had more success than Collins. Still the Sox wound up having the worst season in franchise history—a dead-last-place finish, 64 games behind the first-place Yankees. With 43 wins and 111 losses, a .279 percentage, they were the only team in the majors to have a winning percentage under .300. It was the worst won-and-lost record in franchise history. What else could one expect of a team that scored 518 runs while allowing 915?

A depressed and desperate Red Sox owner Bob Quinn called a press conference on February 25, 1933. His announcement was not unexpected.

"I haven't got the money to continue," he said. Then he informed the press that he had sold the Red Sox and Fenway Park. It was for the same amount of money he had paid almost a decade before for the entire operation: $1.2 million.

It was not the sale as much as the buyer who attracted the attention of Boston's newspapermen, a 30-year-old with a fortune estimated to be more than $40 million. They thought him too young to have that kind of money. "He's just a kid," wrote one wizened scribe who couldn't believe the news.

The "kid" who at first would be called "Tom" and later on in his ownership tenure always "Mr. Yawkey," would remain on the scene for 44 years. Heir to an enormous timber and mining fortune, Yawkey would never own a home in Boston. His time would be spent at Fenway Park, in a suite between May and October at Boston's Ritz-Carlton, in an apartment at New York's Pierre, or on a 40,000-acre game preserve off the coast of South Carolina, where he enjoyed hunting and fishing and entertaining guests between October and April.

Most thought that Yawkey had been taken, paying more than a million dollars for one of the worst teams in baseball and a decaying Fenway Park.

"It was bad," Yawkey conceded years later. "I had to pay off a debt from the Red Sox to Harry M. Stevens, the concessionaire. The team owed $150,000 to the league." And there was also the mortgage held on Fenway Park by the New York Yankees—part of the deal that sent Babe Ruth to New York.

But Tom Yawkey had the courage of youth, a sportsman's zeal, and the money to spare. He figured he could handle it all. And he did.

The young Yawkey hired veteran Edward Trowbridge Collins Sr., the storied former second baseman and veteran baseball man, as general

PAGE 50: In a shot set up by the photographer, a Red Sox player leaps in front of the scoreboard with ball in hand
OPPOSITE: Boston mayor Frederick Mansfield, with hat in hand and Tom Yawkey next to Governor Charles Hurley, watches him throw out the first ball. Also on the field are Red Sox manager Joe Cronin and Yankee manager Joe McCarthy.

SOUVENIR SCORE CARD

Opening Day

New Fenway Park

APRIL 17, 1934

HOME OF THE BOSTON AMERICANS

PRICE 10 CENTS

manager and vice president, giving him the responsibility of transforming the sorry Red Sox into a contender and raising attendance at Fenway Park. The goals seemed wishful thinking, especially in the middle of the Great Depression, but no one ever accused Yawkey of thinking small.

There was a moment of exultation amid all the negatives that season, as the Yawkeymen swept the Yankees in a five-game series.

"The next morning," Yawkey remembered, "my lawyer in New York called to say it was a costly sweep. [Yankee owner] Ruppert's lawyer had just called and they were demanding right now payment on the mortgage. Jake didn't like to lose five straight. So I sent the SOB a check the next day."

BILL WERBER: In May 1933, when I came to the Red Sox from the Yankees, I met with Tom Yawkey about salary. It was for about $2,000 less than what I'd been earning—big money back then. But I signed at his figure. He was the owner.

Then, in a game, I ran after a high foul ball into the Yankee dugout. I missed the first step and went down on my back in the dugout with all the Yankees hollering at me. But I caught the ball.

After the game was over, Johnny Orlando, the clubhouse boy, said that Mr. Yawkey wanted to see me in his office.

"Bill," he said to me, "that was the damnedest catch I've seen in quite a while: you lying on your back with all those Yankees yelling. I am putting the money you wanted back in your contract."

I lived nearby in the Newton Highlands and was really able to experience Boston and all its history. Fenway Park was not that old a park then, and playing in it was a real kick. It had some oddities, though.

RIGHT: Young Bill Werber posing for the camera
OPPOSITE: No instant replay. Safe at first?

Once there were some wild cats in the clubhouse up over the lockers feeding on the pigeons. Somebody said, "Go get Cooke." That was Allen Lindsey Cooke, but everyone called him Dusty.

Dusty didn't like cats because they caught quail. They got him a broom. He started after them. They jumped down off the lockers onto the floor, and Dusty continued to flail them until they all escaped through a window on top of the lockers.

――――――――――

That year, the 1933 Red Sox finished in seventh place and pulled in a home gate of 268,715 — almost 100,000 better than the year before. Tom Yawkey had arranged for grand Fenway Park improvements that off-season.

On January 5, 1934, light snow fell and nasty cold pervaded all of Boston. At Fenway Park the major construction and refurbishment work authorized by Yawkey was under way.

A rapidly spreading fire broke out. Every engine company in Boston was called out. Lines were run through the park from Ipswich Street in an attempt to stop the fire's spread, which already had engulfed Lansdowne Street, where the Seibering Rubber Co., the old Cotton Club, and the Oldsmobile & Pontiac Motor Works were all ablaze.

Inside Fenway Park, the five-alarm, four-hour fire virtually destroyed the recently begun construction and refurbishment project, which was estimated to cost more than $250,000. When it was finally controlled, more than $220,000 in damages had resulted, a fortune in 1934.

Vacationing in South Carolina, Tom Yawkey headed for Boston immediately after getting the stunning news. Shocked at what he saw, the young owner announced, "Opening Day will not be delayed."

The same firms that had partnered to create Fenway Park for $650,000 — Osborn Engineering and James McLaughlan Construction — were involved in the re-creations and repair work. A determined Yawkey wound up paying more than $1 million for the "new Fenway Park," which opened April 17, 1934.

Seating capacity had been increased from 27,642 to 33,817. Wooden seats in right and center field were replaced by concrete stands. The entire grandstand was enlarged and fitted with new oak seats.

The refurbished park now had the highest wall in the major leagues — the replacement for the 25-foot wall made of wood that burned in the fire. The new wall was 37 feet high, sheet metal over wooden railroad ties, and plastered with advertisements.

The steep incline known as "Duffy's Cliff" had essentially been leveled off and removed. There was a warning track in place for outfielders and a hand-operated scoreboard at the base of that left-field wall. State of the art for the time, it created quite a stir with colored lights to signal balls and strikes.

――――――――――

BILL WERBER: New seats were installed, both visitor and home locker rooms and showers were improved, the playing field was put into top condition, and, since Yawkey owned a paint company, the entire park got a fresh paint.

――――――――――

The Senators defeated the Sox, 6–5, in 11 innings on April 17, 1934, in the "new Fenway Park" before the largest crowd to that time in Boston baseball history (interestingly, not one player from the 1931 Red Sox remained on that 1934 team).

A run-scoring double by Washington player-manager Joe Cronin proved the margin of victory.

Tom Yawkey, not pleased with his team's loss but pleased with the way the expansion, refurbishment, and embellishments of Fenway came out, filed away what Joe Cronin was capable of doing for future reference.

Making a farewell appearance at a doubleheader at Fenway on August 12, Babe Ruth drew a record 46,766 fans to the ballpark where he had started his major league career as a pitcher 20 years before. An estimated 20,000 were turned away. Fans stood in the outfield and all over the stands — it was truly jam city to see the Bambino.

Ruth singled and doubled in the first game, but his Yankees lost, 6–4. In the second game, he had one official at-bat.

――――――――――

BILL WERBER: In 1934, I watched the Boston fans mistreat the great Babe Ruth in a way that saddened me. We were playing the Yankees on a Sunday afternoon before about 30,000 folks crammed into Fenway Park.

Ruth was in his last year with the Yankees and just about through as a ballplayer. He struck out twice and popped out in his first three trips to the plate, earning the lusty boos of the Red Sox faithful. Then, in the seventh inning, I hit a sinking line drive that he came lumbering in for. He tried to make the catch, but the ball glanced off his glove and rolled all the way to the wall. I made it to third, giving Babe a three-base error. The fans booed him and laughed at him.

When Ruth next came to the plate, he struck out again. The boos and jeers just swelled up until they practically tore the roof off. It was a sad day for baseball and not just because the game's greatest star was near the end of the line.

――――――――――

PAGE 56–57: Jam-packed Fenway, featuring fans sitting on outfield grass
OPPOSITE: Joltin' Joe DiMaggio slugs another

A week later, 46,995 showed up, shoehorned in—the same SRO frenzy that had been on hand for the Babe—for a doubleheader against the Detroit Tigers. That mob added to the overall attendance of 610,640 for the 1934 season, the third-best in franchise history to that point in time. The Red Sox drew an average of 7,930 into Fenway Park under manager Bucky Harris and finished in fourth place, with a won-and-lost record of 76–76.

The improved place in the standings and the improved attendance at home were both welcome turns of events. But a more dramatic and enduring event would be a decision Tom Yawkey made late in the 1934 season—to eliminate all advertising on all fences at Fenway Park. It was a decision that prepared the way for the "Green Monster."

A little more than a month later, on the 26th of October, Yawkey pulled off the first of what would be many blockbuster deals affecting the fate of the franchise when he purchased Washington player-manager Joe Cronin for a record $250,000 and player Lyn Lary. The new husband of Mildred Robertson (niece and adopted daughter of Washington owner Clark Griffith), the star infielder—who had caught Yawkey's eye on Opening Day—was signed to a five-year contract.

"I was at a league meeting with Griff," said Yawkey, explaining how the deal went down, and I asked, 'What will you take for Cronin?'

"'Oh, I couldn't sell Joe,' he replied. 'I'd want too much money for him anyway.'

"I answered, 'Well, put your figure down on the back of this envelope.' His figure was two hundred and fifty thousand dollars. And so I said, 'Okay, that's it.'"

Joe Cronin was in place for the 1935 season as both player and pilot and stayed on as a player until 1945 and as manager until 1947. On April 16, he made his managerial debut for the Red Sox a successful one—a 1–0 victory over the Yankees. Wes Ferrell fired a two-hitter.

On August 5, Cronin was partly responsible for managing one of the wildest games of the decade. The Red Sox were losing, 8–2, to the Yankees in the top of the fifth inning when rain began to fall. The Sox player-manager instructed his team to keep the game going, hoping it would be rained out. Conversely, the Yanks, under manager Joe McCarthy's direction, tried to make outs to hasten the end of the game.

Fielding a grounder by George Selkirk, Bill Werber threw wildly to first base on purpose. Selkirk ran around the bases for a bit until he was finally tagged out. Yankee Myril Hoag scored from third base with a steal of home with no Sox player paying attention to what he had done. The Yankees ultimately won the farce, 10–2. For their machinations, Cronin and McCarthy were fined $100 each by the American League.

It was the height of the Great Depression; nevertheless, on September 22, for the second straight year, Fenway's single-day attendance record was broken as 47,627 surged into the little ballpark for a Red Sox–Yankees doubleheader. Thousands of fans were turned away and thousands more milled about the ballpark and the field to catch the action.

They had come to witness the lavish pregame Field Day and the ferocious competition for prizes donated by Tom Yawkey. To the dismay of Red Sox rooters, the day turned out to be a Yankee sweep. They took four of the five Field Day events and also both games of the doubleheader.

The Sox finished in fourth place in '35; attendance was 558,568. Tom Yawkey was determined that things would get better for his team. Better meant Jimmie Foxx.

On the 10th of December, 28-year-old superstar Foxx, who had averaged 41 homers over the past

ABOVE: Fans file through iron gates
OPPOSITE: Babe Ruth enjoying the company of kids, and kids enjoying the company of Babe Ruth

seven seasons, who was twice an MVP and had won the Triple Crown in 1933, was acquired by Boston from the Athletics. Two nondescript players went from Boston to the Philadelphia Athletics.

"My dream has come true," Foxx said. So did Yawkey's with the acquisition of "Double X," one of the top sluggers of his day and a perfect fit for Fenway. He would be the regular first baseman for the Sox for half a dozen seasons and average 35 home runs each year.

BILL WERBER: Most of the time I stretched singles into doubles by running hard all the way. We used to get on Jimmie Foxx's ass because he wouldn't hustle to first base. He always remonstrated. "Ah, Bill, you know I'm not as fast as you." But if he had run straightaway, nine times out of ten he would have stretched a double out of a single. Still, he could slug the heck out of a ball, and he was one of the most powerful men I ever saw on a baseball field.

As the 1936 season began, fans entering Fenway were fascinated by the 23½-foot-tall screen installed above the left-field wall that offered enhanced protection for the windows of buildings and cars parked on Lansdowne Street, on the other side of the wall. The screen and the wall together rose to a height of 60½ feet.

Joe Cronin was in place for his second season as player-pilot, assisted by pitching coach Herb Pennock, and coaches Tom Daly and Al Schacht.

On September 6 the Yankees lost a double-header to the Red Sox, 14–5, and 4–2. In the opener, Boston hurler Wes Ferrell had an enjoyable time of it. He gave up 14 hits and from time to time threw lob balls to the plate. The "Maryland Strong Boy," or simply the "Beast," Foxx pounded his 37th homer in the first game. Lefty Grove, who had been acquired from the A's in 1934, won the nightcap.

BOBBY DOERR: It was the spring of 1937 and we'd come up from Florida. Joe Cronin took me out the door at Fenway Park and we stood up back of the stands and he says, "This is what you are

going to be playing in now." What a beautiful site it was to look at Fenway Park for the first time. I don't think I had ever seen pictures of it. That was the start of my first of 14 seasons with the Sox.

In the opener in 1937 in the last of the eighth inning, Johnny Murphy came in as a relief pitcher for the Yankees. I hit a bloop double over first base and got on second base and before I knew it I was picked off. The Yankees had a terrific pickoff play. I could have dug a hole and gone back to the dugout. That was how it started for me.

On May 22, 1937, facing Wes Ferrell in Boston, Hank Greenberg slugged the ball to the right of the flagpole over the center-field wall. It landed 450 feet from home plate and was called the longest home run ever hit at Fenway to that point in time. Ferrell was furious.

BILL WERBER: Wes Ferrell was a marvelous character. I remember after being removed from a ball game once at Fenway, he hit himself in the jaw with both fists and nearly knocked himself out. I saw him crunch the face out of an expensive watch, tear a deck of cards to pieces because he wasn't getting good hands. He was a very determined competitor, hated to lose at anything, the kind of person you like to have on your side.

That 1937 season was a time of progress with Jimmie Foxx and Joe Cronin and Wes Ferrell and Lefty Grove in the house. The Red Sox finished fifth, eight games over .500, 21 games out of first.

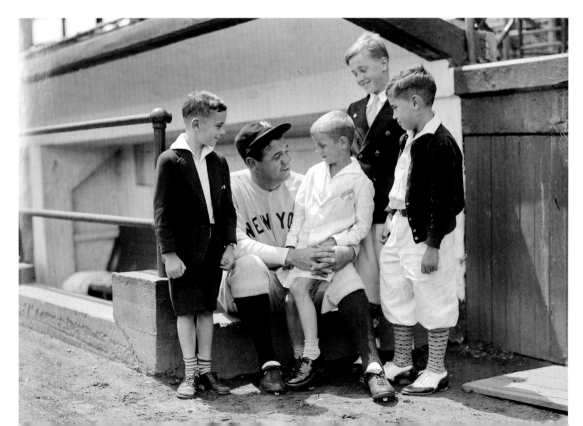

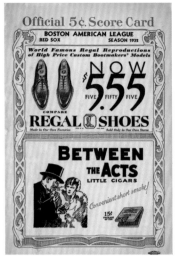

MICHAEL DUKAKIS: The first game I ever saw was in 1938, I was 4½, and Lefty Grove was pitching against the Yankees at Fenway Park. Foxx hit one off the left-field wall, and I tell you, I could hear the smack of the ball against the wall. I mean it was a single, you know, he barely got to first base, it went up there so fast.

My brother was seven. My mother didn't know a bat from a broom handle. But we must have lobbied her intensively until she finally said, "Okay, I'll take you." The next day we asked if we could go again. Mother said, "Boys, if you want to go, you can go, but I won't be with you. I've never been so bored in my life." So from that point on, we went ourselves. We were living on Bolyston Street in Brookline and could take the Chesterfield bus down to Kenmore Square. It was a safe and easy ride to get there.

———

BILL NOWLIN: My father worked at Fenway for two years in the late 1930s, selling hot dogs to raise money to go to the New York World's Fair in 1939. He remembers meeting Doc Cramer and Jimmie Foxx, chatting with them before the game.

They had the same system they have today—they kept a record of the number of hot dogs you check out from the commissary. Then you brought back the money. They didn't count buns. For lunch, my father used to put mustard on a hot dog bun—that was what they called a Depression sandwich.

———

On May 3, 1938, Lefty Grove defeated the Tigers 4–3 in 10 innings for the first of a record 20 consecutive victories at Fenway Park.

Jimmie Foxx flexed his muscles in the nightcap of a doubleheader against the Indians on August 23, slamming a grand slammer in the ninth inning to seal the Sox win. He wound up with 6 RBIs in the game.

On September 7, Joe Cronin Day, Jimmie Foxx did what he did best—fired up the Red Sox offense, powering it to an 11–4 win over the Yankees. He collected 8 RBIs on 3 hits, including a pair of homers—all in just 5½ innings; the game was called on account of rain. Lou Gehrig slapped a pair of singles and collected two stolen bases.

Three days later, Jimmie Foxx hit two home runs for the ninth time in the '38 season. He now had 35 homers at home—the most ever hit at Fenway.

And on October 1, Double X was at it again, setting a Boston Red Sox home-run record by hitting his 49th and 50th home runs of the season in a 9–2 win over the Yankees.

Home attendance at Fenway in 1938 was 646,459—the best for any season in the 1930s. The Sox finished in second place, 9½ games out of the top rung. Yawkey, Collins, Foxx, Cronin, and company were clicking.

The final year of the 1930s saw five future Hall of Famers on the Red Sox roster: Joe Cronin, Jimmie Foxx, Lefty Grove, Bobby Doerr, and a skinny outfielder from San Diego. He had heard about the hitting prowess of Jimmie Foxx and responded, "Wait'll Foxx sees me hit."

The first Fenway Park game appearance of Ted Williams took place on April 16, 1939, in a City Series exhibition game against the Boston Bees (as the Braves were then known). The Splendid Splinter stroked his first single at Fenway; his team won, 1–0.

On April 21, 1939, Ted Williams played his first official game at Fenway, scoring the first run for Boston against the A's on a Frankie Hayes passed ball. The Sox rolled to a 9–2 win. The tempestuous and talented Ted would go on to have at least one hit in every Opening Day game he appeared in.

Two days later Williams homered into the right-field bleachers at Fenway Park, a shot landing 420 feet from home plate. (Before the season was over, he would smash six more into the same area.) He also had a double and two singles in that game. He would have had five hits, but the A's left fielder, Bob Johnson, snared his line drive against the wall.

That was how the "Kid" began, and he never let up. On September 19, in a 6–2 Red Sox triumph over the White Sox at Fenway, Williams homered off Thornton Lee, one of the 31 dingers he would slam in his rookie season.

"From the first day I set foot in Fenway Park," Williams said, "I wanted to show everyone that I was the kind of hitter who belonged with the best in the game—names like Foxx, DiMaggio, and Greenberg."

CHARLIE WAGNER: My second year on the Red Sox we got Ted Williams. One day, Lefty Grove, Jimmie Foxx, and I were sitting at our lockers and Ted comes in bellowing, "Okay, who doesn't smoke, doesn't drink, doesn't chase girls, and goes to bed early?"

Manager Joe Cronin said, "Ted, Wagner's your man." Actually, the Boston writers hung the name "Broadway" on me. People said it was because of the stylish way I dressed. But I wasn't a rowdy.

Ted and I became very good friends. I lived with him, and it was a joy. He got up early, and I got up early. We didn't drink or smoke. No nightclubs, none of that stuff. We were good roommates.

We lived at the Sheraton Hotel on Bay State Road. Ted could look out the window early in the morning and see which way the wind would be blowing at Fenway Park. Sometimes he would say, "Do you see that wind blowing straight in from right field? You lucky pitchers!"

———————————

JAMES "JIMMIE" GREENE: I started to go to Fenway Park around the late '30s. I lived in Lawrence, Massachusetts, and would take the train in to Boston. The Red Sox wouldn't sell out very often, so it was always easy to get a ticket. They were very reasonably priced. I usually sat behind first base or somewhere out in left field with my friends or my brother. I would just be staring at Ted Williams, gaping at him like he was some kind of god.

The lineup was Jimmie Foxx at first. I think I got the idea for writing my name J-I-M-M-I-E because of him. Later I'd see Jimmie Piersall's name written that way, sometimes.

Joe Cronin was the manager and also still playing short. Joe Tabor was on third base, and the outfield was Ted Williams, Dom DiMaggio, and Doc Cramer.

Old "Big Mose," Lefty Grove, would pitch once a week, usually on a Sunday. I don't remember catchers all that well, but I do remember Moe Berg, the third-string catcher, who was often in the bullpen. He spoke seven languages, and people joked that he couldn't hit in any of them.

———————————

Princeton graduate Moe Berg actually spoke a dozen languages, including Japanese and Sanskrit. The joke was that from time to time he'd get the attention of players in the bullpen by giving a lecture on the nineteenth-century Russian novel—in English.

———————————

JAMES "JIMMIE" GREENE: I remember I was with my father one day watching a game against the Yankees. A ball was hit right to Jimmie Foxx, and it went through his legs out into right field. Everyone started booing him. My father turned to me and said, "How quickly they forget."

We quickly found out where players parked their cars and would get there early so we could get autographs. Ted Williams used to put on such a show for us. He'd choreograph the whole thing, line us up, and say, "Now you girls get in front. Tall kids get in the back." He looked very Californian, always in a sport coat. He never wore a tie.

I also remember how wild Jim Tabor was, often throwing the ball right over the first baseman's head. We used to joke about taking your life in your hands when you sat behind first base.

Fenway was such a wonderful place to be. We always went early, saw batting practice. We would go down by the Red Sox dugout and hand out autograph books to whoever would take them and a player would say, "Hey, give me your autograph book, I'll get you some more autographs."

Then he'd go into the dugout and (God knows he may have been writing all of the names himself) he'd come back with a whole bunch of wonderful names for us.

———————————

No one who came to Fenway in the thirties or who followed the sporting scene would forget what the Red Sox accomplished during that decade. From a debt-ridden team with no stars, a decaying hulk of a ballpark, and underwhelming attendance, a miraculous transformation took place.

Tom Yawkey's charges had put the world of baseball on alert: the 1940s were going to be a special time for the "Old Towne Team."

ABOVE: Sox players walking off of the field
OPPOSITE: Red Sox players in clubhouse, 1932
(L to R) Ed Bull Durham, Wiley Moore, Bob Kline, and Paul Ivy Andrews

—FORTIES—

STARS GALORE
BUT NO CIGAR

DOM DIMAGGIO: The first time I walked into Fenway Park was a day in April 1940. It was before the season; there was ice on the field. Coming from California, it was a bit of a shock to me. I was wondering how we were going to start on time.

RED SOX YEAR BY YEAR 1940 – 1949	YEAR	WON	LOST	PCT.	GB	ATTENDANCE
	1949	96	58	.623	1.0	1,596,650
	1948	96	59	.619	1.0	1,558,798
	1947	83	71	.539	14.0	1,427,315
	1946	104	50	.675	—	1,416,944
	1945	71	83	.461	17.5	603,794
	1944	77	77	.500	12.0	506,975
	1943	68	84	.447	29.0	358,275
	1942	93	59	.612	9.0	730,340
	1941	84	70	.545	17.0	718,497
	1940	82	72	.532	8.0	716,234

Tom Yawkey was energetically still calling the shots as owner, and Joe Cronin as player and manager was very much on the scene. A sense of optimism pervaded Fenway Park as the new decade got under way. The Great Depression was a memory. It was a time of new beginnings.

New players such as Dom DiMaggio and construction changes were everywhere. Perhaps the most important change was one made to accommodate Ted Williams. As a rookie in 1939, he had hammered what many deemed a disappointing (for him) 31 home runs.

JON MILLER: "Geez," they said, "we have this great left-handed hitter and he keeps losing home runs out there so we'll pull the bullpens in and make it a little easier for him." They called the area Williamsburg after Louisburg Square in Beacon Hill, a play on that phrase.

Bullpens were moved from the foul lines to the front of the stands in center, creating the center-field triangle. The distance to the right-center wall was trimmed from 405 feet to just over 380 feet.

"With the brought-in fence," Williams remembered, "I was supposed to hit 75 home runs in 1940. I thought I hit pretty good, .344, but I didn't hit the home runs I did before. I got a lot of catcalls. I got a little sour on everything and everybody."

BOBBY DOERR: Ted and I became close friends. We were around the same age; we both liked to go to movies and fish and talk fishing. But the thing Ted especially liked was to talk baseball.

Ted was one of the first hitters to go to light bats. He had a batch of 32-ouncers brought to Fenway.

Some told him, "Ted, you can't get good wood with 32-ounce bats."

Ted's comeback was, "What good is wood if you can't handle it?"

He wanted control of the bat to where he could hit the ball on the fat part. He felt he couldn't do that with a heavier bat even though he was as quick and strong as anybody. But he still went from a 34- or 35-ounce bat to a 32-ounce bat. Now mostly all bats are light, with small handles. Ted brought them into baseball.

The man they would call the "Thumper" saw his home run total drop from 31 in 1939 to 23 in 1940. But Williams was much more than a home-run hitter. He was an all-around athlete, and that was showcased on August 24, when he yielded only one run and three hits in a mop-up two-inning pitching stint as the Sox lost, 12–11, to the Tigers.

SAM MELE: I was going to New York University. My coach, Bill McCarthy, used to drive me up to Fenway Park to work out for Red Sox scout Neil Mahoney. One day, I get in the batting cage. Pitching to me was Herb Pennock, who had been one of the great pitchers in history.

After a few warm-up pitches he says, "Are you ready now?"

I say, "Yeah." Now he throws a screwball, a changeup. Boy, I had a tough time.

They tell me to take five swings. I took four, and I did not swing at the fifth pitch.

"Why didn't you swing at that pitch?" a voice behind the cage says.

"Well, it was kind of low."

"It was, but it was over the plate," the voice says.

The voice belonged to Ted Williams. He called me over and started talking to me about hitting. "You move your feet too far away from the plate," he said. "You got to be able to cover the whole plate when you're batting." I never forgot that.

Throughout the 1941 season, the talk all over Boston was about Ted Williams, who would be the last batter to hit .400.

"Number 9 did that?"

"That's where number 9 hit one."

"He got another hit today, number 9."

It was Theodore Samuel Williams they were talking about—number 9, .406 batting average in 1941.

On May 12 Lefty Grove won the battle of the "lefties," defeating Lefty Gomez and the Yankees, 6–4, for his 20th straight win at Fenway Park and his 295th career victory. A two-run homer by Jimmie Foxx was the Sox victory cushion. Thirteen days later, Grove gave up a single to Joe DiMaggio, giving him the distinction of being the only pitcher to be a part of DiMag's 56-game hitting streak and Babe Ruth's 60-home-run season 14 years before.

On June 21, Lefty Grove finally lost at Fenway after 20 consecutive wins. The Browns pounded him and the Red Sox, 13–9. Grove's streak had begun on May 3, 1938, and lasted through May 12, 1941. He would end the season with a record of 55–17 from 1934 to 1941; his .764 winning percentage remains the highest ever for a lefty at Fenway.

BOO FERRISS: After my sophomore year at Mississippi State University in '41, the Red Sox got me placed in the Northern League, in Vermont. My manager there was Bill Barrett, a former major leaguer and a Red Sox scout. We had an open day. He took me and two players from the University of Oklahoma to our first big-league ball game.

Bill Barrett says, "They're playing the Cleveland Indians. I'll take you in and you can meet the great Red Sox players."

PAGE 64: Boys in the stands hang out with three of their heroes
OPPOSITE: "Splendid Splinter" Ted Williams and the "Yankee Clipper" Joe DiMaggio talking baseball on August 18, 1942

We drove down in Mr. Barrett's car. When we first saw Fenway Park, we were all pretty bug-eyed, I'll tell you that. We were just on cloud nine, you might say — three Southern boys. Then Bill Barrett told us that Lefty Grove was going for his 300th career win that day, July 25.

We walked in the clubhouse and Johnny Orlando, the clubhouse guy, told us to be quiet. We learned that Lefty Grove, who was on the downside of his great career, was in the trainer's room. He always took a little nap before the ball game. "He better not be disturbed or he'll tear up the clubhouse," Orlando said.

So we had to tiptoe by the training room, and my gosh we got to meet Ted Williams, Bobby Doerr, Dom DiMaggio, Jimmie Foxx, Charlie Wagner, and Joe Cronin, the manager, of course.

We shook hands with Red Sox players. Bill Barrett, he knew them all. I didn't think to ask for autographs. Getting an autograph wasn't a big thing back in those days. But I still have the program. It cost five cents.

Manager Joe Cronin told Grove before the game, "Pop, this is a nine-inning game. I'm not coming out to get you." Grove was behind, 6–4, in the seventh inning, tied in the eighth at 6–6. Then Jimmie Foxx hit a three-run homer. Grove had given up 12 hits but he had his 300th and final win.

BOO FERRISS: He struggled, but he made it. We saw it all, sitting in box seats behind the dugout and had royal treatment. An unforgettable day, for sure, for three Southern boys. The ballpark was so compact with seats right down close to the field. The Wall was out there, but it wasn't painted green then. Some called it the Iron Monster.

That was my introduction to Fenway. I had a dream that maybe someday I might be back.

We drove back home, and the next day we were playing baseball.

MONSIGNOR THOMAS J. DALY: I was 14 years old in 1941 when I started working as a [turnstile] boy at Fenway for $1.50 a day. It was a great job. About the second inning or third inning you were free for the rest of the time, and you could watch the ball game. And if there was a doubleheader then you really had a good day for yourself.

Not too many people attempted to sneak into Fenway. There was, however, a note on the bulletin board that I still remember. "Sir, last week I sneaked into the ball game and I'm sending money to pay for the ticket that I didn't buy." The writer was anonymous, of course.

There was no local TV, and radio was WAAB, with Jim Britt and Tom Hussey. All games were in the daylight, and lots of children were on hand. Prices of admission for the grandstands were $1.10, bleachers 55 cents, a reserved seat in the grandstand $1.40, and tickets for the box seats were $3.60. It was a pretty quiet environment. The only music was at the beginning of the ball game, when everybody stood for the national anthem. And there was just the manual scoreboard.

DOM DIMAGGIO: Fenway Park was a quiet place then, but the atmosphere at Fenway heightened a great deal when the Red Sox and Yankees played. I felt that and enjoyed it.

In 1941, when my brother Joe had the hitting streak going, Ted would be talking to the guy in the scoreboard and the guy would keep him posted when Joe got a hit. You couldn't do that at any other park.

There were times at Fenway when Joe would be coming in from center field and I would be coming out. I said very little to him on those

occasions. What the hell was I going to do, stop in center field and have a conversation?

JOHNNY PESKY: Manager Joe Cronin let me play. That was how it all started in 1942 when we went up against the old Boston Braves, an exhibition City Series, one game at Fenway and one at Braves Field.

I made four errors in the exhibition game and felt just terrible about it. I thought Cronin was going to send me down to either Scranton or Louisville. But he didn't say anything to me.

The first time I saw Fenway Park, it was dark and dreary. I was mainly concerned about playing as well as I could and keeping warm.

Opening Day was Tuesday, April 14. I was 22 years old. I came up the runway, up the three steps, and looked out from the dugout. It was an old park even then. But it was very well kept, clean and nice. And right in the middle of the city. I thought it was beautiful.

We lived on Bay State Road, just across from Kenmore Square, and could walk across to the ballpark. I batted leadoff ahead of Dom and Ted.

Ted Williams started his season off against Philadelphia, slashing a three-run first-inning homer, rapping two more hits, and collecting five RBIs, keying Boston's 8–3 romp. He started that way and never stopped.

On May 2, for the second straight game, the Splendid Splinter smashed a ninth-inning home run, this time off Eldon Auker, to give the Red Sox a 10–10 tie with the visiting St. Louis Browns. Bobby Doerr's RBI double won it, 11–10. Pesky pulled off a hidden-ball trick in the ninth, but it was for naught, as Doerr, unaware of the ruse, called time-out before the play. Auker went the distance, allowing 17 hits in the loss.

JOHNNY PESKY: Ted and I lockered next to one another. We always talked baseball. When you're talking to the greatest hitter, it was like talking to the Holy Father.

He said, "Johnny, you've got to hit strikes. Don't be afraid to take a pitch. And you've got to keep that bat on the level." He'd stand up and show me his approach to hitting. And it stayed with me.

————————

It sure stayed with rookie Johnny Pesky as he showcased his lessons on June 13, going five-for-five with a double in a 6–5 win over the Tigers.

————————

JOHNNY PESKY: I hung on Ted and Dominic's [DiMaggio] coattails. At shortstop I made sure I got in front of every ball and tried to catch or knock it down.

————————

Playing without Williams and Doerr in the starting lineup on July 19, the Red Sox lost two to the Indians, 10–7 in 12 innings in the first game of a doubleheader, and 4–0 in seven innings in the second game, called because of darkness. Night baseball at Fenway Park belonged to the future.

The cloud of a world at war hung over Fenway Park throughout the 1942 season, but it was most powerfully felt during the final game, on September 27, the last game for Ted Williams, Johnny Pesky, Dom DiMaggio, and others before they left for active duty.

A crowd of 26,166, including 4,293 youngsters who gained free admission by bringing 29,000 pounds of scrap metal, saw Tex Hughson scatter 11 hits for a 7–6 win over the Yankees. Finishing the game and the season at .356, Ted Williams copped his second straight batting title. Pesky, who had learned his lessons well from a master, was runner-up for the batting championship, hitting .331.

————————

JOHNNY PESKY: I was sitting in the clubhouse with Ted Williams after the game ended when I got a note telling me to go up and see general manager Eddie Collins.

"Well, go up and see what he wants and then come down and we'll go out to eat," Ted said.

So I took a shower, got dressed, and went upstairs. I was scared. I didn't know what he wanted.

"I hope this war don't last too long because we have a relatively young ball club coming on, which can get better down the road," he said. Then he handed me an envelope. "Mr. Yawkey wanted me to give you this."

I waited until I got back to the clubhouse before I opened it. Inside was a check for five grand. I sent it to my parents; it would be the down payment for a house.

————————

With the United States at war, 31 members of the Red Sox organization donated blood as the 1943 season got under way. On July 12, 1943, Babe Ruth managed a service all-star team that pounded out a 9–8 exhibition victory over the Braves as part of Boston mayor Maurice J. Tobin's annual charity Field Day program. The service all-stars put on a good show for the 12,000 fans at Fenway Park. Before the game, Ted Williams and the 48-year-old Ruth were matched up in a home-run-hitting contest. "Teddy Ball Game" parked three balls in the right-field bleachers. Ruth,

bothered by an aching knee, had to be coaxed by the crowd to hit. He swung and flew out to right field. It was to be his final appearance at Fenway in a baseball uniform.

Managing and pinch-hitting Joe Cronin did all he could to keep his Red Sox in the race. He even set an American League record that season with five pinch-hit homers.

On September 12 the first-place Yankees mathematically knocked the Sox out of pennant contention, sweeping a double bill and putting an exclamation point on a five-game sweep at Fenway.

The Red Sox had finished next to last in attendance in the American League in 1943, drawing just 358,275, and next to last in the standings, with a 68–84 record.

ABOVE: Look out! Going for a foul ball.

In 1944 the Bosox played .500 baseball, winning 77 games and losing as many, and drew 506,975, to finish next to last in attendance again. Many stars were away in the armed forces, and the team had to make do with players like Mike Ryba, 41, Bob Johnson, 38, Joe Cronin, 37, and others who were younger but not suitable material for a big-league team.

BISHOP JOHN D'ARCY: During the war, there was a large military presence at Fenway; I think the sailors and soldiers got in for free. I began going by myself around that time when I was 12 years old or so. There was a streetcar that ran from Watertown, by Braves Field, to Kenmore Square in town, and for a nickel (later a dime) you could take that streetcar to Fenway Park.

MONSIGNOR THOMAS J. DALY: I was an office boy in the front office from 1942 until 1946, the year after the war ended. I worked from 10 in the morning until the conclusion of the game for $2.50 a game. For a doubleheader I got $3.75. Cash.

I met Tom Yawkey. To an office boy he was rather formidable, of course. He would come every day to the ball game and speak with Mr. Edward Collins, the vice president/general manager. Mr. Yawkey was rather relaxed in the way he dressed—highly informal, I would say. Mr. Collins always dressed in a very formal style, a suit and tie. He was rather sedate and superstitious. He didn't like people hanging around the ticker tape when the club was away. God help you if you were there and the opposing team got a home run or something. I learned to avoid trouble and stay away from the machine.

Bobby Doerr was very popular with all the girls. I can remember one Ladies' Day when they all crowded around him. "Oh, Bobby, we could kiss you," they cried.

His wife, Monica, was there. "No, you won't," she said.

Fenway Green was the color they used in the ballpark. It came from a paint company in Malden. There was a commotion when they announced that they weren't going to produce that paint anymore, that green. So Mr. Yawkey promptly bought the company. That made sure that that famous green would continue.

I worked for the most part in the business office. Many days I was sent to an office downtown at Filene's Department Store, second floor. I would leave Fenway at about 1:30 and pick up tickets or whatnot and deliver things, too.

Once the game started, I was pretty much free and would sit next to the front office in the grandstand and watch the game. On weekends I was able to sit up in the press box.

One of my duties was to be of help to special players, like making sure that they got into a cab near the end of a game and whatnot. I remember once late in a game with the New York Yankees, I was told to go down and see Mr. DiMaggio—Joe DiMaggio, that is—and make sure he had no problems getting into a cab. He was very popular, and people would mob him, looking for autographs.

There he was, wearing a blue pinstriped suit with a white shirt, red tie, smoking a cigarette. I was rather honored to be in his presence.

"What are you doing to do when you grow up, kid?" he asked.

"Well," I said, "maybe I can do something in baseball, be a player or work in the front office."

Joe DiMaggio shook his head. "No, don't do that. Whatever you do, do something that helps other people."

A kid 14 years of age hearing those words from the great DiMaggio was quite an experience. I never forgot his words. In fact, I think they inspired me to go into the semi-nary to study for the priesthood.

BILL SUMMERS JR. I grew up in the small town of Upton, Massachusetts. My father, Bill Summers Sr., a big man who had played tackle for the champion Green Bay Packers in the early 1930s, was a famous major league umpire for 28 years. When he worked at Fenway, all our family members were able to see the games.

Meeting Babe Ruth, who was visiting the Red Sox dugout at Fenway when I was ten years old was memorable. He put his hand on my head and said, "Nice to know you, kid."

I spent time in the umpires' room watching and talking with my dad and the umpires. I saw clubhouse boy Johnny Orlando there. If the umpires needed anything, he took care of them. There was a bucket of mud, they called it. The umpire behind the plate had the job to make sure the balls were all rubbed up.

Wheaties used to give a case to a player for every home run hit. Well, Hank Greenberg was playing in Fenway and he had hit a couple of home runs. After the game he said, "What am I going to do with these?" My father told him, "I got eight kids." We were eating Wheaties for a long time.

My father was friendly with Yawkey. He was friends with Williams, too, who used to call him "Old Bill."

PAGE 70–71: Ted Williams makes his pitching debut against the Tigers on August 24, 1940. The Sox lose, 12–1.
OPPOSITE: Lefty Grove warming up to pitch

DAVE HUTCHINSON: I remember a tall, skinny kid who batted from the left side. You'd stay at the ballpark regardless of what the score was as long as this man was in the lineup.

You could buy a 25-cent scorecard and get there early and stand down almost on the field and ask for autographs. And if you were lucky you could get one from the tall, skinny kid. You would sometimes come out of the ballpark with maybe 20 autographs.

EDDIE YOST: I was 17 years old in 1944 and playing baseball at NYU. The coach there had an affiliation with the Red Sox. They invited me to spend two weeks at a home stand at Fenway. Every morning I worked out with Hugh Duffy, the old-timer, who hit .438, the highest percentage of any baseball player ever. Then after the major leaguers were done, I'd take infield practice. For a kid, the park, the players, the whole thing was a kick.

The fact that able-bodied performers were in short supply during the war years was underscored by an incident involving rookie pitcher Rex Cecil. The 27-year-old flew from San Diego to Boston on August 13, 1944. Arriving at Fenway—he had never even seen a big-league park, let alone played in one—he was given a uniform and the news that he had better be ready. With the score 6–6, Cecil was pressed into action in the tenth inning against the St. Louis Browns. Not only did he pitch the tenth, he also was on the mound in the eleventh, twelfth, and thirteenth. A Bobby Doerr homer in the bottom of the thirteenth won the game for Boston, and Cecil. With a record of 4–5 in 1944 and 2–5 in 1945, Rex Cecil then called it a career as a major leaguer.

At their major league baseball meeting in February 1945, team owners agreed to cancel the All-Star Game scheduled for July 10 at Fenway Park. The demands of a world at war were center stage.

Each season, the Red Sox had routinely received a waiver from the Boston City Council, permitting them to play Sunday baseball. Now Councilman Isadore Muchnick, who represented the Mattapan section of Boston, teamed with African-American journalist Wendell Smith. They had an offer for Tom Yawkey that they knew he could not refuse. A trade, of sorts.

For the Bosox to keep the long-held waiver going, the team would have to allow three black baseball prospects to try out at Fenway Park.

Yawkey, as the story was reported later, reluctantly agreed to the tryouts of Jackie Robinson, Marvin Williams, and Sam Jethroe but only on the condition that decisions about them would be the province of his baseball people.

Black ballplayers from the Negro Leagues from time to time had played at Fenway when the Red Sox were on the road. The color barrier was firmly in effect at this time, but owners thought nothing of picking up some spare change through this business arrangement. Now they would have the chance to break the big club's color line at Fenway Park, or so was the understanding.

April 16, 1945, began damp and drizzly. At about 10:00 A.M. Muchnick and Smith were in the stands watching as the tryouts were getting under way. Just back from army service in World War II, Jackie Robinson was set to play with the Kansas City Monarchs in the Negro American League that season. Marvin Williams was a member of the Philadelphia Stars of the Negro National League. Sam Jethroe was an outfielder for the Cleveland Buckeyes of the Negro American League.

Red Sox manager Joe Cronin sat in the stands, according to one account, "stone-faced." Eddie Collins, the general manager, reportedly was unable to attend the tryout "because of a previous engagement."

Near the end of their one-hour workout, according to Clifford Keane, a reporter for the *Boston Globe,* someone called out, "Get those niggers off the field!"

Boston Red Sox immortal and Coach Hugh Duffy, 78, was one of those who conducted the workouts. Later that year he would be inducted into the Baseball Hall of Fame. "You boys look like pretty good players," he was quoted as saying. "I hope you enjoyed the workout." Later he remarked, "After one workout, it was not possible to judge their ability."

Later, Robinson said, "It was April 1945. Nobody was serious about black players in the majors, except maybe for a few politicians."

According to United Press International, Jethroe and Williams "seemed tense and both their hitting and fielding suffered."

According to the Red Sox front office, the players were not ready for the majors and would not be comfortable playing for the team's Triple-A affiliate in Louisville, Kentucky.

According to Jethroe, the entire experience was "a sham." The Red Sox front office would never contact the players.

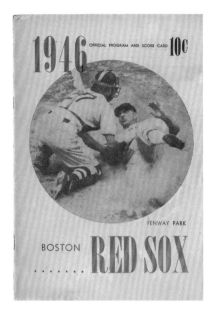

But there was a need for players with the abilities of Jethroe, Robinson, and Williams. As the 1945 baseball season began and the war still raged, major league rosters were stocked with not-quite-ready-for-prime-time players, a few underage ones, and quite a few who were long in the tooth. But the game went on at Fenway Park in 1945 and other big-league venues, as it had always gone on, with white players only.

In place of the canceled All-Star Game, seven interleague games were played on July 9 and 10 for war charity during the break in the major league baseball schedule. On July 9 at Fenway, the Red Sox—in the only day game of the series—ripped the Braves, 8–1. The game featured brother against brother: Jack Tobin of the Red Sox vs. Jim of the Braves. Jack touched up his pitcher brother for a single. Rookie pitching sensation Boo Ferriss had planned to pitch both right- and left-handed but changed his mind.

On the 22nd of July, Boo got his 17th win, 3–2, over the Browns, before a crowd of 34,810—one of the largest crowds of that era. Thousands more were turned away.

BOO FERRISS: My first season, 1945, I didn't have a car. I hardly had a nickel in my pocket. I had a room at a rooming house five blocks from the park overlooking the Charles River. I paid $7.00 a week for that room. Some of the hockey players lived there. I never crossed paths with them. I walked to Fenway Park every day through Kenmore Square. And before games I signed and signed autographs.

I loved pitching at Fenway. The closeness of the Wall didn't bother me. I always thought the Wall could help you as much as hurt you. Sometimes a pop fly would go out. But there's no doubt a lot of times line drives would be hit high up on that wall that in other parks would be a home run where in Fenway they were singles, maybe doubles.

MICHAEL DUKAKIS: I was at a Yankee–Red Sox game when I was in the eighth grade. This was our big excursion toward the end of the school year. We had all saved up our pennies to take the bus and go down there. It was probably 50 cents admission at the time in the grandstand.

Boo Ferriss was the great young pitching star then. Still the Yankees beat him, 14–1. I can still remember the yellow 13 in the scoreboard—13 runs in one inning.

BOO FERRISS: My first-year salary was $700 a month. Since I was there five months in '45, I got $3,500.

After the season was over, Mr. Yawkey called me into his office. I wasn't nervous. He was an easy man to talk to. He handed me a check—a bonus—$10,000.

I'd thought I had robbed Fort Knox. I took the check to the bank back in my hometown in Mississippi, where I grew up.

The season of 1945 may have been wonderful for Boo Ferriss, but not for the Red Sox. Once again they finished in the lower depths in the standings and in attendance—seventh place in an eight-team league, 603,794 at home, next to last in the American League.

DICK FLAVIN: When my father took me to my first game at Fenway, I was a little kid and identified with Eddie Lake, a little shortstop. In 1946, I found out that Lake was traded and they gave his job to someone else who came back from the Armed Forces. I asked, "Who the hell is this Pesky guy?"

My favorite player was Dom DiMaggio. I was the only kid in my grade in Marymount School in Quincy who had to wear glasses. Dom, I believe, in 1946 was the only position player in the American League who wore glasses. Early on, Dom had his own rosin bag, which he kept in his back pocket. Up at bat he sometimes stepped out for a few seconds and used that bag. He claimed that his hands tended to get sweaty squeezing the bat.

Dom also stood in the outfield with his left shoulder toward home plate, facing left field. "You react more quickly to the at-bat if you're facing sideways to the pitcher than if you're head on," he said. He believed he saw the ball better and he got a better jump on it. I think he may have shaded a little bit over to help Ted Williams, but I don't think that Ted was that bad an outfielder. Ted used to say Dom was the smartest outfielder in baseball. Every time a ball was hit to left center he'd yell, "You take it, Dommie."

The first time I saw Dom slide into second base, he did a pop-up slide. "My God," I thought. "It's amazing."

For the 1946 season, upper-deck seats were installed at Fenway. The war was over, and a spirit of optimism was sweeping the nation and Red Sox players. Fans streamed into Fenway into the Back Bay ballpark in numbers that had not been seen in years.

___

JOHNNY PESKY: Coming back from the navy in 1946, I was impressed with how beautiful the ballpark still was. Mr. Yawkey came down and talked to us. He said he felt good about the team. He loved Ted Williams, Dom DiMaggio, and Bobby Doerr. He was very nice to me, too.

Fenway Park was my comfort zone. Very homey.

Fans were close, liking their ball. After the war, we had great crowds. The club now got going pretty good. There was much interest in Red Sox baseball and being in Fenway Park.

___

On April 14, 1946, the home team ripped their crosstown rival Braves, 19–5, before a Fenway crowd of 33,279, the highest attendance in the history of the City Series.

WALTER MEARS: I learned to hate the Yankees in the summer of '46. I was 11 years old, and my dad took me to Fenway. It was my first major league game. We sat a few rows behind the Red Sox dugout, and Joe Dobson beat Randy Gumpert of New York. The crowd around us was growling at the New Yorkers between cheers for Boston. I joined in and became a lifetime Sox fan.

___

ABOVE: Full-color field view of the field of play and distinctive billboards
OPPOSITE: Infield view from the intimate confines of Fenway

The Sox on June 9 took two from Detroit, running their winning streak to 11 games. Ted Williams homered in both games. One shot, off Fred Hutchinson, landed in the right-field bleachers in the 30th row, breaking the straw hat of Joseph A. Boucher, a construction engineer from Albany, New York.

"How far away must one sit to be safe in this park?" asked Boucher. "They say it bounced a dozen rows higher. But after it hit my head I was no longer interested. The sun was right in our eyes. All we could do was duck. I'm glad I didn't stand up."

Judged to have traveled 502 feet, the home run was commemorated by having the seat the ball landed in—Section 42, row 37, seat 21—painted red.

Exactly one month later, for the first time, the All-Star Game was staged at Fenway. Ted Williams once again would be the star of stars. Additional seating that was constructed for the 200 or so members of the press would ultimately become Fenway's roof box seats.

JOHN HOLWAY: Tickets for the game had been sold out for a month. Scalpers were getting as much as $10 apiece. One fan had sent a check for three tickets and received 100 in the mail. He returned them and was rewarded with a season pass.

BOBBY DOERR: It was right after the war had ended, so that made the game special and patriotic.

"I don't think I've ever seen a more festive occasion," said All-Star Frank McCormick, of the Philadelphia Phillies. "Guys who hadn't seen one another in years were crossing back and forth before the game to shake hands and visit."

BOO FERRISS: Eight Red Sox players were on that American League team. Me, Dom DiMaggio, Bobby Doerr, Rudy York, Hal Wagner, Mickey Harris, Johnny Pesky, and of course, Ted.

A bomber pilot during the war, Ted Williams was in his prime of primes—leading the league in batting average, home runs, and RBIs.

BOO FERRISS: Both clubhouses back in those days were side by side. We all came down the same steps by the first tunnel on the first-base side of the Red Sox dugout. I was in the bullpen in the first inning when Bob Feller, who started for us, got in trouble. I couldn't believe that they had me warming up to maybe replace Feller. But he pitched his way out of it and went on to pitch three innings. So I didn't get in the game; they didn't use but three pitchers that day. Still that didn't bother me; I was just thrilled to be there.

BOBBY DOERR: I truly wanted to play in that game, even though a ball took a bad hop and peeled my right thumb nail off days before. I batted the first time. I don't think I hit the second time.

LEFT: 1946 team picture
OPPOSITE: AL Championship flag unfurled, 1946

JOHN HOLWAY: My mother and I were sitting in the right-field stands, second row, near the bull-pen. Finally, it was the moment most awaited. Ted Williams came up in the eighth against Truett (Rip) Sewell, famous for the "eephus pitch"—a high, arching lob. He had developed it after a hunting injury to his leg.

Williams had knelt in the on-deck circle, studying Sewell as he pitched to Vern Stephens.

————————

BOB ALLGAIER: The place went mad when Williams came up against Sewell. I was selling concessions in the grandstand. I could tell the fans wanted that eephus pitch so bad.

JOHN HOLWAY: Williams got his shot at the pitch with the score 9–0 American League and two men on in the eighth.

Ted hesitated on the first blooper, as if deciding what to do. He took a late cut and fouled it on a line into the third-base dugout. National League players scattered.

Sewell lobbed one outside for a ball. Then Rip threw a fastball. It surprised Williams. The count was one ball and two strikes.

Then Sewell launched another blooper. It was a good one, dropping right down the chute.

Actually, it was going to fall short. Ted wrote later that Yankee catcher Bill Dickey had told him to run up into the ball to generate his own power, but photographs show that the pitch was short, and Ted had to hop forward.

Taking two little Fred Astaire dance steps into it, Williams whipped an uppercut golf swing. Sewell gasped.

————————

BOB ALLGAIER: Like launching a missile, it went high up in the air. Everyone went berserk. As the ball went up, almost straight toward me, I groaned, "Pop-up." But it kept rising, like a short high fly. Still it kept carrying. Right fielder Enos Slaughter backtracked until his back was against the bullpen wall, and the ball came to earth behind him just to our right.

Years later Rip Sewell always insisted that "in a regular game" the home run wouldn't have counted, that Williams was that far out of the batter's box. "But I'm glad he hit it; otherwise no one would remember me."

————————

Rapping out two singles, two home runs, and collecting five RBIs, Williams showed off his offensive repertoire. Bob Feller was credited with the win in the American League 12–0 rout.

————————

BOB ALLGAIER: I worked at Fenway from 1946 to 1950, starting when I was 15 years old. Being a little tall for my age, I got a job. My home was in Dedham; I'd hitchhike to and from work.

There were about 50 to 75 of us, high school kids, primarily. We wore white uniforms, white pants, long white jackets. I was what they'd call a "hustler" or today a "vendor" selling in the stands.

When we first got to the park, we had to bag peanuts. A gentleman by the name of Doc Kline had a scorecard stand in the bleachers. He roasted the peanuts and put them out into a big wicker basket. It took three fellows to bag the peanuts—one to open the bag, one to

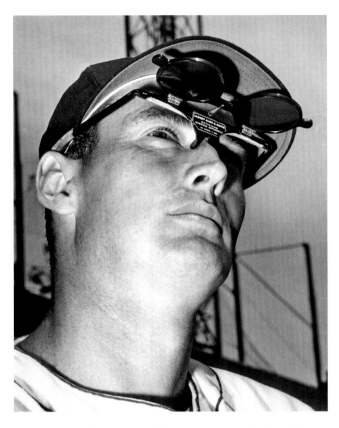

put the scoop of peanuts in, and the other to twist the bag.

They had a seniority system. Anybody new sold the worst possible thing, which was Moxie Tonic. It was heavy work: 25 bottles of Moxie Tonic in a metal container at 10 cents apiece. And you had to open the bottle, pour it in the cup, and pass it in; 10 percent commission, or a penny a bottle.

You would progress to selling souvenirs and then better items, such as Hood's Three Flavored Ice Cream with a little wooden spoon. That was 10 or 15 cents, a penny and a half made per sale. Hot dogs were steamed in a little container with hot water at the bottom. You had a roll, a piece of wax paper, Gulden's

ABOVE: Ted Williams on April 14, 1947, with his sunglasses up, getting set for the next day's opening of season.
OPPOSITE: At the 1946 All-Star Game. Immortals sharing the moment (L to R) Joe Wood, Cy Young, Lefty Grove, Walter Johnson

Mustard, and then a spoon or a stick to put the mustard on. Most usually used a finger to put the mustard on.

Special servicemen were out in right field where it hooks around after the Pesky Pole. Several sections beyond that area were where gamblers sat. We sold a lot of Moxie Tonic there. Very bitter.

We sold beer, but fans could only drink it at the concession stand or the back of the top row of seats. No beer was allowed in the stands.

I progressed to the cigar basket, a stationary spot before the game started. I sold scorecards, peanuts, cigarettes, cigars, gum, candy, and pencils. We sold a lot of 10-cent scorecards and made a penny apiece. Peanuts were also 10 cents. Cigarettes might have been a quarter a pack. Dexter Cigars or JA Cigars were 15 cents each. I sold stuff individually out of the cigar basket. I might have five cartons of cigarettes: Lucky Strikes, Camels, Philip Morris, Chesterfield.

Mrs. Johnny Pesky used to sit with Bobby Doerr's wife, watching the ball game near my station. We thought Mrs. Pesky was great. I really had a boy's crush on her. She was about five-five, with short, curly hair. Not to be disrespectful, but we used to say, "Man, she was stacked." She was very, very pretty.

One day she came over and asked me for a package of Chesterfields. I was out. I told her I could get her Chesterfield but could not leave my basket.

She volunteered to watch it. "I'll need your hat so I'll know what to charge people," she told me. So I gave her my hat and by the time I came back, she had sold a few items.

═══════════════════════════

BOO FERRISS: Bart Giamatti, the former commissioner of baseball, told the story that in

1946, he was eight years old and lived outside of Boston. His daddy and his uncle took him to his first Fenway game. He turns to his dad during the game and says, "Why are they booing the pitcher?"

And his dad said, "Well, that's his name." And my gosh, Bart Giamatti always remembered that.

I got that name when I was just a little toddler. I went through college as "Boo." When I got up to Boston, they called me both David and Boo.

───────────────────────────

There were not too many boos for Dave Ferriss in 1946. Winning 25 of 31 decisions, pitching 26 complete games, he was the workhorse and meal ticket of the Red Sox staff. The team won the pennant, posting a 104–50 won-lost record under manager Joe Cronin and drawing 1,416,944 into Fenway.

The World Series competition was the Cardinals. The two teams split the first two games, played in St. Louis. Then Boo Ferriss spun a six-hitter and blanked the Cards for a 4–0 win. The next day Cardinal bats came alive—St. Louis won, 12–3. Boston won the next day at Fenway, 6–3, sending the series back to St. Louis. The Sox needed one

win for the world championship. It was not to be—the Cardinals won both games in their home park, and with that, the World Series.

The loss to the Cards was to become a recurring theme in the decades ahead—close, but no cigar. But in 1946 and then in 1949, the Sox played at a 61–16 clip at Fenway—two of the best home records in franchise history.

In 1947, Fenway Park's seating capacity increased by 500, to 35,500—the first increase from 1912's 35,000. More importantly, arc lights were installed, making the Bosox the 13th big-league team to light up their home park. That same year, the 240-foot-wide left-field wall was painted with multiple coats of green paint. Tom Yawkey gave the green light to cover up advertising billboards. It was then that the nickname the "Green Monster" was first heard.

The Calvert Owl ("Be Wise"), Gem Blades ("Avoid 5 o'clock Shadow"), Lifebuoy ("The Red Sox Use It") and Vimms ("Get that Vimms Feeling") were now history.

MEL PARNELL: I was 25 years old in 1947 when I went to spring training at Sarasota, Florida, with the Red Sox. There were two spots open on the pitching staff, six of us vying. Harry Dorish got one; I got the other.

I came into Fenway Park for the first time and saw that left-field fence, and I thought maybe I had signed with the wrong organization. But it helped me work on making a change in my pitching style. I came up as a fastball pitcher but soon realized I would have to use a lot more breaking stuff. Pitching at Fenway Park makes you a better pitcher as you move along.

I pitched my first major league game on April 20, against Washington. Frankie Hayes, an old veteran player, was my catcher. I lost that game, 3–2, on a passed ball. I guess that's why I remember Frankie.

It truly impressed me as a rookie kid to see Mr. Yawkey on the field taking batting practice with us. I didn't see him hit any balls out, but he got some close to the wall. The kids who worked around the ballpark would shag flies for him. When he was done, he would give each one a $20 bill.

SAM MELE: I started my major league career on April 15, 1947. It was against the Philadelphia Athletics at Fenway Park. I walked my first time at bat. Then I doubled off the left-field wall. Next I singled. Then I walked again.

I was just thrilled to be there in the outfield with Dom DiMaggio and Ted Williams. "Any ball you can get, you chase me the hell off," second baseman Bobby Doerr would tell me. "But don't yell, 'I got it, I got it' just once. Two or three times and I'll get the hell out of the way." We would never run together, and never did a ball drop in.

DOM DIMAGGIO: Sam Mele wasn't a bad outfielder. Ted Williams wasn't a bad outfielder either, especially at Fenway—he played that wall nicely. I enjoyed a challenge, and Fenway Park did offer a challenge because of its structure. I mastered the ballpark and got along beautifully with the fences; they didn't hurt me and I didn't hurt them.

I did not shoot for the Green Monster. No. I was an all-around hitter, a line-drive hitter, a damn good one, too. I loved to hit in Fenway.

SAM MELE: I was moved around by the hand signals. Ted and Dom were veterans, and I was just beginning my career. Well, every team was different, naturally. Guys hit to right field no power, give me the palm, go in. Go back against the good hitters, like Moose Skowron, go back. He had good power to right field.

Right field, oh, how fucking tough that was to play. The sun came right over the stands. And the carom along the right-field fence . . . you cannot go directly toward the wall for the ball. You gotta surround it because it curves. And if it ever goes by you it would end up, oh, halfway to center field.

At that time they did not have the walls padded. I went into the right-field wall and banged into it. Right after that they padded the right-field wall. I went into the bullpen fence. Later on they padded the bullpen fence.

After every game, everybody—Dom, Pesky, me, Doerr—would all gather around Williams' locker and we would talk about what happened that day. We would talk about what was going to happen tomorrow, and if Ted didn't know about the pitcher for the next day, he would ask every one of us, maybe we saw him and he didn't, maybe we saw him in the minors, maybe we knew something about the guy . . .

I always sat next to Williams in the dugout. Matter of fact, he would call me over if I didn't. "You sit here." He used to tell me about the pitcher: "Look for this, look for that, he's fast, but his ball doesn't move as much as somebody else's."

If he didn't know that pitcher he would go up and down the whole dugout wanting to know: "Has anybody seen this guy? How's his curveball? Slow? Does it go down and in? Has he got a sinker?" Things like that.

On May 13, 1947, Ted Williams more than made good on a promise to a boy in the Malden hospital that he would hit a homer for him. The "Kid" hit two home runs for the kid. Both were pounded to left field, the first pair he'd hit there in his career. The round-trippers paced a 19–6 walloping of the White Sox.

The Red Sox's longtime owner was never enthusiastic about night baseball. As the *Boston*

ABOVE: Pitcher Tex Hughson warms up, 1947
OPPOSITE: Johnny Pesky in the air

Globe's Hy Hurwitz reported, "Yawkey is strictly in the baseball business" and added that Yawkey didn't "believe in fashion shows, nylon hosiery, door prizes and other nonsense."

Finally, bowing to league pressure, Yawkey yielded, agreeing to 14 night games, two with each American League team. The Red Sox became the last club in their league to play under the lights at home.

On June 13, 1947, before a capacity crowd of 34,510 and under a lighting system that was said to equal "the output of 5,000 full moons," Boston nipped the White Sox, 5–3. Chicago committed three errors and left 11 men on base. The Red Sox starter was Boo Ferriss. Way off his game, he gave up 11 hits in five-plus innings.

JOHNNY PESKY: It was like you were walking in daylight. It was great.

"The White Sox, in the role of guests, seemingly were confused by the electrical display," declared the *Chicago Tribune*.

There was no confusion for the Yankees on September 3, 1947. Their bats were on fire. Stroking 18 hits, all singles, the Yanks drubbed the Sox, 11–2, in the first game of a doubleheader. New York won the second game, 9–6, pushing its lead to 12½ games over Boston. Collecting six hits in the twin bill, Joe DiMaggio moved his average to .319. But Ted Williams, the American League's leading hitter, who got five hits in nine at-bats, was able to move his average to .328. "The Kid" would wind up winning the batting title with a .343 average.

BUCKY PIZZARELLI: On Opening Day at Fenway Park, 1948, I was on the field, between first and home, playing guitar with the Vaughn Monroe orchestra. While batting practice was going on and baseballs were bouncing all over the place, we were sitting there, dressed in brown sports jackets and gray pants doing pregame entertainment. Vaughn conducted, played trumpet, and sang beautifully. He was a famous singer then, and his orchestra of 18 was the number one in the United States.

We played songs like Vaughn Monroe's big hit "Racing with the Moon," which the fans loved. Then we finished up with "The Star-Spangled Banner," marched off, and sat right behind home plate, where we enjoyed the game.

On April 18, 1948, the Braves' Warren Spahn pitched a complete-game 3–2 victory over the Red Sox at Fenway Park in the City Series. Less than a month later, on the 12th of May, the first game from Fenway was televised over WBZ-TV.

MATT BATTS: Tom Yawkey and the front-office guys would usually come by the dugout before the game. This day I was warming up Jack Kramer—"Pretty Boy," we called him. He always tried to show off.

I squatted down, gave him a target, and told him to cut it loose. I dropped my glove, caught him barehanded, and Yawkey and them sitting in the stands just fell off, laughing. Kramer got so mad he stormed off into the outfield.

But Kramer could pitch. At one point that 1948 season he had won 11 straight games. He would wind up with an 18–5 record, his most significant triumph coming in the Red Sox's 153rd game of the season on October 2, when he beat the Yankees, 5–1, setting up a crucial contest the next day.

Boston was trailing Cleveland by one game in the standings that day when it was Yankees vs. Red Sox and brother vs. brother, Joe vs. Dom, before 31,304. The DiMaggio family was in the stands, rooting for Boston. Dom had a chance for the World Series. Joe did not.

In the Yankee Clipper's phrase, "They had come to see Yankee blood. We had nothing except satisfaction to play for. And besides, the league standings did not convince us that there were two better teams in the league."

"Joltin' Joe" cracked a first-inning double for one Yankee run. Boston scored five in the third inning. Meanwhile, Cleveland was down after three innings, 5–0, to Detroit.

A charley-horse-hobbled Yankee DiMaggio drove in two runs in the fifth. But by the ninth inning, Boston was coasting with a 10–5 lead. Joe DiMaggio singled—his fourth hit of the game. Knowing the pain that DiMaggio felt, Yankee pilot Bucky Harris replaced his star with a pinch runner.

"I turned and started for the dugout," DiMaggio recalled. "I guess I was limping pretty bad. I'll never forget that crowd. It was standing and roaring like one man. I tipped my cap, but it didn't stop. I looked up at the stands at this ovation they were giving to a guy who had tried to beat them. They were still yelling when I disappeared into the dugout. They didn't stop for another three or four minutes."

Cleveland lost that day. The first single play-off game in American League history was the next day, a Monday.

According to a report in the *Sporting News*, Boston manager Joe McCarthy wanted Jack Kramer to start the playoff game, even though it would be with one day's rest. Kramer passed.

WALTER MEARS: In 1948, the Sox were so far behind I said to my dad, "If they get into a play-off, can I cut school and go?"

"Don't worry about it because they won't," he said.

Famous last words. I skipped school and went on the old rattling subway from Arlington Heights to Harvard Square, where I took the subway to Kenmore Square. I got in line to buy a 50-cent bleacher seat. By the time I got to the window, there were no more tickets. I limped back home, confessed my sins, and stayed after school for two weeks.

Mears had a double loss that day. He missed the game, and his beloved Sox were ripped 8–3 by Cleveland. Incredibly, Boston manager Joe McCarthy could not use Kramer but he had bypassed well-rested starters Ellis Kinder and Mel Parnell and gone with journeyman Denny Galehouse.

A second-place finish and home attendance of 1,558,798, placing the Red Sox fourth among the eight teams of the American League, added up to making 1948 a fairly successful season. And for good measure, the Old Towne Team finished a game and a half ahead of the third-place Yankees. On the friendly turf of

Fenway the Sox were fantastic, playing at a .705 clip, going 55–23.

Baseball's greatest rivalry—the Boston Red Sox vs. the New York Yankees—just kept on going at fever pitch through the 1949 season. On June 28, after missing the first 69 games of the season because of an ailing heel, Joe DiMaggio finally returned to the Yankee lineup. His single and home run helped the Bombers beat the Red Sox, 6–4, in a night game at Fenway before 36,228, the largest night crowd in Fenway history to that point.

The next day the Yankees came back from seven runs down. DiMag torqued the charge with a three-

run homer in the fifth and another home run in the eighth inning.

"You can hate the Yankees," one sign read, "but you've got to love Joe DiMaggio!"

In the final game of the series, after seven innings before another SRO crowd, the Yankees were in front, 3–2. Then the great Joe DiMaggio put the game and the series away for the Yankees with a three-run smash off the left-field light tower, giving his team a 6–3 win and a sweep of the Sox. The Yankee Clipper had finished one of his most incredible series ever—solid defensive play, a .455 average in the three games, four home runs, a single, and 9 RBIs.

That performance at Fenway Park set the stage for the two teams jockeying back and forth most of the season in a frenetic pennant chase.

On September 24 and 25, the Yanks and Sox were at it again at Fenway Park.

WALTER MEARS: I was in the bleachers for the two Yankee games. Boston had slipped about five games behind and then won 10 in a row to catch New York.

Ellis Kinder, shaking off his hangover and pitching a great game—not easy against a lineup of Joe DiMaggio, Phil Rizzuto, Bobby Brown, Yogi Berra, and Tommy Henrich—beat the Yankees, 2–0. Williams hit one out, his 42nd. My favorite play was a foul pop off third base. Berra put his head down and ran at it like a steamroller. Bobby Brown, whose play it was, gracefully positioned himself to make the catch—until Yogi barreled into him, headfirst, and knocked him down like a linebacker. Boston won, 2–0, and trailed by a game.

Next day, Mel Parnell was pitching. I had my bleacher spot where Williams used to hit them, but none came near me. Parnell won his 25th, and the pennant race was tied.

Despite 71 injuries that kept players out of games, crafty Casey Stengel and his Yankees had been in first place all season. Parnell's clutch 4–1, four-hitter over ace Allie Reynolds gave the Boston southpaw a 16–3 record at Fenway.

WALTER MEARS: Each team had one series to go before they met in two final games at Yankee Stadium. Boston went into those games with a one-game lead, with Parnell and Kinder, who had become the entire pitching staff, going against Allie Reynolds and Vic Raschi. I sat listening to the radio in Lexington, Massachusetts.

The result was inevitable: Boston goes ahead, Yankees catch up and win. Tied. Same outcome the next day, and New York wins the pennant.

At 14, it seemed to me like the end of more than just a season. I remember saying to my father, "I think I'll just go for a walk," which I did, so that he wouldn't see me cry. I think that's when I learned that there was no point in mourning the Red Sox. You just take it, knowing that they will come close and fall short.

ABOVE: Elevator man, 1940s
OPPOSITE: Bobby Doerr with an adoring fan

-FIFTIES-

MIDCENTURY AT FENWAY PARK

The Red Sox began the fifties with a great deal of talent, especially Ted Williams. But midcentury at Fenway Park was a mixed bag. Lots of unfulfilled promise, some high moments, but overall it was a challenge to be a Boston Red Sox fan.

RED SOX YEAR BY YEAR 1950 – 1959	YEAR	WON	LOST	PCT.	GB	ATTENDANCE
	1959	75	79	.487	19.0	984,102
	1958	79	75	.513	13.0	1,077,047
	1957	82	72	.532	16.0	1,181,087
	1956	84	70	.545	13.0	1,137,158
	1955	84	70	.545	12.0	1,203,200
	1954	69	85	.448	42.0	931,127
	1953	84	69	.549	16.0	1,026,133
	1952	76	78	.494	19.0	1,115,750
	1951	87	67	.565	11.0	1,312,282
	1950	94	60	.610	4.0	1,344,080

The competition on Opening Day at Fenway in 1950 was the Yankees. When Boston put a five spot on the scoreboard in the fourth inning, driving Yankee ace Allie Reynolds out of the game, pushing their lead to 9–0, Fenway rocked with joy. With Mel Parnell on the mound for the Sox, Boston fans felt confident.

———————

WALTER MEARS: All I wanted for my birthday was an Opening Day seat at Fenway. And I got one. It was grandstand instead of bleachers. I was surrounded by Yankee fans, up from New York. One of them was crowing so much that I bet him a dollar I didn't have that the Red Sox would win. With Boston ahead early 9–0, the Bronx loudmouth left Fenway. Good thing for my unfinanced bet, as the Yankees came back and kept coming. Pitcher Jack Kramer had just come over from the Browns and was supposed to be the next great thing for the Sox. He came in and threw his first pitch into the stands.

A nine-run eighth inning punctuated the Yankee comeback. Billy Martin, making his major league debut, became the first big-league player in his first game ever to record two hits in one inning—that explosive eighth.

That game kind of typified what had been happening with the Sox of that era. Talent alone, the word on the street said, did not win ball games. It was the era of 25 players, 25 cabs, the era of the "Gold Sox," a phrase that underscored the money Tom Yawkey continued to dole out to create a winner. In the fifties the Sox would finish in third place four times, in fourth place four times, once in fifth place and once in sixth place.

Then there was the love-hate affair fans at Fenway Park had with Ted Williams. On May 17, 1950, he dropped a fly ball in the first game of a doubleheader. Raucous razzing followed. In the

second game, a ball scooted past him in left field, and Teddy Ball Game made a halfhearted effort to go after it. Three runs scored. The booing was deafening. The inning ended. Williams came to the dugout, stopped, and made a negative, some would say obscene, gesture—twice.

———————

ROGER KAHN: Every once in a while, Williams would lose his temper and give them the finger. People out in left field would jeer. There was a constant clash between Williams and the customers.

———————

BOB BRADY: But in those years he was the only reason to go to Fenway Park. As soon as his last at-bat, many would depart, especially if the Sox were losing.

———————

ROGER KAHN: At that time, the Red Sox clubhouse closed something like 40 minutes before a game at the request—no, the demand—of Williams, who called reporters the "Knights of the Keyboard."

There were more bodies than you could imagine in the Fenway press box, people from all of the papers. Platoons of reporters. Somebody doing the pregame color—this is when the Yankees came in. Somebody doing the dressing room. Somebody doing the other dressing room. Somebody doing crowd notes. Somebody doing the game itself.

———————

IKE DELOCK: He didn't like the press, and there were a lot of them—he wanted to ban them from the clubhouse. The players said, "You can't do that." So he eased up. But whatever he wanted he damn well got.

———————

At the urging of Williams, Red Sox players agreed to a one-hour interview lag after games before reporters could enter the locker room. The Sox icon would stand outside the door wearing just a towel, counting off the seconds. "Okay," he'd snap, "now all you bastards can come in."

———————

MEL PARNELL: Ted was called out on strikes and came back to the dugout and complained that home plate was out of line. General manager Joe Cronin argued about it but agreed to have home plate checked. At nine the next morning, the ground crew was out there. They checked. It *was* out of line. Ted had the greatest eyes. He was a man with strong opinions about everything, and his own way of doing things.

———————

The Splendid Splinter ordered postal scales for the Boston clubhouse to accurately measure the weight of his bats. He trusted no one. While in the on-deck circle, he would massage his bat handle with olive oil and rosin. The noise, a kind of squeal, did not endear him to disconcerted pitchers.

The eighth day of June 1950 was a perfect day at Fenway for those who loved offense, hot weather, and the home team. Scoring 29 runs in 90-degree heat before just 5,105 fans, the Bosox romped over the St. Louis Browns. Bobby Doerr

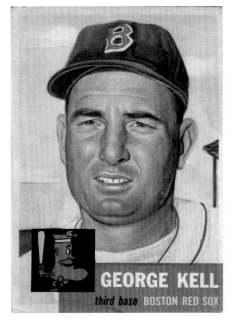

GEORGE KELL
third base BOSTON RED SOX

smashed three homers while collecting 8 RBIs. Walt Dropo homered twice, driving in 7 runs. Ted Williams launched two homers and had 5 RBIs. Half a dozen major league offensive records were set that day by the slugging Bosox.

On the first day of July, Whitey Ford made his major league debut, at Fenway.

WHITEY FORD: I was 21 years old. I wasn't what I would be. I lasted 4⅔ innings, giving up 7 hits, 6 walks, and 5 earned runs.

Another rookie, Boston's Walt Dropo, had a better day than the Yankee southpaw. He slugged a grand-slam home run. Boston won, 13–4.

On August 17, Fenway Park became the site of the American League's first Ladies' Night Game. More than 7,000 women saw the home team down the A's, 10–6. It was the 19th straight loss for Philadelphia at the Fens, dating back to September 12, 1948.

JIMMY PIERSALL: My first day in the big leagues was September 7, 1950. I was 20 years old. And we were playing Washington and I was sitting on the bench. We're down by four runs and

Steve O'Neill, who had replaced Joe McCarthy as manager, said it's time for me to pinch-hit. He called me "pierseraroll"—he didn't know what the hell my name was.

JOHNNY PESKY: A big left-handed pitcher was going against us. Piersall was going up for his first at-bat. "Goddamn, this guy's awful wild, Goddamn it, I'm afraid," Jimmy said.

"If you're afraid," I told him, "you better get a lunch pail and go home."

JIMMY PIERSALL: I walked up. My hands were sweating. I swung at the first pitch and the bat lands beyond the third-base dugout. And I'm standing there without a bat. The on-deck-circle guy gives me another bat. The count goes to 3–2, and I hit a ball between second and third for a hit.

With Pesky, with Williams, with DiMaggio, with Parnell, and now with Piersall, the 1950 Red Sox were a formidable foe at home, where they posted a won and lost record of 55–22; on the road they barely played .500 ball.

On April 15, 1951, exactly four years to the day after Jackie Robinson broke baseball's color line, almost exactly six years to the day after he and Marvin Williams and Sam Jethroe were passed over by the Red Sox in the "tryout" at Fenway in 1945, "the Jet Jethroe" returned as a member of the Boston Braves in the preseason City Series game—Boston Braves versus Boston Red Sox. The speedy Jethroe showed the Sox what they had missed in not signing him. Going four for five, homering, and driving in two runs, Jethroe dominated. But the Braves lost the game, 6–3.

A month later the Red Sox celebrated the 50th anniversary of their first game in Boston. On hand

were 29 old-timers who had played, managed, or umpired in the American League in that first season, including Connie Mack, Dummy Hoy, Cy Young, Hugh Duffy, and Clark Griffith. In the game that followed, Ted Williams slammed his 300th career homer.

On July 8, Red Sox fans rejoiced as a Yankee pitcher failed to complete a game for the 20th straight time at Fenway Park. Five days later, Sox fans rejoiced even more when Mickey Mantle struck out four times in a doubleheader.

Just before the 1952 baseball season got going, the last City Series game between the Boston Red Sox and the Boston Braves was played at Fenway Park on April 13 before a tiny and chilled crowd of 3,813, who braved 40-degree weather. Pitcher Gene Conley, then a Boston Celtic and future member of the Sox, started for the Braves. Faye Throneberry (the brother of "Marvelous Marv") homered with two outs in the seventh. The Sox won the game, 2–1. The Braves moved to Milwaukee the following season, and that ended the City Series with the Boston Braves.

GENE CONLEY: That April 13 was the first time I saw Fenway Park. "My goodness, what a small ballpark," I thought. Some of the minor league parks I had played in were bigger.

Seventeen days later, before 24,767 on "Ted Williams Day," the Kid played his last game before heading to Korea as a Marine fighter pilot. Fans and players sang "Auld Lang Syne" in a pregame ceremony, and Williams was given a Cadillac. Always one in the moment, the Sox outfielder in his final

PAGE 88: Banner saluting "Teddy Ballgame," who went 4 for 4 in the 6–5 Boston victory over the Yankees, August 17, 1958
OPPOSITE: Jackie Jensen signs autographs

at-bat of the game hammered a two-run shot off Dizzy Trout—the frosting on the cake of the 5–3 Red Sox triumph over the Tigers.

Fighting at Fenway during the 1952 season seemed contagious. Hyperactive Jimmy Piersall and Billy Martin got into a shouting match before the Red Sox–Yankee game on the 24th of May in the tunnel beneath the stands. After the game they were at it again. As the story goes, Boston pitcher Ellis Kinder accompanied Piersall, and Bill Dickey accompanied Martin as seconds. Martin sucker-punched, throwing the first blow. They got into a clinch. That ended the "fight." Piersall supposedly changed his bloody shirt in the clubhouse and was verbally on Martin from the bench during the rest of the game.

JIMMY PIERSALL: It wasn't a real fight, just pushing and shoving. The only guy that got hurt was Bill Dickey. Heck, the way the media played it up it was like a real brawl. You know, writers would hang their mothers for the Pulitzer Prize.

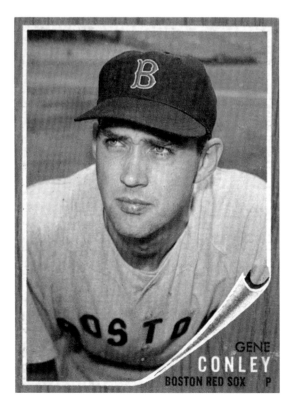

GENE
CONLEY
BOSTON RED SOX   P

Less than a month later, on June 11, in a game against the Browns, Piersall led off the ninth inning against Satchel Paige, announcing that he was going to bunt. He laid down one safely. Then the Sox outfielder began imitating the ageless hurler's moves, yelling "Oink! Oink! Oink!" An infield hit moved Piersall to second base. Mimicry and "Oinks!" continued.

Exasperated and unnerved, Paige walked the bases full. Another walk, to Billy Goodman, scored a Red Sox run. Ted Lepcio singled, reloading the bases. Sammy White slammed a grand-slammer. Then, seemingly influenced by Piersall's behavior, the Red Sox catcher rounded third base, crawled home, and kissed the plate. It was a bizarre day at Fenway.

That 1952 season was a sad one for Jimmy Piersall. He wound up playing in just 56 games. Then he was away for treatment of his behavioral problems.

On June 3, 1952, Walt Dropo was traded by Boston along with Don Lenhardt, Fred Hatfield, Johnny Pesky, and Bill Wight to the Detroit Tigers for Dizzy Trout, Johnny Lipon, Hoot Evers, and George Kell.

GEORGE KELL: I was traded for an idol, Johnny Pesky. But I did get a wonderful reception. Mr. Yawkey called me up to his office and told me how proud he was to have me there. Then later he sent me some silverware that I treasured for a long time.

Fenway was sort of made for me. It was just baseball, baseball. My first day playing for Boston I homered over the left-field fence and I hit a double off of it and I thought: "My goodness, I'm liable to hit a lot of home runs and a lot of doubles." But it wasn't that way, it wasn't that easy. They pitch you a little different. They're not going to keep bringing the ball inside to where you can pull it all the time.

At first it seemed like I would never go into a slump at Fenway Park, like I could always reach that wall out there. I couldn't, but that's how I felt. I also felt like I could hit .300 there, which I did both years I was on the team, and I made the All-Star team.

It was tough to play the infield at Fenway, especially third base. Almost everybody was aiming for the left-field fence. Everybody was trying to pull the ball. I don't think I ever had so many hot shots hit right at me by people just like myself trying to reach the left-field wall.

Ted Williams came back from the Korean War and played at the end of my career with the Red Sox. When I was a member of the Tigers I won the batting title on the last day of the '49 season. I won it because Ted went hitless that day and I had a couple of hits. I won it by two thousandths of a point and boy, I tell you, to me it was tremendous. But it was a tremendous loss for him because he was the all-time great hitter.

The next year at Fenway a man asked me if I would pose for a picture with Ted Williams. I agreed and started over to the Red Sox dugout.

"No," Ted came out, "we are going to make it in front of your dugout because you won the batting title from me fair and square."

And I thought, "What a wonderful and honorable man he is." We became good close friends from then on.

JIMMY PIERSALL: By 1953, I was back with the Red Sox. At first, players on other teams would call me "Gooney bird" and go "Coo coo, coo coo."

I finally said to myself, "I'm a pretty good player. So if I hit a home run or make a good play I'll give them the finger."

On May 8, 1953, Boston snapped a 13-game losing streak to the Yankees. A Billy Goodman homer off Johnny Sain was the game-winner in the bottom of the eleventh inning. The next day the first-place Yankees nipped Boston, 6–4. Mickey Mantle homered off Bill Werle. But the Mick's bid for a second home run was denied as Jimmy Piersall made a great catch in front of the Sox bullpen in right-center field. There is no report of his giving the finger.

DAVE HUTCHINSON: It was incredible how many times Jimmy Piersall was able to do that. Defensively, for so many years, he was something else.

LEIGH MONTVILLE: I grew up in New Haven, Connecticut. My parents gave me three things in life: the Catholic Church, the Democratic Party, and the Boston Red Sox. One time, in the early 1950s, when I was eight or nine years old, we stopped in Boston on the way back from a vacation trip because I was such a Red Sox wacko. The game got rained out, so we stayed overnight. The next night the game got rained out, too. I was a little disappointed by the rain and the way Fenway Park looked from the outside—it looked like a factory.

BILL NOWLIN: Curt Gowdy was with the Red Sox from about '53 on, the main guy when I was growing up. I remember the advertisements like Narragansett Beer and Atlantic Richfield: "Atlantic keeps your car on the go, on the go, on the go, on the go." And as it faded out: "Hi neighbor—have a Gansett."

FRANK SULLIVAN: I went up from A ball in '53. I was 23. I saw buckshot wounds all over the walls and learned that Ted Williams was out shooting pigeons in the park. I heard Yawkey also shot along with him.

BILL LEE: The longtime guy in charge of the groundskeeping, Joe Mooney, told me that the cops came to Williams and asked, "Ted, didn't you worry about your stray shots going to Kenmore Square?"

Ted was supposed to have said, "You know, I was thinking about that."

FRANK SULLIVAN: The tunnel from the clubhouse to the dugout would be empty of players when I went out to warm up. That tunnel echo got to me. I pounded on my glove, yelled as loud as I could, did whatever it took to rise to the occasion.

It was an old ballpark but the locker room, the clubhouse was really nice. Terrific shower, big tiles. Our lockers weren't much, just steel lockers. The clubhouse wasn't rectangular. It was broken up a lot. There would be guys you could hardly see sitting by lockers. Ted Williams was kind of hidden all the way over in the left corner.

Teddy Ball Game's first morning chore was a call to Fenway Park to determine how the flag was blowing. He had become an expert on all kinds of New England weather experiences and always wanted to be prepared. There were times when gale winds transformed lowly pop flies into high-flying homers. There were times when the gales tore the big hand from the clock and bent the foul pole in left.

——————————

IKE DELOCK: Most of the time Ted Williams arrived very early for games. I was like two lockers away from him. He had so many bats in his lockers. There was a certain respect for him from the other players. He was a good-looking guy. He could be loud; you couldn't miss him. Pleasant when he wanted to be but pretty scary when he wanted to be.

——————————

In 1953, Red Sox pitcher Mickey McDermott punched reporter Bob Holbrook in the face in the locker room. "Terrible Ted" congratulated the Sox hurler.

——————————

DAVE HUTCHINSON: I had an interview set with Ted Williams. He said, "Five minutes." Well, it ran close to 40 minutes. I started with questions on hitting. And he moved the chair away and went in the batting stance, showed me how you could hit a ball better swinging up than swinging down. And he talked about so many of the great ballplayers and the way they hit.

——————————

FRANK SULLIVAN: The warm-up area for the starting pitchers was between the dugout and the backstop, not out in the bullpen. When people saw the starting pitchers come out, they knew the start of the ball game was only half an hour, 20 minutes away. As I started to toss I always stopped for a moment and looked up at Mrs. Yawkey, who would be in her box alone. I would tip my cap to her and she would wave at me with crossed fingers.

The attendance wasn't bad. A good crowd would be around 20,000. We rarely played in front of a few thousand. Fenway was right in town. They often closed businesses during games. It was nothing to go down Washington Street and see a shop closed at one o'clock.

I was a ground-ball pitcher. I threw sinkers and sliders, so the Green Wall didn't bother me a minute. It helped me a lot because so many hitters try to pull the ball and if you're throwing sliders on the outside for strikes and then you come back inside, they're going to go for it. I thanked God for Frankie Malzone at third. And Williams was not a bad left fielder at Fenway Park. He knew how to play the wall, and he always had a decent arm.

MICHAEL DUKAKIS: Williams was a much better fielder than people gave him credit for. There was nothing relaxed about him, but there seemed to be a casualness about the way he fielded.

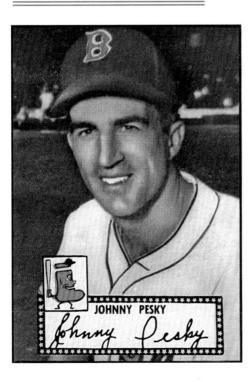

IKE DELOCK: We didn't chart the games other pitchers pitched. We talked to them between innings only if they wanted to talk to us. I sat in the dugout when I pitched and dropped my glove down in a certain way. That was my signal I wanted to be left alone. As long as I was winning, the glove did the trick.

CHARLIE PATTERSON: In June 1953 I traveled with two friends and my family to Boston. My dad worked for our North Carolina hometown paper and was attending a newspaper convention. He got us in the Red Sox clubhouse and dugout before the game with the Indians.

We got baseballs autographed by Gene Stephens and Tommy Umphlett. We had seen both play in D ball in our hometown. We got quite a few other autographs, including George Kell's, Lou Boudreau's, and Mel Parnell's.

We were very innocent, small-town, Southern 12-to-14-year-olds. Our ears really got big when we heard a player yelling madly at a guy in a suit. He was using language we had never heard before, and we kept saying to each other, "What does that mean?" That was the first time we ever heard the "f" and "s" words. That player gave his autograph, too. Jimmy Piersall.

On August 6, 1953, in his first game back after his stint as a Marine fighter pilot in Korea, with the Sox trailing by one run to the St. Louis Browns in the ninth inning, Williams pinch-hit. It was his first official plate appearance in 15 months. He popped up to first base.

"It was a good ball to hit on the ground, but I wanted to get it into the air and not hit into a double play," said Williams after the 8–7, ten-inning loss. "I got under it too much."

A highlight of the 1953 season for the fans at

Fenway took place on September 19. Winning his 20th game of the year, Mel Parnell trimmed the Yankees, 3–0. It was Parnell's third shutout of the New Yorkers that year.

The Red Sox 1954 Opening Day lineup:

Billy Goodman	2B
Jimmy Piersall	RF
Jackie Jensen	CF
George Kell	3B
Harry Agganis	1B
Charlie Maxwell	LF
Sammy White	C
Ted Lepcio	SS
Bill Henry	P

On Opening Day, April 15, 1954, before 17,272, Boston defeated the Senators, 6–1. Harry Agganis made his major league debut at Fenway with two hits. Boston University's first All-American football player, he was drafted by the Cleveland Browns in 1952 and offered a $25,000 contract. Red Sox owner Tom Yawkey offered $35,000.

ABOVE: Ted Williams signs contract in Red Sox office while a seated General Manager Eddie Collins and Manager Joe Cronin look on
OPPOSITE: A well-dressed and orderly crowd lines up at the advance ticket sales office in 1955

STEVE RYDER: The "Golden Greek" was from Lynn, Massachusetts. He played first base. He just had everything—a beautiful swing, he could run, had good mobility. He played first base. He was majestic.

Before 15,683 against the Yankees in the first game of a doubleheader on April 19, the Red Sox won, 2–1. Harry Agganis again had two hits. In the second game, before 27,762, the Yankees topped Mel Parnell, 5–0, and Agganis managed the only hit of the game for Boston off Jim McDonald. Mickey Mantle homered for New York.

"I loved to play at Fenway Park," Mickey Mantle remembered. "But center field there was kinda tough. There were all those angles and the short center-field fence. At Yankee Stadium you could run for two days in the outfield. There you had to watch it. You'd turn around and smash into the fence."

ROGER KAHN: A Red Sox pitcher got something in his eye. They had sent out the trainer and eight other people and they finally got the speck out. Bobby Brown was leaning on his bat. I said after the game, "There's a guy in distress with his eye and you're a doctor. What about the Hippocratic oath?"

Brown said, "If I'm the hitter and the guy with the eye problem is the pitcher, screw the Hippocratic oath."

Brown was a pretty good third baseman, a very good hitter. But when a residency in cardiology became open, he took it. There was a little ceremony at Fenway for him, and Brown was always regarded as kind of an unemotional guy. Still, he stood at home plate brushing a tear from his eye as he said good-bye to all of his buddies: Jerry Coleman, Yogi Berra, and all of the rest. As most know, Brown would go on to become a very successful cardiologist and then president of the American League.

TERRY GUINEY: I went to the park for the first time in the midfifties. There were five boys in our family, and the tradition was that each of us went with our father to their first game.

A lot of afternoon games were during that era, so it was easy for kids to turn up at Fenway after school. City kids would go to the park by themselves, hang around the players' entrance, and often get autographs. Sellouts were a rarity. You probably could buy a bleacher seat for a buck or two and move around to another section.

The crowd was mostly Irish and Italian; there were very few blacks. Not many women. Food presentation was peanuts and Cracker Jacks and hot dogs and Cokes and beer.

JIMMY PIERSALL: On August 16, in a Jimmy Fund charity contest, I hurt my arm throwing against Willie Mays. He had a great arm, but I could throw as good as he could. I made a throw to the plate and my shoulder burned. After a while I learned to throw more with my wrist and to follow through with my body.

Hurting my arm was a freak thing. I very seldom got hurt. I didn't dive for balls. When you dive for balls, you lose a step. You had to know the runners, how your pitchers were pitching, what kind of stuff they had in order to play in that Fenway Park outfield, especially with all the odd angles.

I would position my guys in right and left for the different hitters. I would whistle over to right field and take my guy off the line. I stood sideways like Dom DiMaggio, sometimes. He played deeper than me. But he had a great arm, good hands, and he could run. He ran like a hop, skipping, and a hop. You didn't want to kid him about that either, because he didn't like that. He was a very low-key guy.

LEFT: Wearing skis, Mel Parnell gets set to throw a snowball on April 14, 1953. A freak snowstorm postponed opening day against the Senators.
OPPOSITE: Lights on at 4:30 P.M. because of a forest fire in Canada and a foggy, eerie night in and around Fenway

One thing about that Green Monster was that you would have balls coming directly off, balls that would hit the middle and go one way, balls that would hit in the bottom and go to the right. I would take balls off the wall in practice and without looking fire them into second base. I just knew where it was.

The fans were close to the field. You'd get acquainted with a lot of them. They would ask for my autograph and I would sign about 100. Coming in and going out from the outfield, I would always step on first base. It was just something I came to do to please the fans at Fenway.

———————————

JAMES "JIMMIE" GREENE: The last time I was in Fenway was probably '54. I sat in the grandstand reserved seats. A ticket cost two dollars. Ted Williams didn't swing at one pitch and was called out on strikes. The bat never left his shoulder. That stuck in my mind that with the eye he had that was not a strike.

———————————

In 1954, the Old Towne Team won 69 games and lost 85 and finished 42 games behind Cleveland, in fourth place. Even at home Boston had trouble, posting a record of 38 wins and 39 losses.

The team was never in first place all season long, and only 931,127 came to see them play, placing them sixth in an eight-team league. Lou Boudreau was out as manager; Pinky Higgins was in.

It was Yankees against Red Sox on April 14, 1955. The lone black player on either team was rookie Elston Howard of New York. Appearing as a substitute for Irv Noren, who was tossed for arguing with an umpire, Howard singled in his first career at-bat.

Less than a month later, on May 7, Howard cracked his first big-league home run. A dead-center-field shot by the "Mick" broke a tie, enabling the Yanks to outlast the home-team Sox, 9–6.

TED SPENCER: I grew up in Quincy, Massachusetts, and many times I would take the bus, subway, and trolley to Kenmore. If I had a buck and a quarter or 75 cents I'd sit in the bleachers. The two biggest people in Boston from my perspective then were Ted Williams and Cardinal Cushing.

My real name is William Thomas Spencer. Family legend has it that I held my rattle in my left hand when I was about two weeks old. "Hey, he's going to be a lefty like Ted Williams," they said. And that's how I got to be called "Ted."

It was a Sunday, a doubleheader. My best friend, Fred Goduti, and I were sitting by the far corner, where the "triangle" is—virtually right behind, the first or second bench there, behind the bullpen.

Ted Williams hits a shot. The thing came right down. At the last minute I realized the ball was going to hit me in the face. I ducked. The ball bounced behind me, and a whole group of kids converged on it, including Goduti, who came out grinning, clutching something under his shirt. He subsequently sent the ball to the Red Sox, and Ted Williams signed it and sent it back. To this day, Fred still has this ball.

———————————

BILL MONBOUQUETTE: The day I signed a Red Sox contract in 1955, I finished pitching batting practice and joined my mom and dad in the right-field grandstand to watch the game. Two drunks behind us spilled their booze on my mother. They were swearing. I turned. "I don't appreciate your language or spilling your beer on my mother. No more!"

"'What are you going to do about it?" I looked at my father and he nodded and we sure did a job on them. We cleaned their clocks. The next thing was that my dad and I were cuffed behind the back and put in a holding cell. We had to call Johnny Murphy, the Red Sox farm director, to get us out.

———————————

BILL NOWLIN: When I was a young teenager, I'd often go to the park, by myself or with one other kid. Sometimes we'd have a little bit of fun. There's that brick wall that serves as the back of the bleachers in center field. You used to be able to stand, look down over the wall, and watch people walking down the street. We'd get a cup full of water and pour, trying to time it so the water landed ten feet in front of them. Sometimes the timing didn't work. At least one time somebody actually bought a ticket and came charging into the park to try to get us. Fortunately, we had moved to another part of the bleachers by then.

There certainly were some inebriated types. But I never saw any fights break out. The ushers used to be brawny types from Boston College and so forth. The stories were that they would just beat up people under the stands if they were causing too much trouble.

———————————

STEVE RYDER: On June 27, 1955, Harry Agganis died. We were devastated. He started spitting up blood in Kansas City when the team was on a road trip. They sent him back to Boston and the Santa Maria Hospital in Cambridge, the hospital of choice for the team. Some type of a pulmonary embolism developed, and it just took him very quickly.

———————————

Pinky Higgins remained as manager as the 1956 season began. His coaches were Del Baker, Jack Burns, Boo Ferriss, Mickey Owen, and Paul Schreiber. The team would be better (but still mediocre) than the season before, draw 1,137,158—an average of 14,579 per game—into Fenway, and finish in fourth place.

PAGE 98–99: Fans watching a game from billboard supports
OPPOSITE: Ted Williams nervously toeing the dirt on April 30, 1952, at a pre-game ceremony honoring him before he would join the Marines on May 2

This was the lineup on April 27 that lost to the Yankees, 5–2, and that appeared quite often that 1956 season:

Billy Goodman	2B
Billy Klaus	3B
Mickey Vernon	1B
Jackie Jensen	RF
Dick Gernert	LF
Jimmy Piersall	CF
Don Buddin	SS
Sammy White	C

DON KOSAKOWSKI: It was the 14th of July 1956. I was 10 years old, coming back to Connecticut from a week's vacation on Cape Cod with my parents. My mother went shopping in Boston. My father decided it would be a good time to take me to my first game at Fenway Park.

We got tickets right at the window and walked in. We sat behind third base. Boston was not a powerhouse team by any means in those days. Mel Parnell was the starting pitcher against the White Sox. About the fifth inning, people started talking about the no-hitter.

MEL PARNELL: In the seventh inning, my right fielder, Jackie Jensen, came to me in the dugout. "Look, you're going for a no-hitter." He says, "Don't let them hit the ball to me. I don't want to be the guy to mess it up."

I said, "Jackie, forget it. If it happens, it happens. All I'm looking for is a win."

The dugout was very quiet. I never did reach a state of nervousness because I just didn't expect it to happen.

JIMMY PIERSALL: The count went to 2–2 in the eighth and Mel went [pitched] away from the right-handed hitter [Luis] Aparicio [of the White Sox] and I went over to right-center and made the catch.

DON KOSAKOWSKI: The last batter was pinch hitter Walt Dropo. He was a big guy, and everyone had this fear that this guy was going to pop one. But he hit back to Parnell. **JIMMY PIERSALL:** Mel Parnell ran all the way to first base. He got his no-hitter and his 4–0 win.

MEL PARNELL: When I got to the clubhouse door, Mr. Yawkey was standing there with a new contract in his hand and a pen. He says, "Here, sign this."

I said, "Mr. Yawkey, you don't have to do that. You pay me to do these things."

He said, "Son, sign the contract, will ya?"
I said, "I sure will."

DON KOSAKOWSKI: When the game ended, my dad and I collected my mother, had something to eat, and then drove back home to Ansonia, Connecticut—160, 170 miles.

Three days after Parnell's no-hitter, Ted Williams homered off Kansas City's Tom Gorman for number 400—the only run in the Red Sox victory. The shot was slammed in the second game of the double-header and landed six rows deep into the right-field

grandstand. Crossing home plate, the Splendid Splinter spit in the direction of sportswriters.

A "repeat spit" took place on August 7. A crowd of 36,350, a record for a night game at Fenway Park till then, was locked in for Red Sox vs. Yankees. With two outs in the eleventh, Williams misjudged Mickey Mantle's windblown fly ball, dropping it for a two-base error. Fans loudly voiced their displeasure, some called it disgusting. Williams then made a neat catch of a shot by Yogi Berra, ending the Yankee inning. Fans still booed.

Approaching the dugout, Williams spit at the fans. And exiting the dugout to come up to hit in the bottom of the inning, Williams spit again.

In the bottom of the eleventh inning Teddy Ball

the ball to your right, to your left. It was good practice hitting the baseball. Ted used to love that. It gave you a feel for hitting the ball, watching the ball. Ted said it was a sad thing when we couldn't have it any more. That was when they put those signs in: "No pepper."

MEL PARNELL: Ted and I used to work out together. I pitched batting practice to him and so did Mickey McDermott. He saw very few left-handed pitchers. We wouldn't tell him what we were going to throw. So we're trying to figure out Ted Williams and Ted Williams is trying to figure out us.

New York's Bill Skowron had five hits, but the Yankees stranded a record 20 base runners, losing to the Red Sox in Boston, 13-7 on September 21. It was baseball's greatest rivalry again but also Mantle vs. Williams. The "Mick" drove the ball 480 feet into the centerfield bleachers. The home run landed a foot from the top. Mantle's three hits put his average at .352, just four points behind Ted Williams. At year's end Mantle would best Williams .353 to .345 to win the American League batting title.

Game worked a bases-loaded walk, giving Boston a 1–0 win. Heading to first base, he tossed his bat about 40 feet in the air. For his expressiveness, the tempestuous talent was fined $5,000 by the league, the largest fine levied since Babe Ruth broke curfew in the 1920s.

"I'd spit again at those booing bastards," Williams griped—a reference to what he called "those wolves in the left-field stands."

JIMMY PIERSALL: "What are we going to do with Ted?" Mr. Yawkey asked me.

"Mr. Yawkey, I have my own troubles."

He loved Ted. Ted was like a son to him.

Some fans booed Ted because they figured it would make him play better. Eventually they closed off the bleacher seats by left field so people couldn't holler down at him.

Usually I batted first or second. Ted would talk hitting with me all the time, but not in the locker room. When I used to ask him, "If you were me,

what would you do?" he'd tell me, "I would try to hit the ball to right-center or left-center."

You know, he's the one player that the opposing team would come out for to watch take batting practice.

When I was a runner on first base and Ted was hitting, it always made me more alert than ever because the ball would get there so quick, always with a hook on it.

BOBBY DOERR: Ted got a bad reputation. But he didn't deserve it. After ball games he would sit in the stands with the kids. They'd come in the clubhouse and ask, "Will you talk to the kids?" Ted would say, "As soon as all the fans are all out of the ballpark, and I don't want anything in the press about it."

In my time, games started right around 1:30 or 2:00. I'd get to the ball park about noon, plenty of time to get batting practice. Back then we played pepper. As the bunter you would hit

BILL NOWLIN: I started going to Fenway in 1957 on my own when I was 12. I'd get into the bleachers for 50 cents. I always sat in the bleachers.

A grate blocked off the bleachers from the rest of the park to prevent people from moving from the bleachers to the higher priced seats. After the sixth inning, you could pass through for 50 cents or whatever the difference was between the unreserved grandstands and the

ABOVE: Jimmy Piersall slides home
OPPOSITE: Ted toweling off and enjoying it

bleachers. When the ushers were gone near the end of the game, I'd move around and sit in one of the better seats.

Ted Williams was my favorite. I thought he was going to hit a home run every time up. And '57, of course, was the year he hit .388. I got to see a lot of great play by him as I sat in those bleachers. I touched his home run ball — I can't remember if it was Number 494 or 497 — after it had been caught by somebody else.

CARL BEANE: The first time I went to Fenway was in 1957. We lived in Western Mass., and my dad didn't drive so we took the bus. We'd eat lunch in Bickford's and then we would walk about two miles from the bus station to Fenway. My dad was always able to get seats in Section 18, right between home and first; we'd have a clear view of everything. He had been following the Red Sox since 1933 when he was about nine years old, the year Thomas Yawkey bought the ball club.

On April 15, 1958, 35,223 — the largest Red Sox crowd ever for an opener — saw Don Larsen and the Yankees win 3–0. Yogi Berra slammed a two-run homer in the seventh inning. Official seating capacity now was 34,819.

JERRY CASALE: My first major league win was on September 14, 1958. To me Fenway looked so small, especially from the mound. You turned around and it seemed like that wall was on top of you. I beat the Senators 7–3. I also hit a three run home run off Russ Kemmerer. It cleared the right centerfield fence, landing on the street.

But later that season I lost my first ballgame in Fenway Park. Hoyt Wilhelm, the best pitcher I ever faced in my life, beat me. He was so tough.

I faced Gus Triandos with the bases loaded. He hit a high fly ball to left field. I was ready to walk off the mound when I turned around and saw Williams going back, back to the wall. The wind blew it right up into the damn screen and I lost the game 5–2. That wall helps and it hurts you.

The unusual through the decades seemed to always be a part of Fenway action. Case in point was on September 21 as the Red Sox completed a three-game sweep of the Senators all by 2–0 shutouts spun by Tom Brewer, Frank Sullivan and Ike Delock.

The final shutout showcased one of the ways Williams earned the nickname "Terrible Ted." Disgusted by a called third strike, he flung his bat into the stands striking Joe Cronin's housekeeper bloodying her head. Fortunately, 60-year-old Gladys Heffernan was not seriously hurt. When a contrite Williams rushed to her seat, the crowd booed. American League President Will Harridge fined Williams for the "bat-throwing." And come Christmas, "the Kid" sent Heffernan a $500 diamond watch.

On April 12, 1959, in 42 degree temperature, the Yankees and Red Sox played their season opener in front of 22,559. New York was the victor, 3–2, on Bob Turley's two-hitter.

STEVE FOLVEN: The team always broke my heart because I grew up in the '50s and early '60s. My father used to take us always to "Family Day" once a year. We'd get seats in the grandstands, adults a buck fifty, kids 75 cents. We would bring food because we couldn't pay. I'd just get

one hot dog and one Coke. Hot dogs were 35 cents, the sodas maybe 25 cents. They also sold peanuts. And that was about it. Crowds were workingclass fans, really into the game.

We were in left field. The announcer Sherm Feller made announcements as if they were from God. Just before the first pitch when the umpires and everybody was walking out to the field, you would hear him: "Attention, Attention Ladies and Gentlemen, boys and girls, we call your attention to the following American League rules. There's no fans allowed on the field. Anyone on the field will be subject to fines. Thank you. Thank you."

There were no message boards in those days. The scoreboard on the left-field wall was

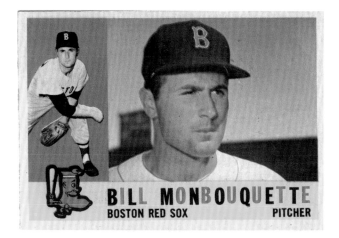

BILL MONBOUQUETTE
BOSTON RED SOX   PITCHER

not visible to us. Sherm Feller was our only link then to American league scores.

My friend's father had tickets to one of the last Red Sox games in 1959. He invited me and my father. It was the first time I ever sat in the box seats. It was freezing, but it didn't matter. Our seats were in the front row, right next to the Senator dugout. They were the old brown folding seats. An usher would show you the way to them, brush them off, and stand there waiting for a tip. My father didn't know why he was hanging around.

I was transfixed for all nine innings. It was the first time I'd seen Williams that close. I felt

like I could almost touch him as he walked by. I remember his swing, how he would coil and grind the bat. This was the season that he didn't do that well. He had a pinched nerve in his neck. I just remember when he swung I never had seen anything before like it. I expected him to swing real violently, it seemed like he wasn't really moving the bat and the ball would just shoot off the bat. He had two hits and one of them was a long fly ball to center field. In those days, they had this huge flagpole in center field in front of the wall. It was like a little alcove there. He smashed a long fly ball that hit off the top of the flagpole, and it bounced down. It should have been a home run, but it was only a double.

———————

JERRY CASALE: I was a small fry. I lockered next to Teddy in '59 and '60. When Teddy had big days with the bat he was always flying high. Teddy was always there, helping me out, telling me how to pitch, how to do this and that. He never kept quiet. He was always trying to talk to somebody all the time.

Teddy was just wonderful to me. I was a young guy coming out of the army. He knew I didn't have any money. I'd made $90 a month for two years; I was always broke. Ted was making a film on hitting, and he said to me, "Come to the ballpark the next few days early and make some money."

One day I threw 10 pitches, the next day 20. It was nothing. He handed me $200. And $200 in those days—wow! It was like $4,000 today.

———————

JOHN MORTON: It was 1959 and I was 13. A classmate's dad acquired several tickets to take his son and a few friends to Fenway. It was a big deal in those days to go to Boston, to say nothing of seeing the Red Sox play.

I didn't realize it then but my classmate's father had impressive connections. We were in box seats ten rows behind the Red Sox dugout.

Midway through the game Ted Williams, looking serious, strode to the plate. We all agreed, the only thing to make it a totally perfect day would be to see him hit a home run.

But he struck out. I saw his bat launched at us like a rocket.

The bat had clattered across the metal pipes which divided the box seats, coming to rest at my feet. Like every other kid at the game, I had brought my glove, hoping that a foul ball might come within reach, but I was looking down at Ted William's bat.

I reached for it and was mystified by the tar-like goo smeared on the handle. Suddenly, an usher appeared, yanked at the bat and shouted: "Gimme that!"

———————

DON GILE: I came up in 1959. I was just going to help in the bullpen. When they told me to go in and pinch-hit, I was absolutely flabbergasted. There were less than 10,000 in the park. I do not remember running in from the bullpen to the dugout, but I made darn sure I didn't pick up one of Ted's game bats.

———————

PUMPSIE GREEN: In 1959, I was playing for the Red Sox farm team in Minneapolis and having a great year, hitting about .330 or .340. On July 21, I got a call to report to Chicago. I suddenly became weak. I just couldn't believe the news.

LEFT: Lefty Mel Parnell styling his pitching pose
OPPOSITE: Lolly Hopkins, rated number one Bosox fan–and also the loudest–wields her megaphone in a game against the White Sox on August 2, 1955

Now I was making my major league debut. I came in as a pinch runner and remained in the game to play shortstop. We lost the game, 2–1, to the White Sox. I will never forget my first at-bat. I faced Early Wynn, who really shook me up. He had a big name. It was near the end of his career and the start of mine.

It never crossed my mind to have a room-mate, since I was the only black on the team. It wasn't a rule. But it was unwritten that blacks did not room with whites. I roomed with no one until Earl Wilson came along.

Before Elijah Jerry Green appeared on the scene, the Red Sox did not have a single African-American employee at Fenway—not a vendor, usher, groundskeeper, ticket-taker, player, or coach.

PUMPSIE GREEN: The Red Sox got me a room in a hotel. I didn't even know if I had to pay for it or not. I got to meet Mr. Yawkey the second day that I was in Boston. He was a very gentle, short, round man. He said he wanted to get to know me, and wished me well.

"If you run into any problems or need any advice on something, you don't have to go to the coaches or manager. Come directly to me," he said. I thanked him, and we shook hands.

I was a Californian and got in touch with guys from the University of San Francisco—Bill Russell and K. C. Jones—stars on the Boston Celtics. Russ would later take me around and talk to me. He told me where I should and shouldn't go.

My first night in Boston was July 24. Fenway Park just felt small. Even Minneapolis, where I played for two years, seemed bigger. There was now more media pressure than ever. "I can't fail. I can't make a mistake." That was how I felt.

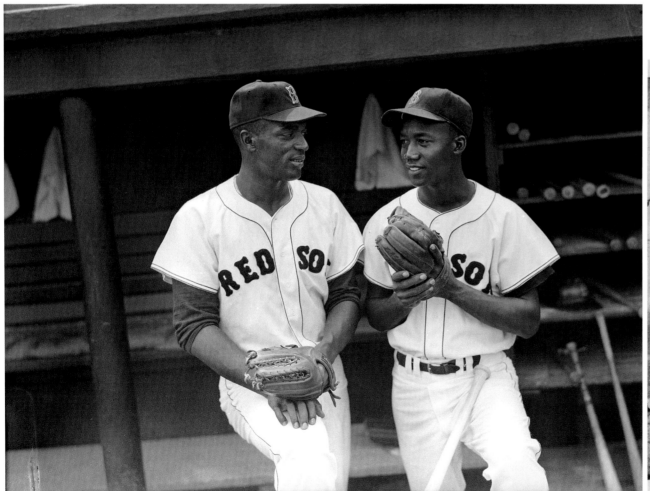

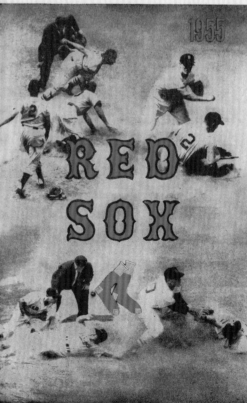

On Tuesday, August 4, Green, 25, batted lead-off, played second base, and made his Fenway Park debut in the first game of a doubleheader against Kansas City. Boston won, 4–1.

PUMPSIE GREEN: There was such a crowd, the park was full. A lot of blacks wanted to come to the game. They didn't have seats, but they were accommodated. The Red Sox roped off a corner part of center field.

I got a rousing ovation when I got up to the plate—a standing ovation. I can remember thinking to myself, "I really don't want to strike out right now. I really want to hit the ball." I tripled off the wall.

I made good friends on that team—Pete Runnels, Frank Malzone. Jackie Jensen and also Ted Williams. They were fellow Californians. Williams was one of the nicest guys I've ever met around baseball or any other time. He'd say, "Hey, Pumps, let's go warm up." Me warming up with Ted Williams. I loved it.

Some people said he was making a statement. But it wasn't just he who befriended me; it was he and a bunch of the guys. It was just that after the ball diamond, they went their way and I went my way.

Sometimes terrible things would be yelled out, racial epithets, at Fenway and at other ballparks. Some people said I must have felt like killing somebody. I got to where I could divorce it from my mind. I told people I had enough troubles trying to hit the curveball. I wasn't going to worry about some loudmouths.

JERRY CASALE: It's September 7, 1959. We were playing the Yankees. Bottom of the second inning. Don Buddin hits a three-run home run into the center-field seats and we knock out their pitcher, Duke Maas. I'm the next batter. Casey Stengel comes out of the dugout. He waves to the bullpen to bring in this guy Bob Turley. He could throw hard, real hard.

I start digging in. Yogi Berra asks, "Jerry, how's your wife? How's the kids? Nice year you're having."

All that bologna, you know. So I got taken up into that. The great Yogi talking to a peon like me.

The pitch went right by me; I never seen it. I said right then and there, "I'm never trusting a little fat, little Italian catcher again."

I dig in again. "C'mon, Bob. Give me that fastball again, this time on the inside of the plate." Turley gives me that pitch I want and I hit it over the screen, across the street. When I got to the plate trotting out the home run, I said to Berra, "I'm not married."

The next batter was Pumpsie Green. He hits one into the right-field seats, his only home run that year. We hit three home runs in a row. That was a nice moment in Fenway Park, especially beating the Yankees.

But my biggest thrill was being next to Ted Williams in the clubhouse. From time to time I think of Teddy and Fenway. How many times we sat in that little locker room and he would take off his pants coming in from a game, rip off his shirt, throw them, and hit me with them. Thousands of dollars right in my face. Who thought of it then?

The decade of the fifties at Fenway closed with a three-game series against the eighth-place Washington Senators. Managing the Sox now was Billy Jurges, who replaced Rudy York, who replaced Pinky Higgins. Attendance for game one was 9,089, the middle game drew 5,428, and the final game 9,110. Still the gate for each contest was better than the game against Baltimore that preceded the Washington series: only 2,199 showed. It was a depressing way to end the fifties.

ABOVE: The classic "Splendid Splinter" doing what he did best
OPPOSITE: First black players on the Red Sox team (L to R) Earl Wilson and Elijah "Pumpsie" Green, August 1959

—SIXTIES—

THE IMPOSSIBLE DREAM

On April 19 the new decade began at Fenway Park: Playing before 35,162 against the Yankee team of Roger Maris, Mickey Mantle, Bobby Richardson, Elston Howard, Bill Skowron, and company, the Red Sox disappointed the Fenway faithful, losing, 8–4.

	YEAR	WON	LOST	PCT.	GB	ATTENDANCE
RED SOX YEAR BY YEAR 1960 – 1969	1969	87	75	.537	22.0	1,833,246
	1968	86	76	.531	17.0	1,940,788
	1967	92	70	.568	—	1,727,832
	1966	72	90	.444	26.0	811,172
	1965	62	100	.383	40.0	652,201
	1964	72	90	.444	27.0	883,276
	1963	76	85	.472	28.0	942,642
	1962	76	84	.475	19.0	733,080
	1961	76	86	.469	33.0	850,589
	1960	65	89	.422	32.0	1,129,866

BOB SULLIVAN: I grew up in Chelmsford, Massachusetts, in the '50s and early '60s. It thought of itself then as a farm town.

My early games on TV from Fenway had everything to do with Curt Gowdy. I can to this day regale one with the Narragansett Jingle. Games on the radio from Fenway were as resonant to me as going to the ballpark. My grandfather used to sit on the back porch in Lowell, Massachusetts, in his Mount Vernon Street home. I must have been four or five.

I remember his cigar smoke and sitting on his lap and listening to the Red Sox.

I remember coming home one night with my brother from catching crappies, coming into the house, Dad sitting on the couch. "Hey, come here and listen to this."

Home run call:
Ned Martin: *"Long drive, left field. Way up, and gone. Mercy!"*

═══════════════════

CARL LOVEJOY: We'd park in the same spot in the area which is now for Boston University fraternities. We would walk past the wooden cart with the old wagon wheel and the black guy who was the salesman with an apron and a hat, sort of a bender's hat, the change maker on his belt. You'd hear the crack of the bat as you were buying peanuts and wanting to get inside, wanting to get to your seats to see batting practice, hoping to catch that foul ball.

I loved it when the foul ball would come down the screen and everybody would "whoooop!" and the batboy would catch it.

Going into a public men's room for the first time was to be intimidated. The urinals were troughs. And there were all these men and boys lined up.

PAGE 108: Summer at Fenway: A white-shirted crowd in right field bleachers under the Gruen clock, and Yankee players in the bullpen
ABOVE: Yankee manager Casey Stengel shakes hands with Joe Cronin, American League president, back at his Fenway Park stomping grounds

HARRY BAULD: Fenway was a place that you could go to the same way you went to the movies. I paid 50 cents to sit in right field. The ushers were all those incredibly florid-faced old guys. They'd dust the seat for you. I never did give them a tip. We were working-class kids. It was hard enough for us to scrape up the 50 cents admission.

On July 22, 1960, Ted Williams homered in a 6–4 Sox win over Cleveland. In the seventh inning he stole second base, to become the first major leaguer to steal bases in four straight decades.

BOB SULLIVAN: Dad wanted my brother Kevin and me to see Williams play before he retired, so he planned a big day. We were going to go in early and we were going to come back relatively late, considering we were so young.

So we drove down in the Oldsmobile with my brother and I on the back couch in the days before seat belts, and my mom sitting up front as terrified of 128 as Dad was back then. The way Dad would have driven, I'm sure it took an hour and a quarter. He parked under the Common. We took a taxi up, the first taxi we had ever taken in our lives.

Fenway was such a dungeon down underneath that you came out of the darkness and into the light. This was like, oh my goodness, it was like sending you to heaven. It was like a religion. Ted Williams. Fenway Park. I, of course, was a young Williams fan. And Dad was a World War II veteran, a master sergeant, and he was a Williams devotee. There's a myth now that all of the Boston fanship booed Williams. He was a prickly character. But it was the sportswriters who had problems with him, personal problems, that they took out on him in the pages of the newspapers.

He played hard. The fans in left field would heckle him and he'd spit and all the rest of it, but mostly the fans loved the guy. And Dad, as a veteran, was eternally devoted to this guy. His military background, his patriotism, his heroism.

We sat behind first base. It was just some game in August. There was no one in the park; they had given up on the team for every good reason.

Afterward, we got a taxi and Dad took us to Bailey's for enormous ice cream sundaes, served in silver cups with gooey, dripping marshmallow.

Falling asleep on the back couch of the Oldsmobile, curled up back there with my brother, it was just great.

On the 25th of September, Casey Stengel clinched his tenth pennant in a dozen seasons as manager of the New York Yankees as Ralph Terry edged Boston, 4–3.

"I drove into the ballpark," Curt Gowdy recalled, "parked the car, went into the clubhouse, and Johnny Orlando, the clubhouse guy, said, 'Gowdy, Gowdy, come here, this is the Kid's last game ever.'

"'What do you mean? We have a series in New York this weekend.'

"'Mr. Yawkey told him to take the last two games off and go fishing. This is his last game. You have to promise me you won't mention it to anyone.'

"I said, 'I promise I won't.'"

BOB KEANEY: I was a Lynn, Massachusetts, kid who loved Ted and trembled that his final game might be rained out that damp, drizzly, dark Wednesday. I sat with my friend Bruce Jackson on the third-base side, where John Updike sat collecting notes for his prize-winning essay on Ted's farewell game.

Ted warmed up with a pregame catch near the dugout with Willie Tasby and I loved that because Tasby lived in Lynn, too—ironically, Williams Avenue.

FRANK MALZONE: It was a cold day, the wind was blowing northeast in from right field, the kind of day you say nobody is going to hit one out.

September 28, 1960, Red Sox vs. Orioles. Overcast, dank, chilly, the final day of the final home stand of the 1960 season. Only 10,454 showed up. The game was not televised locally or nationally. "You Made Me Love You," playing over the loudspeaker, created a melancholy mood.

The Red Sox lineup on September 28, 1960:

Pumpsie Green	**SS**
Willie Tasby	**CF**
Ted Williams	**LF**
Jim Pagliaroni	**C**
Frank Malzone	**3B**
Lou Clinton	**RF**
Don Gile	**1B**
Marlan Coughtry	**2B**
Billy Muffett	**P**

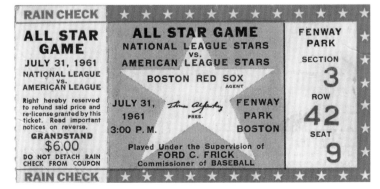

FRANK MALZONE: I wish there was more people there. They didn't realize, you know.

Curt Gowdy, Red Sox radio and television voice, began the spare ceremony: "Twenty-one years ago, a skinny kid from San Diego, California . . ." Boston mayor Collins, seated in a wheelchair, presented a $1,000 check to the Jimmy Fund, the favorite charity of Ted Williams, 42, who was given a plaque by the local sports committee. The inscription was not fully read. Williams hated a fuss.

He even was annoyed by the news announced to the crowd that his uniform number, 9, would be permanently retired. It was the first time the team ever honored a player that way.

"In spite of all the terrible things that have been said about me by the Knights of the Keyboard up there," Williams said over the loudspeaker, "and they were terrible things, I'd like to forget them, but I can't . . . I want to say that my years in Boston have been the greatest thing in my life."

FRANK MALZONE: Ted hit two balls good, the first one got into the wind in the right-field corner and was pulled back and caught by the right fielder, the next one the center fielder caught.

In the fifth inning, the Splendid Splinter clubbed the ball 380 feet, but the center fielder caught it in front of the visiting bullpen. "Damn,"

an annoyed Williams said to first baseman Vic Wertz. "I hit the living hell out of that one. If that one did not go out, nothing is going out today."

BOB KEANEY: In the eighth inning, Tasby, a black center fielder obtained from Baltimore, led off with Ted's last at-bat seconds away.

CURT GOWDY (game call): "Everybody quiet now here at Fenway Park after they gave him a standing ovation of two minutes knowing that this is probably his last time at bat. One out, nobody on."

BOB KEANEY: Ted dug in, wiggled his fanny, and glared at pitcher Jack Fisher. Everyone stopped breathing. Ted swung as hard as he could, but he missed the fat pitch and nearly sprained his arms. Some dreamers said later that Ted missed on purpose, so that Fisher would be fooled into throwing that fastball again.

CURT GOWDY (game call): "Jack Fisher into his windup, here's the pitch. Williams swings—and there's a long drive to deep right! The ball is going and it is gone! A home run for Ted Williams in his last time at bat in the major leagues!"

FRANK MALZONE: He hit one a little lower and a little bit better, and the wind didn't hurt it, and it made the bullpen.

JERRY CASALE: I was in the bullpen with Bill Monbouquette and Mike Fornieles and others. We were all up front looking over the railing. The ball went over our heads.

Williams circled the bases as he always did, in a hurry with his head down, trotting out number 521, his final homer. The crowd stood and cheered the man and the moment.

FRANK MALZONE: When he hit a home run, it was usually high—it wasn't no line drive. This time he got it all. When he hit a home run, he had a way of loping. This time his running was like a hop.

TED SPENCER: Williams hits the home run. I hear it on the radio. I said to myself, "Damn, I should have been there."

STEVE RYDER: I'd broken my knee in June when I was playing baseball in the Milwaukee Braves system and was in a recovery stage. I was a left-handed hitter and the amazing thing was seeing how he held through right to the last moment.

BROOKS ROBINSON: I was playing third base. He went running around the bases, and I looked at him as he passed second base. I had my arms folded as he passed me. That was absolutely a magical moment to be a part of that history.
STEVE RYDER: He had that regal trot around the bases. Didn't tip his cap, didn't look at the stands, just right into the dugout.

The inning ended and Williams went out to play left field in the top of the ninth. Just before the inning began Carroll Hardy replaced him. The Kid ran in. The crowd had one more standing ovation in it.

"We want Ted! We want Ted!" The fans chanted. But he refused to come out for a curtain call. Later

PAGE 112: In the sixties there were lots of bleak days at Fenway like this one on July 5, 1961, Red Sox vs. Tigers
PAGE 113: Aerial view of Fenway, 1968
ABOVE: (top) Ted Williams talks to Yankee catcher Yogi Berra, 1960; (bottom) Mickey Mantle and Roger Maris find some time to socialize at Fenway, 1960
OPPOSITE: Yaz takes a big swing in a 1964 game

it was reported that players and umpires tried to get him to come out. No dice.

FRANK SULLIVAN: We all wanted him to stop and at least take his cap off but that sonofabitch, he just ran into the dugout. He didn't stay around or let us say anything. You know that was the way that Ted was. He went down the dugout steps straight into the tunnel. That was it, aloha. We didn't know that that was his last game but we all suspected it. We were out of contention, so he wasn't robbing the team. It was just Ted was Ted and it was tough at times.

FRANK MALZONE: Typical Ted. Whoever was close by, he shook their hands and waved his hands to everybody else. "See you, gang." That was it.

In *My Turn at Bat,* Williams wrote, "You can't imagine the warm feeling I had, for the very fact that I had done what every ballplayer would want to do on his last time up, having wanted to do it so badly, and knowing how the fans really felt, how happy they were for me. Maybe I should have let them know I knew, but I couldn't. It just wouldn't have been me."

JERRY CASALE: At that moment, all we knew was that it was his last time up at Fenway. We didn't know if he was going to be coming back.

"Now Boston knows how England felt when it lost India," wrote Ed Linn.

Afterward Teddy Ball Game announced that he would not make the trip to New York for the Red Sox's final games of the season.

DON GILE: Two years later almost to the day that Ted hit that home run, I hit a home run in my last time at bat at Fenway. Ted was the 18th player in baseball history to hit one his last time at bat. I was the 19th.

No wonder Teddy Ball Game called it a career. Even with Ted Williams, the 1960 Red Sox were a poor excuse for a major league team. Posting a 65–89 won-and-lost record, finishing in seventh place 32 games out of first, they drew a million plus into Fenway Park. They would not reach that mark again for the next seven years.

Ted Williams was gone, but the talk was about the "new Williams" waiting in the wings.

Back on November 28, 1958, two days after receiving a $125,000 offer from the Cincinnati Reds, he arrived with his father in Boston to negotiate with the Red Sox. Scout Bots Nekola recalled the experience.

"They drove up to Boston in the middle of this damn blizzard," Nekola said. "It was dismal, snowing like hell, and Fenway Park was the last place in the world you'd try to entice anybody with."

The young prospect walked around the park while the scout waited nervously. He studied the fences. Finally he came back to Nekola. "I can hit in this park," he said.

Red Sox farm director Johnny Murphy offered the boy $100,000 plus college tuition. The father wanted $125,000 but dropped to $115,000.

"We'll give you $108,000 plus a two-year Triple-A farm contract a year plus the rest of your college expenses," Murphy counteroffered.

The contract was signed. They all went to meet general manager Joe Cronin, who sized up the five-foot-eleven, 170-pound young man. "He doesn't seem very big" was the baseball legend's reaction.

"He walked out shaking his head like a man who had met a midget when he expected a giant," the youth recalled.

—————————————

TED SPENCER: Over the winter the story was about Carl Yastrzemski, the new Ted Williams. "Well, I'm not going to miss this," I said. I missed Williams's last game. Three guys in high school with me wanted to go, too. It was April 11, 1961, my 18th birthday. I went down to the basement ticket window in Remick's department store in Quincy, Massachusetts, and bought four tickets, $3.50 each. Great seats—about four rows behind the on-deck circle behind the dugout on the visitors' side.

Yaz hit a bloop single to left field in his first at-bat and went 1-5 that day. That first hit came off A's hurler Ray Herbert. The Sox lost to Kansas City, 5–2.

—————————————

"I came to love Fenway," Yaz said. "It was a place that rejuvenated me after a road trip; the fans right on top of you, the nutty angles. And the Wall. That was my baby, the left-field wall, the Green Monster."

JOHNNY PESKY: I think Yaz was as good as any outfielder that ever played there, and I'm not taking anything away from Ted. Yaz was like an infielder from the outfield. He threw well; they couldn't run on him. And he knew how to play that Monster.

══════════════

DAN SHAUGHNESSY: Yaz could decoy better than any outfielder and routinely pretended he was ready to catch a ball that he knew was going to

carom off the Wall. Sometimes this would make runners slow down or stop altogether.

Memorial Day weekend 1961 showcased Red Sox versus Yankees, but it also spotlighted the Mickey Mantle–Roger Maris home-run battle. On May 29 the Mick slammed his first home run in two weeks, the only Yankee run as the Sox won, 2–1. Ike Delock was the victor over Whitey Ford. The next day Mantle and Maris hit two home runs each in a 12–3 Yankee romp over the Red Sox. On May 31 Mantle and Maris homered again in New York's 7–6 win.

Two big-league All-Star Games were staged each season from 1959 to 1962. In 1961, the second game was played at Fenway on July 31. Six dollars got one a seat in the grandstand Section 3, row 42, seat 9.

Don Schwall, who wasn't on a major league roster on Opening Day; Mike Fornieles; and manager Mike Higgins, as a coach, represented the Sox.

DON SCHWALL: I struck out John Roseboro and Stan Musial with a man on third. Heavy rain stopped the game in the ninth inning, making it the first All-Star Game to end in a tie. Detroit's Rocky Colavito homered for the American League for the only All-Star home run ever hit over the Green Monster.

Schwall was swell in the midsummer classic. His team, however, was mediocre at best. The Sox drew just 850,589 at Fenway in 1961 and posted a 76–86 record for a sixth-place finish.

JOHN SHANNAHAN: The summer of 1962 my uncles Patrick and Teddy took me to my first game, a weekday afternoon against the Minnesota Twins. We sat on the third-base side, upper box seats. I asked my uncles which team is which. Red Sox are in the white uniforms and the Twins in the gray, they said. But in the bright summer sunny afternoon they all looked white to me.

It was Nuns' Day, and it looked like there were thousands of nuns in front of us dressed in their old black habits with the white coifs around their faces. In the early '60s, Richard Cardinal Cushing would hold a Nuns' Day at Fenway every year. Later on, when I went to my second game at Fenway, I wondered, "How come the nuns aren't here?"

BISHOP JOHN D'ARCY: Nuns' Day was a big day at Fenway. The nuns wore the old long habits, and Cardinal Cushing—a great, bigger-than-life Boston figure and a big baseball fan—would come along. He'd wear a straw hat, which was common in those days, and a black suit. Back then the priests always wore black to the games, and there were a lot of priests at the games.

SISTER ANNE D'ARCY: There were probably hundreds of nuns at the game, from all different communities, and it was such a treat to meet the other sisters and take in the game from seats in the grandstand. It was kind of like an outing where everyone could enjoy this treasure of a Red Sox team even if they were not that good.

Earl Wilson had joined the Red Sox on July 29, 1959, eight days after Pumpsie Green broke the color barrier on the team. The scouting report on Wilson described him as a "well-mannered colored boy, not too black, pleasant to talk to, well educated, very good appearance."

The six-foot-three, 215-pound, right-handed pitcher's marker moment took place on a rainy June 26, 1962, before 14,002. He pitched a no-hitter against the Angels and also hit a home run in the 2–0 win.

ABOVE: Carl Yastrzemski supports Lonborg with his second home run off Cardinals pitcher Joe Hoerner on October 5, 1967
OPPOSITE: Jim Lonborg pitches against St. Louis in World Series, October 5, 1967

Johnny Pesky, on the scene as manager since the end of the '62 season, got his "country club" group off to a hopeful 1963 start. At the end it would be the same sad story—a 76–85 record, a seventh-place finish, 28 games off the pace.

Dick Stuart and Dick Radatz were two "cult figures" who performed in the sixties for the Sox. Richard Lee Stuart was with the team in 1963 and 1964. Richard Raymond Radatz had a longer tenure, 1962 to 1966.

On June 23, 1963, first baseman Stuart, known as "Dr. Strange Glove" for his challenged ways as a fielder, established a major league fielding record by grabbing three first-inning grounders and tossing them to pitcher Bob Heffner for putouts. The Yankees, unfortunately, bombed the Sox, 8–0.

Sox fans delighted in giving Stuart the mock cheer. There was a game when wind was whipping about Fenway, as was customary at times. Stuart, also known in some circles as "Cement Glove," without losing a step, deftly snatched up a piece of paper that had blown his way. That effort provoked the crowd into rising and giving him a standing ovation.

Radatz was a top relief pitcher and a powerful presence on the mound. In 1963 he entered a game against the Yankees with the bases loaded. Reaching back for a little extra, he struck out Mickey Mantle, Roger Maris, and Elston Howard—all American League MVPs at one time—on a total of 10 pitches. Mantle complained afterward, as the story goes, about what it was like to hit against that "monster." Dick Radatz became "Monster" Radatz.

Another symbol of those down mid-1960s years at Fenway Park was right-handed hurler Jack Lamabe, who posted a career 16–20 won-and-lost record for Boston. He did strut his stuff, how-ever, for all to see on Opening Day 1964—Friday, April 17—pitching a complete game and knocking out two hits. That game honored the late John F. Kennedy. Tony Conigliaro, out of Revere, Massachusetts, homered in his major league debut.

STEVE FOLVEN: I went with my friend Billy Brooks and his uncles by car. We drove down Commonwealth Avenue, parked on a side street across from BU [Boston University], and walked to the park.

The Yankees were winning, 1–0, in the last of the ninth. Stottlemyre was still pitching. And Yastrzemski led off that inning with a triple. And then the Sox filled the bases with one out. And I said, "They're finally going to win." Malzone hit like a line drive to third. Clete Boyer, the vacuum cleaner, just scooped and made an incredible play, threw to second—the ball went to first, double play. They lost, 1–0.

Leaving, you just went under the bleachers. It was like the solemn march. Nobody said too much. I just remember Billy Brooks's uncles, as we would go back from these games, saying, "Yeah, and every time we go, we lose. Every time we go, they lose." These guys are like 50 or 60 years old and I'm going like, "Don't take it so seriously, will ya?"

Many fans took it seriously. Johnny Pesky was sacked as manager with two games left in the season. The Sox finished 1964 in eighth place in a 10-team league and drew 883,276 to Fenway.

The Citgo sign in Kenmore Square is a fixture outside left field. It officially debuted in the 1965 season. Composed of 5,878 glass tubes adding up to more than five miles of neon, the 60-foot-by-60-foot, high-voltage sign is lit up from dusk to midnight. Its ruby red, blue, and white neon is a sight to see at night.

1967
WORLD SERIES
AMERICAN LEAGUE vs. NATIONAL LEAGUE
FENWAY PARK

GRANDSTAND
$8.00
DO NOT DETACH THIS COUPON FROM RAIN CHECK

GAME
1

RIGHT: Marching band, Opening Day 1962
OPPOSITE: Keeping the faith in the rain on Nuns' Day at Fenway

Like the Citgo sign, lanky Jim Lonborg also made his debut in 1965, on April 23, and recorded his first major league win on May 10, 3–2 over the ninth-place Yankees. Yaz slugged two homers and a sacrifice fly. Mantle went three for four, with a homer. The Mick's ninth-inning double with two outs triggered Lonborg's exit, but the Monster, Dick Radatz, entered the game and got the final out.

SAM MELE: I came into Fenway a lot when I managed Minnesota from 1961 to 1967. My home was still in Quincy, Massachusetts. So I slept in my own bed. It was funny. I was managing against the team that I loved.

In 1965 we beat Boston 17 out of 18 times, 8 out of the 9 at Fenway. It actually hurt me to beat them. I felt sorry because in my heart I was a Red Sox fan. I had played for them, I had scouted for them. Tom Yawkey would come in my office. And we would talk a lot. Oh, yeah, geez, he had me in his will.

FRANK MALZONE: I used to marvel at the way Tom Yawkey came around to say hello to everybody. They say he sat up in his box and not only watched our game but had two TVs going on watching two other games. This is how much he loved baseball.

Yaz loved baseball, especially on the 4th of May, 1965, when he hit for the cycle, blasted two

home runs, and drove in five. Nevertheless, the Old Towne Team went down, 12–8, to Detroit.

Tony C. (Conigliaro) also put together a "day" for himself, on the 27th of July at Fenway. He stroked three home runs, two in the opener of a doubleheader, and a grand slam in the nightcap. Boston, however, was the loser in both games to Kansas City.

The losing, the miserable attendance, the doom and gloom that pervaded Fenway were on parade big time on the 16th of September. The tiniest crowd of the season made its way into Fenway Park—just 1,247 paid and 1,123 in on passes. Dave Morehead opposed Luis Tiant of the Cleveland Indians.

BILL NOWLIN: That day, I was sitting in Section 8. I was a student at Tufts College at the time, but I guess I didn't have any classes then.

Cleveland batted in the top of the ninth. Morehead had struck out eight, given up a walk, and was one out away from a no-hitter. He got two fastball strikes on Vic Davalillo, a pinch hitter. The next pitch was a curveball hit back to him.

DAVE MOREHEAD: I went to catch it, and I was going to run over to first the way Mel Parnell did in his no-hitter, either step on the bag myself or hand it to the first baseman. In my haste, the ball hit the heel of my glove, and I started to run without the ball, which lay on the mound. I went back to pick it up and threw it to first base real quick. The throw was low in the dirt, and "Mad Dog" Lee Thomas scooped it out. I had my no-no.

After the game the news came out that Tom Yawkey, as was his practice, would rewrite

Morehead's contract and give the 22-year-old a $1,000 bonus. That was the good news. The bad news was for general manager Pinky Higgins. He was let go and replaced by Dick O'Connell.

Fenway was a ghost town of a ballpark in 1965, when the team drew but 652,201, an average of 8,052 a game. The worst came late in the season. On September 28, against California, only 461 showed to watch the sad Sox. The next day was even worse against the same team—just 409 in the house. Finishing ninth in the 10-team American League, the Sox lost 100 games and won 62.

Managers kept coming and going. Top prospects somehow never made it for one reason or another. Billy Herman was in place as the 1966 season started. Early on Dave Morehead, just 24, regarded as a brilliant future star, suffered an injury to his arm and was never the same. Posting a 1–2 record in a dozen appearances, he symbolized the Red Sox of that era—promise but pathos.

Mickey Mantle, a key figure in the Boston–New York rivalry, slammed his 37th and 38th home runs at Fenway on June 29, when the Yankees edged the Red Sox, 6–5. With these dingers, Mantle tied Babe Ruth's record for most homers by a Sox opponent.

MIKE ANDREWS: In 1966, I was playing for Toronto, the Red Sox AAA franchise managed by Dick Williams. After the playoffs I drove down with Dick to Boston. He thought he was coming for meetings about players. He actually was to be offered the manager's job.

My first game in the big leagues was September 18, against the California Angels. I was 23 years old. I came up with the bases loaded, hit a ball really hard in the hole to Jim Fregosi, who backhanded, jumped up in the air, and threw to first. "Welcome to the big leagues."

I never adjusted to a liquor sign on a billboard outside of Fenway, though. It was almost outside

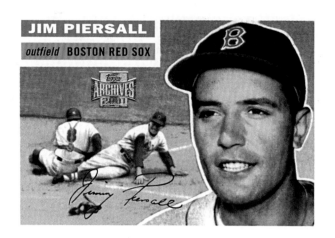

JIM PIERSALL
outfield **BOSTON RED SOX**

of center field. People would climb up and stand on the platform of this billboard, which was higher than the left-field wall, to watch the game.

Fenway was pretty empty. Maybe 6,000-some-odd people. There was no one ever in Toronto, either. So I was kinda used to that type of crowd.

The Jimmy Fund sign was the only advertising at the park. The environment wasn't very luxurious. Going up and down that dingy runway from clubhouse to dugout, it was dark, dank. There were little 40-watt bulbs that angry ballplayers would break occasionally. You walked on old wooden slats and had to watch that you didn't step on one that was broken.

At day games, what fans there were sat in the center-field stands. I always thought it gave us an advantage. Opposing players complained that they had trouble picking up the ball against a mainly white-shirted background. But playing there all the time, you get adjusted to it.

In 1966 the Sox lost 90 games and finished ninth. Attendance at Fenway Park was 811,172, an average attendance per game of 10,095. It was pitiful.

LEIGH MONTVILLE: I was a sportswriter at the *New Haven Journal Courier* and convinced my boss to send me to Opening Day of the 1967 season. "Okay," he said, "you can take the train but you

have to come right back after the game is over. I don't want you staying overnight."

I had my matching sport coat and my tie and my new portable typewriter. I took the train up and got off at Back Bay. It was cold. I tell the cabdriver, "Fenway Park."

"Why are you going there?"

"Because I'm a sportswriter and I'm covering Opening Day."

"The game is postponed. Too cold," he said.

I had to get a story, so I went in the locker room and talked to Dick Williams. I was terrified because I had read all this stuff about how gruff he was.

MIKE ANDREWS: Dick was a tough manager, very, very tough. He wasn't one who gave you a lot of accolades.

LEIGH MONTVILLE: I didn't know they had a press room, so I went across the street to a grill to type up my story while knocking back a couple of beers.

Rookie Bosox pilot Dick Williams realized he had a tough job ahead. Coming off a 90-loss season, the Red Sox were a 100–1 shot to win the American League pennant in 1967.

The young, crew-cutted disciplinarian promised that the team would win more than it lost in 1967. He vowed changes, and said that if blowing up the country-club atmosphere was what was needed, he would do that, too.

"There had been tremendous teams at Boston," Williams said, "but they had won just one pennant in twenty-one years. At home they were excellent, but they just could not win on the road because it was a team manufactured to play at Fenway Park."

Williams said he would not allow the dimensions of Fenway to influence his managing style and the play of his ballplayers. "I made it clear," he said, "the Green Monster was not going to be a factor. I had seen too many players ruining themselves taking shots at the Wall. I made my pitchers concentrate on pitching to right-handed batters, who always came up there looking for the ball away, thinking we'd get them to avoid pulling. I knew that the way to pitch at Fenway is to get the ball inside and gradually back the batter up a little."

The Opening Day lineup for the Red Sox at Fenway in 1967:

Jose Tartabull	CF
Joe Foy	3B
Carl Yastrzemski	LF
Tony Conigliaro	RF
George Scott	1B
Reggie Smith	2B
Rico Petrocelli	SS
Mike Ryan	C
Jim Lonborg	P

JIM LONBORG: It started off as a typical Red Sox season. There were 8,324 fans on a cold and dreary April 12, Opening Day. We beat the White Sox, 5–4. Petrocelli hit a three-run homer. And I got the win.

BOB SULLIVAN: I went to Dartmouth, and we used to road-trip down to Fenway and get standing room without any trouble. It was $8 for grandstand seats. But so many seats were empty. You would flip an usher a quarter and you could

OPPOSITE: Lou Brock loses his cap as he steals a base off Jim Lonborg in the 1967 World Series

move down into the seats. Then it changed. What happened was '67.

A lot of the buzz in Boston was about rookie Billy Rohr, who on April 14 one-hit the Yankees and Whitey Ford at the Stadium.

ED MARKEY: Billy Rohr in the early part of that season became the symbol of our renaissance—the lefthander we so needed over all those years.

Markey and thousands of other Red Sox fans were at Rohr's next start, on April 21.

ED MARKEY: Fenway Park was electric. This was our chance to vanquish the Yankees. He won that game, too, 6–1, subduing the Yankees a second time, beating Mel Stottlemyre.

Despite his promise, Rohr never won another game for the Red Sox and finished the season in the minors. Although Rohr wasn't in a Red Sox uniform for all of Boston's "Impossible Dream," he helped set the pace for it.

"Billy Rohr was 1967," Peter Gammons wrote, "even if he only won two games and was out of town by June."

MIKE ANDREWS: My 1967 salary was $11,000. And in July Tom Yawkey called me into his office and gave me a $4,000 raise. I was told he was always doing things like that.

After the All-Star break, Boston took off on a 10-game winning streak. In July, crowds topped 25,000 a game.

In August, they numbered 30,000 or more.

In September, there would be standing-room sellouts.

BISHOP JOHN D'ARCY: There was a tradition that every rectory in the immediate Boston area would get a free pass to Fenway. It was indeed a wonderful perk. The rectory was the priests' home, but if somebody worked there and was not a priest, he could probably use it as well. I think you had to pay 50 cents or a dollar to get it. You would go in and find your own seat, but it was not hard to find a seat in those days. In 1967, when the crowds came back, that was the end of that.

A crowded Fenway Park in that era before '67 was an anomaly. Weird weather conditions were not. Fans from the start of play in 1912 brought umbrellas, jackets, blankets with them—even in midsummer. On April 25, 1962, the ocean breeze dropped the temperature at Fenway from 78 to 58 degrees in 10 minutes. One August day in 1967 pea-soup fog caused a couple of stoppages of a game—outfielders could not see.

But an even stranger sensation was at Fenway Park on the 18th of August: pennant fever. The Red Sox were in fourth place and were hosting the fifth-place California Angels in a four-game series.

Tony Conigliaro singled his first time up off Angels starter Jack Hamilton. In the fourth George Scott led off with a blooper to short left-center field and was cut down trying to stretch the hit into a double. A fan in the left-field grandstand tossed a smoke bomb onto the outfield grass, delaying play.

When play resumed, Reggie Smith stroked a line drive single. Conigliaro batted next.

—————————————

DAVE MOREHEAD: I was sitting on the top step of the dugout, charting pitches, right there by the corner closest to the on-deck circle. I was talking to Fitzie, the clubhouse man. I was watching Tony. Jack Hamilton threw the pitch.

—————————————

An inside and high fastball hit Tony C. flush on the cheek below the left eye. Dropping to the ground, his cheekbone crushed, his eyeball imploded, Conigliaro writhed in pain.

—————————————

DAVE MOREHEAD: He had to have lost sight of the ball. It was frightening. His left eye was closed before our trainer, Buddy Le Roux, got to him.

Coaches and players raced out to the unconscious young star. A silent and stunned crowd watched as one of their favorites was taken off the field on a stretcher.

More than a year and half later, Conigliaro would return to play baseball for the Sox. He had some small successes. But the injury left him with some brain damage and vision problems and ended what should have been a brilliant career.

Two days after the "beaning," there was a doubleheader against California. The Sox lost the first game, 8–0. They won the second game, 9–8. Reggie Smith homered batting left- and right-handed. Yaz popped two three-run homers, one in each game of the doubleheader.

On the 30th of September, Carl Yastrzemski slugged his 44th home run as the Bosox nipped the Twins, 6–4, to tie for first place.

—————————————

BRUCE TUCKER: That 30th of September was my first time at Fenway. I was 18. I paid a dollar to an usher at the gate to get in. It was the end of the '67 season. Fenway was jammed with people. The "grown-ups" in the stands. Guys wearing shirts and ties.

We had no seats. We just went from place to place, sat on the stairs until some usher would come over and tell us to get out of there, and then we'd sit on the stairs somewhere else until another usher told us to move. But we saw the game.

—————————————

Senator Ted Kennedy; his father, Joseph P. Kennedy; his brother, New York senator Robert Kennedy; and Minnesota senator Hubert Humphrey were at the game. Winning Red Sox pitcher Jose Santiago gave Senator Ted Kennedy the game ball.

JIM LONBORG: I was on the mound on October 1, the winning pitcher as we clinched the pennant. All of my teammates and thousands of Fenway fans seemed to run at me. It's what you dream about in Little League. I was trying to get back into the dugout. Thank God for the Boston police—they were able to control the crowd.

—————————————

The Red Sox beat the Twins, 5–3, but the Impossible Dream was still a dream until Detroit lost to California to finish one game behind the Red Sox. Listening intently to the radio in their locker room, Boston players and officials reacted with glee as California nipped Detroit, 8–5. Inside Fenway Park loyal fans rejoiced.

—————————————

BRUCE TUCKER: The Sox finished 20 games ahead of the ninth-place Yankees. Boston was going into the World Series. People started tearing apart the scoreboard, ripping the sod off of the field, just trashing the place.

—————————————

The attendance at Fenway Park that Impossible Dream season jumped from 811,172 in 1966 to 1,727,832. Winning 20 more games than in 1966, Boston was 49–32 at Fenway, 43–38 on the road.

———

BRUCE TUCKER: We went back for the World Series, all of us taking the day off from school, taking the bus into Boston, asking the usher to let us in.

"How much you got?" he asked.

"Well, we got change."

"Gimme what you got!"

One at a time, we gave him whatever we had in our pockets and he let us through the gate.

———

The fall classic matchup was Boston versus St. Louis. Cardinals ace Bob Gibson irritated Red Sox management, fans, and players. Looking around Fenway Park prior to the Series, the power pitcher asked, "Where's the upper deck? Where are all the seats?"

Gibby was disappointed that Detroit was not the competition. "Their bigger ballpark would have meant more fans, more money," he said. "I don't know about you, but $1,500 is a lot of money to me."

Game one, on the 4th of October, Lou Brock of the Cardinals collected four hits and Gibson fanned 10 Red Sox. Jose Santiago pitched a beauty for Boston and even homered. But St. Louis won, 2–1, scoring on two RBI ground balls from Roger Maris.

Two home runs by Carl Yastrzemski, Jim Lonborg's masterful pitching (no-hit ball for 7⅔ innings and a one-hit 5–0 gem) evened the Series for Boston. Sal Maglie, the Red Sox pitching coach, said that Lonborg's performance was "a better pitching effort than Don Larsen's perfect game in 1956" against him and the Dodgers.

The next three games, two of which were won by the Cardinals, were played at Busch Stadium. That set up games six and seven at Fenway Park on October 11 and 12. The Sox won game six, 8–4, setting up the decisive seventh game.

Jim Lonborg, with a lot of mileage on him from a long season, started with two days' rest. He was ineffective. Bob Gibson was more effective. Fanning 10, yielding only three hits, the Cardinal ace led his team to a 7–2 victory and the world championship.

LEIGH MONTVILLE: I started at the *Boston Globe* in '68 and I spent a lot of time at Fenway. The press box was fabulous because it was right at the end of the foul ball screen, and you were right on top of the game. Still there were a lot of those old-time baseball writers, and there was a huge press crew that most other cities did not have. Not only Boston guys, but guys from Lynn and Quincy and Bedford and Fall River, the Cape, Worcester.

You'd get to Fenway Park early and leave late. The earlier you came the earlier you got the stories, so you showed up at three and then two and then even earlier for a seven-thirty game.

After games, it was "open bar" in the press room. A lot of drinking. You could go home at three-thirty in the morning after covering a night game. There was some great conversation. Billy Martin would come up. Managers and coaches would come up. Drinking and talking was the big thing.

It was a long, long day. You'd be around for a while and you'd eat a meal in the press room before the game and pound out your story and then you'd pound out something during the game and then you'd pound out something after the game.

You'd leave the ballpark and, you know, it would be totally quiet and you'd be climbing down a kind of fire escape with stairs that were welded on. It was an age we'll never see again. All that drinking stuff—and everybody drove home.

Tom Yawkey was kind of aloof and away from the whole thing. He was in his box with his wife and Haywood Sullivan or whoever was his person at the time.

A lot of the players were terrific. Bill Lee was great. He pointed at Yastrzemski one day,

LEFT: Watering down the seats and aisles
OPPOSITE: The 1965 Red Sox broadcast team in open stands for the first time in Fenway history

who was near the end of his career and still going strong, and asked me, "You know what his secret is?"

I said, "No."

He said, "He wears his uniform when he goes to bed at night. Lying down he has the symbol for infinity on."

It was always good in those years at Fenway, but I was amazed that the manager's room was always very sterile—none of those guys ever seemed to decorate their office.

Fenway in that era was people going to a lot of games, knowing baseball. It was like being in a speakeasy or something like that. Everybody knew somebody. Everybody had a connection to someone. Everybody was involved with the game and the players and the park.

———

SISTER ANNE D'ARCY: In the late '60s I used to bring the fifth-grade class to Students' Day. It cost 50 cents for right-field grandstand seats. Parents would come to chaperone. The students would be wearing all that Red Sox stuff, having a fine time of it. They were well behaved, but they ate a lot.

———

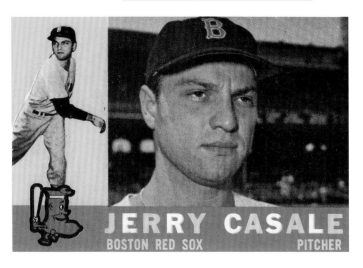

JERRY CASALE
BOSTON RED SOX   PITCHER

ERICA TARLIN: I grew up in Brookline. My first game was '68. We always sat in the bleachers because that's all we could afford. Fenway wasn't the most well-maintained ballpark and part of that was because from time to time ownership was lobbying for a new stadium and one way to do that, of course, was to keep the place looking decrepit.

———

MIKE SCHAFER: During 1968 my brothers and sister and I saw over 30 games from the $2 bleacher seats. My hero was Joe Foy. My sister was 12 and she took us on the subway. My older brother was almost nine. My twin brother and I were six going on seven. A gaggle of kids.

We stood and held the handrail and leaned in on the turns on the Green Line subway car, each of us with a dime in our sneakers. I remember the rush of the subway, the push-out door at Kenmore Square, and the excitement of the walk-up to the park. I had one hand in the glove we carried for foul balls and the other in my brother's.

We stuck together, bought a program, paid attention, and kept score. We always stayed through the ninth inning, and we ate until we had only enough money left to get us back on the train.

———

"September Song" at Fenway Park in 1968 saw two legends of the game in action. Mickey Mantle on September 27 flew out in his final at-bat at Fenway. Andy Kosko replaced him and homered, tying the score in the eighth inning. A Joe Pepitone ninth-inning home run gave New York a 4–3 win.

Two days later, before 35,209, Carl Yastrzemski went hitless in the season finale, against the Yankees. Yaz won the battling title with a .301 batting average—the lowest to ever lead the league

with those numbers. No one else hit .300 in the American League that "Year of the Pitcher."

Even though Boston finished in fourth place in 1968, 17 games out of first, attendance that season was 200,000 more than in the time of the Impossible Dream.

———

JOHN PIZZARELLI: My father, Bucky, was playing up in Boston, and we all drove up on a Friday early during the 1969 season. I was a Yankee fan then and had my Yankee hat on. The division in the stands was so interesting, and I remember somebody playing "Taps" as they convinced a guy in back of me to take off his Yankee cap. I was able to keep mine on.

———

It was a very bad day for Red Sox pitchers, June 14, as the Oakland A's clubbed them for a 21–7 rout. Reggie Jackson hit 2 home runs and drove in 10 runs.

———

BILL LEE: I got called up from Pittsfield in '69 because Jim Lonborg had gotten hurt falling off a motorcycle. I had never been to Boston before. I had my dad's car, a 1962 Chevy, the hot car for the time. It was white, two doors, red stripe down the side. They said come down the turnpike and you'll see Fenway Park on your right, you'll see the lights and stuff and just get off at the first exit and head back. You'll be at the park in no time.

It took me frickin' 45 minutes to get there. Finally I parked over on Boylston and walked probably a half of a mile.

This was June 25, 1969. Against Cleveland. The doubleheader crowd was already settled in. I just walked in and then they took me through the corridors down to the locker room. You come out through one of the tunnels and you can't believe this beautiful jewel of a diamond in the middle of the city. I think Bart Giamatti summed it up best when he described where the Persian worked for Paradise in a closed green place where you least expect it, or something like that.

They sent me out to the bullpen. In the third inning of the second game I'm in the ball game. My first batter was Duke Sims, a left-handed hitter. He rips a ball down the right-field line, past first, and he thinks it hits chalk. It caroms off the wall into right field and is called a foul ball. I walk him on a 3–2 count. The next hitter is big, strong Tony Horton. I throw him a changeup and he hits a deep, hard line drive foul and wrenches his back and the trainer comes out and takes his time checking. Finally, they decide Horton can stay in the ball game. I end up walking him. First and second, nobody out.

Next is Ken Harrelson, who hits a hard ground ball between third and short. George Scott at third makes a great play on a half hop. All in one motion he throws to O'Brien at second, who throws to Dalton Jones at first. Double play.

Next guy is Max Elvin. I strike him out on three pitches and bang, I'm out of the inning.

Bobby Doerr told me, "Don't unpack your bags, you ain't gonna be here long." I did unpack my bags, and I was there 9 years, 142 days.

On July 20, Sherm Feller announced that astronaut Neil Armstrong had made history setting foot on the moon. The news rippled through the crowd. The umpire called time. Baltimore's Brooks Robinson somehow had not heard Feller's announcement and came to the plate ready to hit. The umpire gave him the news. Robinson dropped his bat and began to applaud. Spontaneously, the crowd broke out with "God Bless America."

JEFF IDELSON: It was Red Sox against Orioles. We were sitting in the grandstand beyond the first-base line. I remember how rich and blue the seats were and that I was sitting in a wooden seat—I had never sat in a wooden seat other than in school. But mostly I remember how I felt the excitement and aura of being in a palace.

BROOKS ROBINSON: The Red Sox and the Orioles had a lot of good battles in that ballpark. I played at Fenway 23 seasons. Fielding third base wasn't really any different at Fenway. I just played where I thought they were going to hit the ball, depending on who was hitting and who was pitching, and I didn't really take into consideration the left-field wall.

It was a terrific park to hit in. I think, however, you learned after a while to not try for the Green Monster and just let your natural tendencies take over.

With nine games left in the 1969 season, third-base coach Eddie Popowski replaced Dick Williams, the outspoken hero of the Impossible Dream, as manager. The deposed skipper had been caught in several cross fires, and those did him in.

There were disagreements with his best player, Yaz, who threatened to fight Williams on a couple of occasions. There was a loss of rapport with the front office. And most significantly, there was a feud with Tom Yawkey.

"I didn't think your coming into the locker room as often as you do helps," Williams told the longtime Sox owner. "Too many times I've eaten someone out for a mistake and then seen you put your arms around his shoulders as if to comfort him."

There was no one comforting Dick Williams.

The 1969 Red Sox drew 1,833,246 into Fenway—tops in the league—but they finished in third place in the American League East, 22 games behind Brooks Robinson's Baltimore Orioles.

Overall, it had been a Fenway decade that started with the retirement of one legend, Ted Williams, and ended with the presence of another legend-to-be, Carl Yastrzemski, in left field for the Fenway Faithful to cheer for.

The Sox had not won the World Series in 1967, but they had appeared in their first one since 1946, their second since 1918. Everyone around the ball club and Fenway Park had high hopes as the 1970s beckoned.

BELOW: Bat boys in the 1960s making small talk

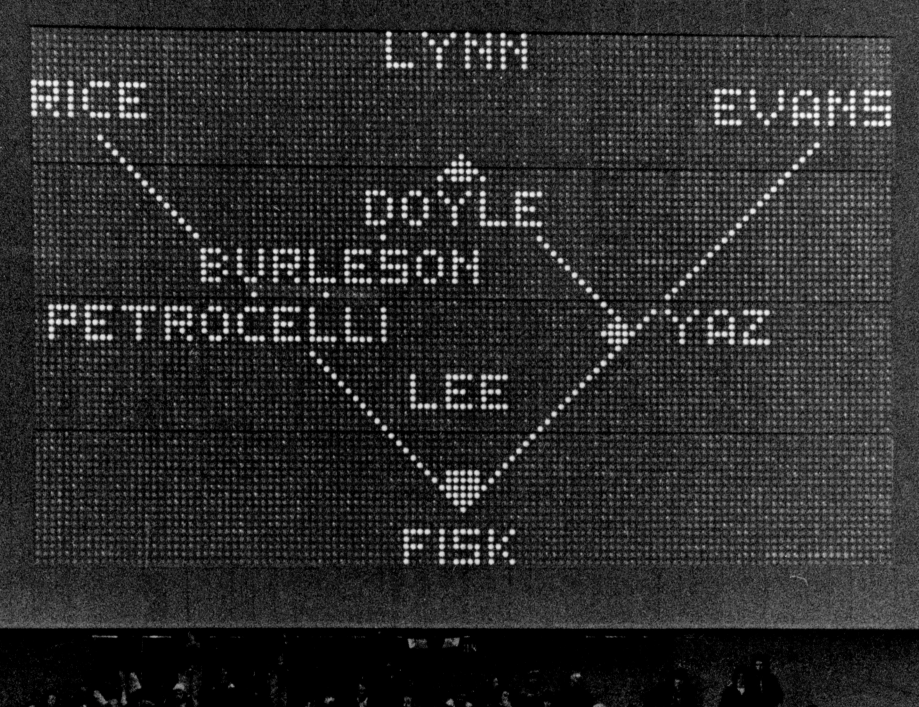

-SEVENTIES-

ALL THAT YAZ, AND MORE

The Red Sox decade of the seventies began on April 14 at Fenway: Yankees against Red Sox. There were 34,002 in the house. New York manager Ralph Houk was pitted against new Red Sox skipper Eddie Kasko. Another Opening Day. Missing was a longtime fixture, the center-field flagpole. No one seemed to notice. Old Towne Team rooters exited happily after watching their team, behind Ray Culp, win 8-3, aided by homers off the bats of George Scott, Tony Conigliaro, and Reggie Smith.

RED SOX YEAR BY YEAR 1970 – 1979	YEAR	WON	LOST	PCT.	GB	ATTENDANCE
	1979	91	69	.569	11.5	2,353,114
	1978	99	64	.607	1.0	2,320,643
	1977	97	64	.602	2.5	2,074,549
	1976	83	79	.512	15.5	1,895,846
	1975	95	65	.594	—	1,748,587
	1974	84	78	.519	7.0	1,556,411
	1973	89	73	.549	8.0	1,481,002
	1972	85	70	.548	0.5	1,441,718
	1971	85	77	.525	18.0	1,678,732
	1970	87	75	.537	21.0	1,595,278

The Red Sox Opening Day lineup at Fenway, April 14, 1970:

Mike Andrews	2B
Reggie Smith	CF
Carl Yastrzemski	LF
George Scott	1B
Rico Petrocelli	SS
Tony Conigliaro	RF
Luis Alvarado	3B
Jerry Moses	C
Ray Culp	P

Old Towne Team fans reveled in the potential of their team, which blended depth, youth, and experience, a powerful offense, and some strong pitching. And more help in the form of Luis Tiant, Fred Lynn, and Jim Rice was in the offing.

With Carl Yastrzemski, the Red Sox were always exciting, never out of a game. Fans at Fenway came to see "Yaz" as they had come to see "Teddy."

RED SOX

CARL YASTRZEMSKI   of

JOHN KENNEDY: It seemed everybody thought Tom Yawkey kowtowed to Ted Williams and Carl Yaz because a lot of times people would come into the locker room and see him sitting with them. But he didn't ignore anyone. My locker was right by the clubhouse door, and he would always stop and ask how were the kids, was there anything I needed?

━━━━━━━━━━━━━━

EDDIE KASKO: My first day on the job Mr. Yawkey came into my office. "Listen, if you don't want me to come down to the clubhouse just tell me and I'll stay out of here."

"Mr. Yawkey, you own the team. You can come here any time you want."

"No, no, but I don't want to get in the way of your running the ball club or managing it or doing anything like that."

I said, "No, that's going to be no problem."

He says, "Well, you know I just like to come down and talk to the players. I like to know about their families and their outside interests."

In those years, there was a longtime nucleus in place at Fenway—a special fan, the organist, the PA guy, the switchboard operator, the head groundskeeper, the top PR guy.

Sherm Feller was the PA guy. He'd always hold court in the press room. He had hearing aids that you tuned in with a dial. You'd be hearing the "eeeeeeeeeeerr, eeeeeeeeeeerrrrr." He'd reach in and say, "Hold it, hold it, I'm getting Shanghai."

━━━━━━━━━━━━━━

STEVE FOLVEN: I was on the cleanup crew with my brother Ray, a time when the program and scorecard cost a dollar and 25 cents. It was like being in the Promised Land. You got a ticket for free. After the ball game ended, they'd give us a bag and we'd pick up papers and stuff until four or five in the morning. We'd get paid $2.50 an hour.

There were probably about 10 to 15 guys picking up and half a dozen or more guys blowing the stuff. We'd just walk like mummies. We'd pick up old cups, straws, leftover food, newspapers.

My brother Ray and I went on the field, into the dugout. We weren't going to steal anything, didn't even try and get to the locker room.

Perching like Sox manager Dick Williams in the dugout, my brother Ray gave the signal to the bullpen: "I want the lefty." He touched the left arm. Then he left the dugout, and started walking to the mound, pantomiming Dick Williams, the deadpanned look.

━━━━━━━━━━━━━━

The brothers Folven had their times at Fenway. The brothers Conigliaro were center stage on the 19th of September 1970. Tony and Billy homered in the nightcap of a twin bill, and the Red Sox romped, 11–3, over the Senators (managed by Ted Williams).

An attractive team that drew better at home than any other American League team, 1,595,278 at Fenway, the Red Sox were 52–29 at home but just 35–46 on the road. Had they been a bit better away from Fenway, who knows what they might have accomplished that season? They finished in third place in the American League East.

On April 6, 1971, before 34,517, the Red Sox won their second straight home opener against the Yankees behind Ray Culp, 3–1. Reggie Smith had a banner day for the Sox with three hits.

More Sox power was on display on the 9th of August as they slammed six home runs, beating Detroit, 12–11. Four of the Sox runs came on a grand slammer by Bob Montgomery.

PAGE 130: Fans listen to the announcement of the Red Sox starting lineup as it is displayed on the new electronic scoreboard on April 13, 1976
OPPOSITE: Grainy black-and-white aerial shot of the empty park waiting for action, 1976

RICK MILLER: I made my debut with the Red Sox on September 4, 1971, coming in late in the game as a pinch hitter. I was really nervous. I swung at the first pitch. It was a high fastball. It went for a double off the Green Monster.

I loved Fenway, loved to play there. But as an outfielder you were challenged. I had to learn the tricky configurations and angles, how to get great jumps, how to play players. I would cheat, I knew the counts and moved on each pitch according to the count.

ERIC PORTNOY: The great thing about moving from Rhode Island to Brookline, Massachusetts, was our proximity to Fenway Park. It was nothing for my brother Bobby and me to make the ten-minute trolley ride to the ballpark. Our grandfather Sam Skoler encouraged us. He had been a big Sox fan since he came to this country in the 1920s. He remembered everything about going to Fenway—all the old stars, even when Babe Ruth played for Boston.

BOB SANNICANDRO: In '72 I was a clubhouse attendant. I had just graduated from high school. I wore just shorts and a T-shirt. The only time I wore a uniform was when I was a ballboy down the right-field line.

If a new team was coming in for a series we'd have to be there bright and early to unpack their gear and put it in their lockers. If their laundry wasn't done, we did it. We'd clean and polish their spikes. "Clubhouse kids," they would call us.

Tom Yawkey would come in the clubhouse and be dressed up nice. Then he'd switch to flannel grays, pants and top and sanitary socks. He would go on the field and play pepper games. He would know you by name. He would slap you on the back and say, "How's it going, Bobby?" Every so often there would be an extra check. It was called "gratuity from Mr. Yawkey." A lot of money for those days.

We were discouraged from taking tips, but there were some players that were more tip-giving than others.

Bill Lee was always talking about our place in the universe and stuff like that. He was very intelligent. I listened to a lot of his philosophies. Great curveball. Great heart.

It was hard to believe that Yaz was only 32 at the time. He was very good to me and a motivator to the team. One day Nolan Ryan, who had an aura, was scheduled to pitch.

"We can beat this guy," Yaz said, "nothing to worry about. You know he throws everything straight."

I'd always idolized Joe Namath, who had a Fu. And I'd always say to Luis Tiant, "Grow it down. Grow it down like a Fu." He grew the Fu and that year Luis had some real success when it looked as if he was done. He became "El Tiante" toward the end of that year—famous for that Fu.

I would take bats home and use them in my Legion games. I liked Aparicio's. I was a 17-year-old kid, and it wasn't that heavy and it was a thin-handled bat. I remember Richie Allen's bat, how big and heavy it was.

Eddie Kasko was a very quiet manager, very businesslike. His office was pretty much off-limits. We'd go in to clean it, vacuum it, but that was it.

RIGHT: Southpaw Bill Lee pitches to Pete Rose of Cincinnati to open the seventh game of the World Series, October 22, 1975
OPPOSITE: In Game 2 of the 1975 World Series against Cincinnati, Boston center fielder Fred Lynn makes a diving catch of Johnny Bench's fly ball in the sixth inning

It was very common for players after the game to sit down and have a couple of beers and unwind and then maybe take a couple of beers, put them in a sanitary sock, throw it over their shoulder, and leave the ballpark.

I autographed baseballs for players. This was before sports memorabilia really hit. If it's a Yaz ball, it might not be Yaz. If it's a Reggie Smith ball, it might not be Reggie Smith. There was one player, I'll leave him nameless, showed me how he signed his name. He told me to go home and practice. I went home and the next day he says, "Not bad, keep working at it."

A tough job was to get two dozen baseballs signed from each player. Some of them would get very upset, especially since they were honed into preparing for a game. Sometimes those

balls would get flicked up into the air; I'd end up picking them all up off the floor.

"Fuck them balls." You'd get that. But, if you went up to a player and said, "These are for the front office," it was understood that they had to sign those balls, that they were for somebody "upstairs."

Most players had their ritual. They would go over to the table where they would fill out the number of tickets that they would need for the day, look at their mail, take some time to sign their baseballs. And then they'd get ready for infield, outfield, and batting practice.

In those days we took the polish and shined the shoes. We used a wire brush to clean off spikes. It was very common for a player to have six pairs of spikes. Many times I would be in the

spikes and they'd have a beer pulled for me. I'd have two beers, watch them pull the tarp off the field, be back in time, and never miss a pitch.

In the bullpen Sparky Lyle worked in a strange way, throwing his first pitch real slow, just a lob. And the second pitch he'd throw 90 plus miles an hour. Because they weren't expecting, he'd hit catchers in the chest and worse a lot of times. Around the fifth inning, Sparky would go to the Triangle, get a cheeseburger, and be ready to go.

=====

DICK BRESCIANI: June 1972. I was with the team for about a month working as assistant to Bill Crowley, the director of public relations. He told me that there was going to be a special Jimmy Fund Night in August with Texas in town, with Ted Williams as the manager. In those days, Mr. Yawkey would donate the proceeds from a game to the Jimmy Fund.

"We want to make sure this is a sellout." Bill Crowley said. "We're going to have the disc jockeys around town hype this game for the next two months. We'll have a pregame hitting contest between former Red Sox players and the DJs.

"We'll give prizes. For the grand finale, we want it to be a big surprise, we want Ted to come out to hit. He hasn't swung a bat in Fenway Park since the day he left. Then on Saturday afternoon after the game we are going to have a surprise party for Mr. Yawkey—in celebration of his 40th anniversary owning the team. We're going to have a special event in the press room. We've got many former Red Sox coming as well as the current team. So we want Ted to get Mr. Yawkey to come up to the press room after the game. He doesn't do that much anymore. So Ted's going to somehow get him up there."

I had never met Ted Williams. So we get to Texas. We were out at the ballpark, and I'm with

clubhouse working, laundry, vacuuming, and a pitcher taken out of a game would come in and explode. Doors would get mashed in and more.

One time I was invited to a party upstairs. I sat at a table having dinner and Ted Williams was directly across from me. I just watched and listened as Teddy Ball Game held court. He was so charismatic; his booming voice could just drive a conversation.

I got paid decent money for a part-time job; those gratuity checks from Mr. Yawkey did help. And at the end of the year, I received a sixth of a share voted by the Red Sox players. It was like $400, even though the Red Sox came in second.

=====

BILL LEE: I started out as a reliever and became a starter in '73. Old guy Gene Clines was in the pen and he asked to see my grips. I showed him my curveball grip. "No, no, no. That's how you hold a cocktail."

So I learned what you learn out in the bullpen is bad habits. You learn how to smoke, chew tobacco, and waste your time.

But it wasn't a bad environment at Fenway. Fans would bring you anything you wanted. During rain delays, I would sneak out with an usher named the "Whale." We would run out the back entrance down Ipswich Street, cut back through the back alleyway, and end up in the Eliot Lounge. They'd hear the clicking of my

a whole bunch of the Boston scribes. There he is in the dugout all by himself. I follow along with the group and he's standing there with a fungo bat, his foot up on the step, and yells, "Here comes the G-D Boston writers."

So they start chitchatting and kidding around and now they all turn around and leave and I figure, okay, he's in a good mood. I'll have to introduce myself and tell him what is planned.

He looks at me and says, "Who the hell are you? And what the hell do you want?"

I tell him and he says, "Oh, cripes, I'm not doing it. You think I'm going to go out there and swing a bat in front of all those people? I have not swung a bat in Fenway Park in 12 years."

"It will be a great thrill for everybody," I said. "Pitching coach Lee Stange will throw some soft ones to you."

And he goes, "Aaaaahhh. You tell that Crowley I'll do it. But goddamnit he better not have other things he wants me to do, too. I'll do those two things and we'll get it done for Mr. Yawkey."

Williams almost hit one into the bullpen. He got one to the warning track, and the crowd went berserk, and then the next day even though his team blew a lead late and we won, he got Mr. Yawkey up to that press room and it was a great surprise party.

───────────────

JOHN SHANNAHAN: Old-time Red Sox players as well as local personalities took batting practice, and depending on where they hit the ball, they'd win money for the Jimmy Fund. Guys like Frank Malzone, Ted Lepcio, Walt Dropo, a lot of guys from the fifties took swings.

Things were starting to end when the crowd started to chant, "We want Ted. We want Ted." And he emerged from the visitors' dugout, bat in hand, and went to the plate. He took his cuts and he had sort of warning-track power. But

the last ball he hit was right down the right-field line, and whether it was fair or foul nobody seemed to care; it was close enough. It was the last home run, unofficial as it was, that he ever hit at Fenway.

───────────────

DON LENHARDT: As first-base coach under Eddie Kasko from 1970 to 1973, we'd go to Mr. Yawkey's office after games. It had a nice bar and a barman. We would talk about the game, the roster.

Once I told Mr. Yawkey, "We need to get rid of Yaz and Reggie Smith." Of course it was just a joke. But to tell the truth, they wore me out game after game at Fenway. Everybody wanted to go home when the games were over. But those two always wanted more batting practice, and I was usually the guy who obliged and pitched it to them.

───────────────

THOMAS DONAHUE: In 1972 I went with my mother and a friend of hers and her son. I had a glove; we sat in the bleachers. A ball was hit by Carl Yastrzemski. It came straight at me. I reached out to get it. But I was too little; it went over my head. A gentleman in front of us scooped it up crying, "I got it!"

Another man yelled out, "You saw the kid reaching for it. Give him the ball." And he gave it to me. My mother still has the ball; I guess I'll inherit it one day.

───────────────

Tommy Harper and Rico Petrocelli on September 7 paced a 10–4 Red Sox victory over the Yankees with three-run homers, putting the Sox in first place. Nine days later Dwight Evans, who would become a Fenway favorite, made his major league debut, replacing Reggie Smith in right field as the Sox humbled the Indians, 10–0.

Attendance that 1972 strike-shortened season was 1,441,718, second in the American League. Boston posted an 85–70 record and finished in second place just half a game behind Detroit, who played one more game than the Sox in the American League East.

On April 6, 1973, the first ball was thrown out on Opening Day in a game against the Yankees by Ed Folger, a Sox minor leaguer, whose legs had been amputated that past September as a result of a farm accident. The game was the first in major league history to feature the "designated pinch hitter," as the position was first called.

Ron Blomberg was the first to bat in that spot. He faced Luis Tiant and walked in the first inning.

OPPOSITE: 1975 team picture

Red Sox

FRED LYNN

RON BLOMBERG: I was left at first base when the inning ended and was going to stay there because normally that was my position. First-base Coach Elston Howard said, "Come on back to the bench, you aren't supposed to stay out here."

I went back and asked, "What do I do?"

He said, "You just sit here with me."

Blomberg finished the game one for three. Boston's DH, Orlando Cepeda, went nothing for six. The Bosox rapped out 20 hits and ripped the Yanks, 15–5. Four runs came across the plate on Carlton Fisk's first career grand slam.

HOWIE SINGER: Summer of '72 or '73. My first game. Section 11, toward the back of the grandstand. It's the eleventh inning and my dad says, "Hey, kids, I'm sorry. It's getting late and we got to drive back. If it's still tied after this inning, we go."

Bottom of the eleventh and Reggie Smith comes up. I'm up and screaming, "C'mon, Reggie! Hit it right here." And he hits a walk-off home run.

With the score tied 2–2 in the top of the ninth on August 1, 1973, Yankee catcher Thurman Munson tried to score from third base on a missed bunt attempt by Gene Michael and crashed into Red Sox catcher Carlton Fisk. The two got into it, triggering a 10-minute bench-clearing brawl. Both players were ejected; the game resumed and Boston eked out a 3–2 win.

The ever tart and observant Bill Lee quipped to Fisk after the game, "I can see by the scratches on your face you've been in a fight with Gene Michael."

On Opening Day at Boston against Baltimore in 1974, Luis Tiant lasted 6⅔ innings and was touched for four earned runs. The Boston 7–6 loss, however, was charged to fellow Cuban Diego Segui, 36.

"El Tiante" on the mound was a bear of a man, a workhorse, one tough pitcher whose windup also elicited lots of attention and commentary.

EDDIE KASKO: Luis Tiant's windup? Oh, that was him. And the funny thing was there were some who tried to imitate it and tried to hide the ball like he did.

There was a game against California. Tiant started. We were ahead like 5–1. You could tell that he wasn't really that sharp but you're trying to get him through the inning with the lead. He got into the fifth inning and pitched himself into trouble. A base hit, and a run was scored. Jim Spencer was coming up.

I went out to the mound. My mistake was not motioning to the bullpen ahead of time. "Give me one more hitter," he said, "I know I can get him out."

"Well, okay, I'm going to give you the one more hitter." I was barely back at the dugout when Spencer ripped a base hit up the middle. I just turned around and went back out to the mound. "You left me in one hitter too long," Tiant said. I think he smiled.

That was Tiant, you know. Just being comical. But he was a guy you could count on. In between starts he loved to shag balls in the outfield. He'd catch them behind his back. I wouldn't have hesitated to play him defensively in center field if the need arose.

DWIGHT EVANS: When that bullpen door at Fenway was unlatched and Tiant came out, people would go crazy.

CHRIS WERTZ: I was two years old at my first game. We sat in the bleachers on long aluminum benches that burned your bare legs. Tiant was pitching and my mother had me screaming, "Looie! Looie! Looie!"

LUIS TIANT: The more they called my name, the more they were behind me. You want to show what you can do, to give your 120 percent every time. Here I was between the middle and the end of my career, but it worked out pretty good for me.

On August 19, 1974, in his major league debut, Jim Rice appeared in the Sox lineup as a DH and went 0–2. He did drive in a run with a sac fly. Boston hammered Chicago, 6–1.

OPPOSITE: Fred Lynn in his classic batting stance

A sad moment for bird lovers took place in a game against the Tigers in 1974. Willie Horton's foul ball hit a pigeon who landed on home plate, dead.

Sad also for Sox zealots were injuries to Carlton Fisk and Rick Wise. Notwithstanding, the Bosox persevered. They were in first place with a seven-game lead on August 21.

___

FRED LYNN: I got called up in September of '74. And I couldn't get over how everything at Fenway was so old. If you were over six-one you could dome yourself pretty good, so you had to watch your head when you came out of the dugout.

Playing the outfield at Fenway was a lot of fun for me. But playing center field you had a lot to worry about—the door to the equipment area, the bullpen that jutted out way in the back, a rod-iron fence with gothic spikes on it at the 420 sign. Lots of things out there gave caroms. You just had to learn how to play them. I just threw balls off of everything and saw how they would bounce.

Sherm Feller became a good friend. Being a center fielder, all the speakers were right behind me. I could hear him clicking the microphone on and off and sometimes he would forget and I'd hear him mumbling stuff.

The players' parking lot was as big as a postage stamp. Fans had access to it. So it was very difficult to get your car out. Either they were beating on your car because you had a good game or they were beating on your car because you had a bad game. Either way your car got beat to crap. Most days, they had mounted police trying to push the people back.

Ted Williams came by quite a bit. He kind of liked our club. Lots of times I would talk to him in the clubhouse about hitting. He liked my swing but didn't like my thought process very much.

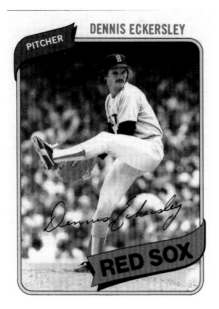

In those days ticket prices were very affordable, the cheapest seats being in the bleachers. Usually there were college kids sitting there, having a few beers, relaxing, watching the games. Instead of having law enforcement on hand for when fights broke out, they had the BC football team. And they would stop all the fights. You would see those guys running!

The Yankees trimmed the Red Sox, 6–3, on September 9 for their first victory in Boston since July 31, 1973. Since 1972, the Yanks had won just 2 of 24 games at Fenway.

With the "Gold Dust Twins" excelling—Jim Rice, who recorded his first big league homer on October 1, and Fred Lynn—and other young talent, the future seemed solid for the Red Sox. By season's end, 1,556,411 had flocked to Fenway, tops in American League attendance. Losing 24 of their final 38 games, the Sox finished in third place. Out was Eddie Kasko as manager, and in came Darrell Johnson.

In 1975, Fenway opened with a remodeled left-field wall, an electronic scoreboard installed, and the manual scoreboard changed to show only out-of-town scores from other American League games.

The lineup Boston put out in '75 was powerful and versatile, featuring players such as Fred Lynn,

Jim Rice, Rico Petrocelli, Dwight Evans, Rick Burleson, and Carl Yastrzemski. Tony Conigliaro was back, too.

TERRY GUINEY: Opening Day was very cold. What was extraordinary is that Tony Conigliaro was in the lineup as the DH. Tony was a hero from just over the bridge. He had been out of a Red Sox uniform since 1970 as a result of the devastating injury. Coming up to the plate, Tony received an ovation that went on and on and on. He got a hit, and the place went crazy. Just chills up your spine. Tony lasted another 20 games and then he was done.

BOB SULLIVAN: Patriots Day. Nobody else in America knows what we're talking about. We'd get this odd day off. As a kid, I used to go out to Lexington to see the reenactment before dawn, when they came out and reenacted the battle on the Green. We'd always go out for the parade in Concord. I can't believe how many times I saw Bill Lee lose that 11-o'clock game. And he was one of the greatest lefthanders in the Sox uniform. Well what kind of management would ever pitch Bill Lee before noon?

On Patriots Day, April 21, 1975, "Spaceman" Bill Lee was hammered. The Yankees romped, 12–1. That was a bad day that season at Fenway.

But there would be more good days than bad, like a 9–3 win over the Kansas City Royals on July 18, when Jim Rice slugged a monster shot over the center-field wall, becoming only the sixth player to accomplish the feat.

One of the more poignant moments at Fenway took place on August 26, 1975, when the parents of Luis Tiant were announced to the crowd at Fenway

and Luis Sr. threw out the first pitch. The family reunion resulted from a letter Senator George McGovern brought from Massachusetts Senator Edward Brooke to Fidel Castro asking him to allow Luis Tiant's parents to travel to Boston and watch their son play ball. Castro approved the visit for "as long as they wanted."

LUIS TIANT: I had not seen my father for 17 years. My parents didn't even know my wife and their grandkids. For about 25 years, my dad had been a great pitcher for the New York Cubans in the Negro Leagues. When I played winter ball, coaches and managers who had played with my father used to tell me, "You're good. But your father was better."

This day, my parents sat in Section 14, right behind first base. When I looked to the catcher for signs, I could see my father with a noise-maker. I was pitching for the Red Sox, but I was also pitching for my parents and relatives.

I lost that game. But it was a great day just to be around my father and mother. I had thought I would never see them again.

PAGE 140–141: Carlton Fisk jumps on home plate after hitting the twelfth-inning homer to win Game 6 of the 1975 World Series against Cincinnati, October 21, 1975
OPPOSITE: Master at work: Luis Tiant on the mound

FRED LYNN: In 1975, it seemed like it rained every day. This day it was the "Game of the Week." Bill Lee was pitching. Rain delay. With today's pitchers, no chance the starter comes back. But Billy comes back. Then there is another rain delay. He is out there helping the grounds crew with the tarp. And then he comes back and pitches again. He was the '75 Red Sox, and the fans at Fenway loved it.

Toward the middle part of the season, people really started to take notice of what was happening with the club. With Yaz and Fisk and Lee and Jimmy Rice and me and Dewey Evans and Luis Tiant and Rico Petrocelli and the others—we had a colorful group of guys and also a lot of talent.

I would make a play and they would go crazy out there in the outfield seats. They would be yelling my name, especially the girls. I was young and they were young, so it was nice.

———

LUIS TIANT: Fenway is a ballpark for the pitcher; whoever makes the less mistakes is the one who's going to come out with a victory. You have to be a pitcher there; you can't be a thrower.

———

On September 16, El Tiante bested Baltimore's Jim Palmer, 2–0, in an old-time pitchers' duel. Solo shots by Carlton Fisk and Rico Petrocelli accounted for the scoring, pushing the Bosox lead over the Orioles to 5½ games, virtually clinching the American League East title. Boston swept the Oakland A's in the American League Championship Series.

The World Series competition was the Big Red Machine. Led by likable manager Sparky Anderson, the Reds had won the National League West race by 20 games over the Dodgers and swept the Pittsburgh Pirates in the Championship Series.

The first two games were played at Fenway before 35,205 on both October 11 and 12. The teams split, Boston winning the opener, 6–0, but losing the next game, 3–2. Luis Tiant, an 18-game winner in the regular season, pitched a five-hit gem for Boston in the opener.

———

LUIS TIANT: I saw my father in the stands. He smiled and he put his hands up and he was happy. That was the pinnacle of my baseball career. It was a great family moment for me and my wife and the kids, my mom and dad.

———

The Reds won two of three at Riverfront Stadium. Trailing 3–2 in the Series, the Red Sox were happy to get back to Fenway. Game six was delayed by a travel day and three straight days of rain. The World Series resumed on the 21st of October. Sox manager Darrell Johnson had rested star pitcher Luis Tiant for the game.

———

FRED LYNN: In the fifth inning with two on, Ken Griffey drove a ball into left center. I ran it down. I went up and I just missed it. I just had run out of real estate, basically. The base of the Monster was concrete. The tin started maybe 15 feet up or so. I hit the wall and crumpled, losing all

feeling from the waist down. But I was entirely conscious and lay still because I thought I had seriously injured my back.

Charlie Moss, the trainer, comes out and Darrell, the manager. I was already starting to get some tingling. They helped me up. I stayed in the game, but it was pretty scary.

———

Griffey ended up with a triple, driving in two runs. Then Johnny Bench singled Griffey home to tie the game at 3–3. Bottom of the eighth, Cincinnati was ahead, 6–3. The Red Sox had two runners on base, two outs.

———

LEIGH MONTVILLE: Mike Barnicle was sitting in the box seats next to the press box. I was sitting near the end of the press box. We "talked" back and forth through glass. I wrote the words "Bernie Carbo" on a piece of paper and held it up, and he nodded.

———

LENNY MEGLIOLA: Rawly Eastwick was throwing BBs for Cincinnati. Bernie Carbo had two pathetic swings, and it sure looked like he was going to strike out. I closed my eyes. All of a sudden I hear the roar of the crowd and I turn my head quickly and right toward the center-field bleachers, exactly where the home run went.

———

NED MARTIN (game call, NBC Radio): *"Two strikes. The pitch . . . Carbo hits a high drive to deep center, way back, home run!"*

———

RICK WISE: I was out in the bullpen. All the pitchers were out in the pen. It could have been the last game of the Series. When it landed in the stands, it was absolute bedlam.

———

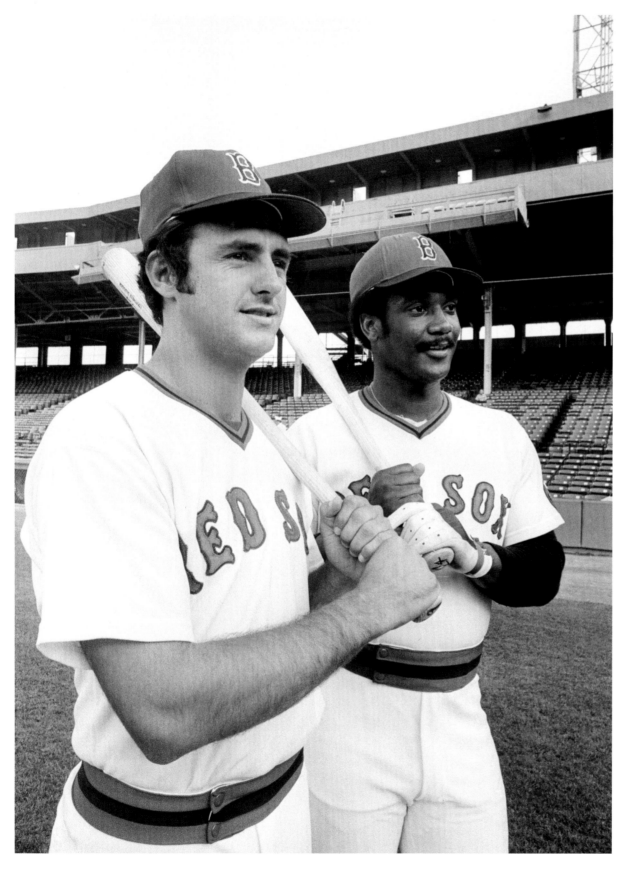

Rawly Eastwick was a strike away from ending the inning before Bernie Carbo hit the three-run home run. "That was one of the most unbelievable at-bats I've ever seen," said Reds catcher Johnny Bench, who dropped Carbo's 2–2 foul ball. "He looked so bad, it was unbelievable."

BERNIE CARBO: Getting to home plate after that home run, my teammates mobbed me and the fans went crazy. I heard them screaming my name. I found that I tied the game after I got to the dugout. Batting, I was so focused on keeping the inning alive that I hadn't paid any attention to the score.

The game moved to the top of the 11th inning. With Griffey on base and one out, Joe Morgan smashed a drive toward the right-field seats. Dwight Evans, a 23-year-old outfielder now in his third full season with the Red Sox, raced to the front of the stands and made a leaping, one-handed catch. Griffey, who had run himself into an out going well past second base, was doubled up at first.

FRED LYNN: We were in the twelfth inning, still tied. It felt like it was two o'clock in the morning. That game had lasted forever. I was in the on-deck circle in a front-row seat. Pudge [Carlton Fisk] and I were watching [Pat] Darcy warm up. We didn't know much about him except that he threw sinkers. He wasn't even supposed to get in the game. Sparky

---

OPPOSITE: Red Sox pitcher Luis Tiant Jr. is reunited with his father, Luis Tiant Sr. after 15 years
LEFT: Sensational rookie outfielders (L to R) Fred Lynn and Jim Rice, August 4, 1975

[Anderson] had run out of pitchers.

Pudge says to me, "I'm going to get on, knock me in." It was a perfect pitch for Pudge, down and in—Pudge was a low-ball hitter.

NED MARTIN (game call, NBC Radio): *"The 1–0 delivery to Fisk. He swings . . . long drive, left field . . . If it stays fair, it's gone . . . . Home run! The Red Sox win! And the Series is tied, three games apiece!"*

FRED LYNN: As soon as Fisk hit it, I knew it had enough to get out. I had a real good angle and I could see it was going to make it. It didn't take long to get out. I was the first one to congratulate him.

His body language, everyone claimed, helped it go.

Well, he was doing that. And I was jumping up and down.

NBC had positioned a cameraman inside the Green Monster. A rat scared the cameraman, who had the camera frozen on Fisk, waving his arms and using body English, willing his fly ball fair and off the left-field foul pole.

"The ball only took about two and a half seconds," recalled Fisk. "It seemed like I was jumping and waving for more than two and a half seconds."

BILL NOWLIN: I had standing room. They let us sit in the aisles. I sat between Section 17 and Section 18. Basically where I was sitting I could look directly down the left-field foul line. So I was perfectly positioned to see that ball arc. It looked like it was starting to move a little more, a little, a little more toward the foul pole.

FRED LYNN: I was happy I didn't have to hit again. I was thinking we have game seven at our place and things are looking good.

LENNY MEGLIOLA: Fisk was kind of standoffish but more approachable than Yaz. Fisk would just let the questions assimilate and he would answer in a drone. But then he would go on and on. Fisk didn't necessarily seek attention, but he didn't send out vibes like don't come next to my locker today. After that game he was swarmed over by media, as you would expect. He did not seem to mind.

BILL NOWLIN: That night for hours, people were honking horns driving around Fenway and around town, just so excited about it.

Game seven was played at Fenway on Wednesday, October 22. The pitching matchup was Bill Lee and Cincinnati's Don Gullett. The Red Sox southpaw had a crowd of reporters around him before the game and was asked to compare himself to Gullett.

BILL LEE: I told them that after the game Gullett was going to the Hall of Fame, and I was going to the Eliot Lounge for a few beers. That gave them something to write.

DON ZIMMER: Darrell turned to Lee, with no input asked by me. Lee was the most logical choice and all we really had left. He had handled the Reds well in game two.

The Red Sox jumped out to a 3–0 lead. Tony Perez's two-run homer off Bill Lee with two outs in the sixth got the Reds close. A Pete Rose single tied the game in the seventh. Jim Willoughby replaced Lee, and Darrell Johnson brought in rookie Jim Burton to pitch the ninth.

With Ken Griffey on third and Rose on first, Joe Morgan blooped a single to center. The Reds won, 4–3, and were world champions.

RICK WISE: It was a mistake pitch. It was a good pitch, and it was a good piece of hitting on Morgan's part. It's just the way it goes.

FRED LYNN: In those days you didn't have 40 pairs of spikes. We only had two or three and they were waterlogged, leather, and weighed about five pounds apiece. Morgan hit that little blooper and I'm just sloshing through the mud and I got the ball on one hop. Had we been play-

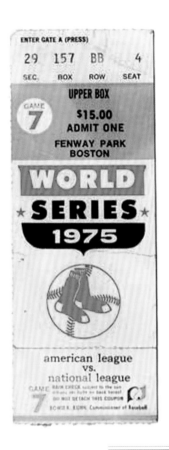

ing on dry turf, I would have caught it easily. The ground didn't drain well in those days. It was a swamp. And I just couldn't get there.

At the very start of what would be a stellar career with the Sox, Fred Lynn was already a fan favorite and someone owner Tom Yawkey embraced. He had already won Rookie of the Year and MVP during the regular season.

Lynn's crash into the concrete outfield wall in game six had moved the fans and motivated Yawkey to act.

JON MILLER: When Lynn smashed into the wall, Yawkey, who was in his later stages—not only as team owner but of his life—turned to Haywood Sullivan and said, "We have to put padding up. That has to be done as soon as the Series is over."

They put the padding in after the 1975 season basically re-covering the left-field wall, taking out all the old tin.

MIKE ANDREWS: All the tin that was taken down was donated to the Jimmy Fund. Little paperweights with an authentic piece of the tin on them were created. Some pieces had big dents.

As the 1976 season got under way, Fenway's first message board was added over the centerfield bleachers. The railroad tin panels in the wall were replaced by Formica-type panels, resulting

in more consistent caroms and less noise when balls hit the wall. Manager Darrell Johnson was in place. Much was expected of him and the team. He would however, win 41 games and lose 45 and be replaced by Don Zimmer.

BILL LEE: He was definitely a noncommunicative type, Zimmer. He was a belligerent terrier, a Gila monster, a great third-base coach. It was the Peter Principle one more time: "Always keep dumb-assed people below your general manager."

On Opening Day, April 13, fans at Fenway saw the Red Sox beat Cleveland, 7–4.

On June 29 Rick Wise, the winning pitcher in relief in the sixth game of the 1975 World Series, spun his second one-hitter of the month. The Red Sox nipped the Orioles, 2–0.

Attendance on July 8 reached 1,007,491, the earliest date in history that the franchise topped the million mark. The next day brought the announcement that an ailing Tom Yawkey had died of leukemia at age 73 in New England Baptist Hospital. There was no funeral service. He was cremated. Team ownership was then taken over by a trust headed by his widow, Jean.

BILL LEE: The winter before, I used to go in to get my mail at Fenway Park. Mr. Yawkey was always stealing my *National Geographics*. I had to go up to his office to get them; he was going through chemotherapy at the time. We had long talks.

Butch Hobson had played in a couple of road games in 1975. On July 28, playing in his first game at Fenway, he doubled off the center-field wall and smacked an inside-the-park homer. Boston beat Baltimore, 12–8.

Special milestones at Fenway took place for Jim Rice and the Red Sox on August 30. The solid outfielder launched a fifth-inning home run against Texas, the 100th homer of the season for the team—giving the franchise 100 homers or more for 31 straight years.

Boston posted an 83–79 record and finished 15½ games behind the Yankees, in third place in the American League East. If they had just been better on the road there would have been another first-place finish. At home, the Sox had been a sensational 46–35; at other ballparks they were a mediocre 37–44.

Don Zimmer was still on the scene as manager as 1977 began at Fenway Park. His coaches included Walt Hriniak (batting), Al Jackson (pitching), Johnny Pesky (first base), and Eddie Yost (third base). Ferguson Jenkins, affectionately known as "Fergy," started Opening Day for the second straight year and lost both starts.

BELOW: John Kiley, longtime organist for the Sox (and Bruins and Celtics), making music
OPPOSITE: Jim Rice swinging away

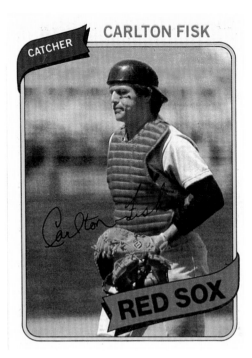

CATCHER — **CARLTON FISK**
Carlton Fisk
RED SOX

BISHOP JOHN D'ARCY: What a thrill it was to go with my Irish-born father to Fenway in 1977 and sit in the center-field bleachers and have hot dogs. By then he understood the game. To see how he had gotten interested in it and understood it, and was sitting with me in the bleachers, was very special.

LENNY MEGLIOLA: I'd been at the *Metro West Daily News* about ten years and was now sports editor. I took my five-year-old son and my father, who was in his late seventies, to their first game. My father had had eight mouths to feed. An Italian immigrant, he didn't quite understand baseball.

We were in Section 17—very good seats, behind first base. The JumboTron scoreboards were just coming into effect. My dad looked at that like it was the eighth wonder of the world.

Mid-June: Red Sox vs. Yankees, a battle for first place, a three-game series at Fenway. The Sox humiliated the Yanks 9–4 in the Friday night game on June 17, shelling Catfish Hunter for four homers in the first inning.

The next day, the park was jammed with the largest Saturday afternoon crowd (34,603) in a couple of decades. It could not have been a better day for Sox fans.

Self-possessed Reggie Jackson nonchalanted it in the outfield as Jim Rice blooped a double. Yankee pilot Billy Martin removed his egocentric star from the game, a move that triggered loud booing and no small smattering of profanity throughout the park. Some of the cursing came from Martin and Jackson, who almost exchanged blows in the dugout. National television cameras recorded the moment, showing Martin being restrained by coaches Elston Howard and Yogi Berra. Sox fans with a view into the dugout cheered wildly.

Boston cruised, 10–4, popping five home runs.

"When they don't hustle, I don't accept that," the hyper Martin said later. "When a player shows the club up, I show the player up."

The next day was even sweeter for the Old Towne Team fans. The Sox humbled the visitors, 11–1. Boston slugged five home runs, including Carl Yastrzemski's 460-foot shot off Dick Tidrow, the only ball ever to reach the right-field-roof facade.

The win gave Boston a three-game series sweep on a windy weekend that was truly the "Yankee Massacre."

Some Yankee zealots claimed that Boston's rout was due to the strong wind blowing in Fenway. Elated at the sweep that gave Boston a 10–1 home stand record and the division lead, Bosox rooters snapped back, "The Yankees had the same wind blowing all weekend, and they didn't hit one home run."

The age-old rivals drew 103,910 for the series into the not so comfortable confines of Fenway, but no one who was there complained.

In the end Boston made a spirited run for the division title that season but finished 2½ games behind the first-place Yankees, tying with Baltimore for second place. The team had its best attendance ever at Fenway, 2,074,549, the first time it drew two million, just the fourth American League team to hit that mark.

DENNIS ECKERSLEY: I came to the Red Sox as a 23-year-old in 1978. The setting was just old-time baseball. You come into the park out of the middle of the city. Opening Day, I pitched against the Texas Rangers before a packed house with a team behind me that included Jerry Remy at second base, Rick Burleson at short, Jim Rice, DH, Yaz in left, Fisk catching, Freddy Lynn playing center field, big George Scott at first base, Dwight Evans in right field, and Butch Hobson playing third. Some lineup!

I came off the field in the tenth inning with two outs and they gave me a standing O. And I was like, "Oh, my God." That was my first taste of it.

Carl Yastrzemski would turn 39 years old in 1978. Despite constant back pains, he played on. "Captain Carl" had a talented supporting cast that "had his back," including Dwight Evans, who stroked a pair of homers; Jim Rice, who hammered his 16th dinger; and Bill Lee, who went nine innings for his seventh win, his 91st with the Sox, as Boston drubbed Detroit, 6–3, in an early-season game.

Another who thrived that 1978 season, especially at Fenway Park, was newcomer Dennis Eckersley.

DENNIS ECKERSLEY: I was 20–8 in that first season, 11–1 at home. I loved pitching at Fenway. It played right to my emotions. They scored me a ton of runs. I pitched well, too.

There is a major edge pitching at Fenway for the Red Sox. It is an intimidating place for the opposing team. And if you're not pitching well for the Sox, it's a tough place to pitch. A bad energy can come your way.

Vinnie Orlando, the equipment manager, was an old-school guy who ran the place. It was almost like you had to be nice to him in order for him to take care of you.

I asked him: "Hey, when are they going to put our names on the back of our uniforms?"

"Never," he said. "Let them buy a scorecard."

On July 3, Carl Yastrzemski hit a run-scoring double, his 2,800th career hit.

DENNIS ECKERSLEY: That day I beat the Yankees, and my record went to 9–2. Then on the 25th of August, I beat the Angels 6–0. My record was 15–5, 8–0 at Fenway.

BILL LEE: This game was against the California Angels. I was in the bullpen with this lefthander who had been warming up and he had a bad meal and he ran back to the potty. Zimmer walked out to the mound. The next batter was left-handed, and Zimmer calls for the lefthander, who isn't coming out of where he is. I hadn't even thrown a warm-up pitch, but I take off my jacket and I come out the door and start running in.

Zimmer says, "I didn't call for you, Lee, goddamnit."

I said, "Well, he's in the shitter and he ain't coming out. Gimme the goddamn ball. I can get this guy out on one pitch."

One pitch. Batter hits a ground ball to second. We're out of the inning.

The Yankees came into Fenway for a crucial Thursday-to-Sunday four-game series that started September 7. Boston was in first place, four games ahead of the team from the Big Apple; however, most of its 14-game July lead over the Yanks had evaporated.

New York won the first game. New York won the second game.

DENNIS ECKERSLEY: I was 4–1 against the Yankees that year. I took the mound in game three. My record was 16–6, and I had won my last nine games at Fenway. They had beaten us badly the first two games. The pressure was really on me, the team, the fans. I pitched against Ron Guidry, who was 20–2. It was a Saturday, a nationally televised game. I lost, 7–0. There was a pop-fly ball with the wind blowing that somebody dropped, and they got seven runs. That's what I remember.

We got swept the four games. They outscored us, 42–9. They left Boston tied. And then the last month of the season was back and forth. Everybody said we choked, but we won 12 out of the last 14 just to tie. I don't call that choking.

BOB SULLIVAN: The last game of the 1978 season the Yankees were one game ahead of the Red Sox. Everyone was so disgusted with the lead we had blown that only 29,201 showed up for this most important game.

It was a balmy 73 degrees. Tiant threw like 140 pitches; he was such a warhorse, heroic out there. He pitched like a guy possessed, giving up just two hits, complete game. We scoreboard-watched and saw Cleveland ahead of New York by quite a few runs. We got some runs against Toronto and won our eighth straight to tie the Yankees and force a one-game play-off.

The next day my friend and I got in line. They were selling two tickets at a time, so we picked up two tickets at a go and just kept getting in the back of the line. We got 28 tickets—all bleacher seats. Then we went to the Dugout bar on Commonwealth Avenue. We made a pledge, like Huck Finn and Tom Sawyer. "We will scalp

ABOVE: Don Zimmer, in his first home game as manager, scans the crowd on July 26, 1976, prior to a game against Cleveland

RAIN CHECK
OPENING DAY

1975
AMERICAN LEAGUE
CHAMPIONS

GAME
1 APR 12 1976
* DAY *
RESERVED $4.00

20	13	6
SEC.	ROW	SEAT

none of these tickets." We started calling our friends from all over who were Sox fans. People brought their parents, girlfriends. People flew in from out of town.

———————

On October 2 at two-thirty in the afternoon, a one-game playoff got under way inside Fenway Park before 32,925. It was the two teams with the best records in baseball after 162 games—winner take all for the American League East title. Former Yankee Mike Torrez was on the mound for Boston; Ron Guidry, the best pitcher in baseball that season, for the Yankees.

The Red Sox lineup that day:

Rick Burleson	SS
Jerry Remy	2B
Jim Rice	RF
Carl Yastrzemski	LF
Carlton Fisk	C
Fred Lynn	CF
Butch Hobson	DH
George Scott	1B
Jack Brohamer	3B
Mike Torrez	P

STEVE RYDER: Four of us went. We expected to win that game, absolutely. The Sox had a good year, they'd come through. I was seven rows from the field on the third-base side directly up from the on-deck circle.

———————

DENNIS ECKERSLEY: It was electric that day. I had pitched Saturday and won number 20 and was glad I wasn't pitching that play-off game.

I was in the dugout. I was in the clubhouse. I was all over the place. I was more nervous watching than pitching. It was 2–0 in the seventh. They were setting up this little stage for the celebration.

———————

STEVE RYDER: Then all of a sudden:

———————

BILL WHITE (game call, WPIX): *"Deep to left! Yastrzemski will not get it—it's a home run! A three-run home run for Bucky Dent and the Yankees now lead . . . Bucky Dent has just hit his fourth home run of the year and look at that Yankees bench out to greet him . . ."*

"I've always loved Fenway Park," Yastrzemski said. "But that was the one moment I hated the place, the one moment the Wall got back at us. I still can't believe it went in the net."

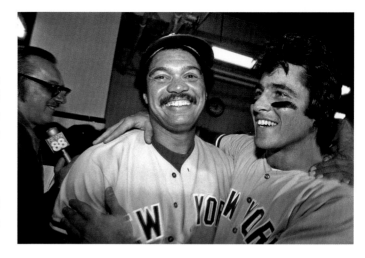

BILL LEE: Torrez threw that horseshit slider that is still sitting there in middle of the plate, and Bucky Dent hit, right near the end of the bat. I couldn't believe he hit it out, but he did.

———————

ROGER KAHN: My memory is Dent slamming a foul ball into his foot and hobbling around and there was a delay of several minutes. During that whole delay Mike Torrez did not throw a single pitch. Normally, you just throw to keep loose. Dent got a new bat from Mickey Rivers. And the first pitch Torrez threw after the break that may have been five minutes, was that shot to left field. You could see Yastrzemski thinking he could play the ball and kind of crumpling when the ball went out.

———————

LEIGH MONTVILLE: It was a ball that everyone thought was going to be caught, a nothing kind of hit.

———————

ABOVE: Reggie Jackson and Bucky Dent, joyous in the locker room after their home runs beat Boston, 5–4, to win the pennant on October 2, 1978
OPPOSITE: The Bucky Dent pop fly home run that sent Red Sox rooters into shock and despair

DICK FLAVIN: I was in a box seat right behind the Red Sox dugout. You could put your beer right on the roof. So I had a great look of Yaz coming off the field right after he popped up. He had his head down, anguish.

STEVE RYDER: I saw that pop-up up close. It was a fairly high one, you could say it was a home run in a silo. It just ended the game, and the people left in kind of a dejected attitude and demeanor. Whipped.

DON ZIMMER: Instead of going into the clubhouse, I sat in the dugout and watched their team celebrate.

DON ZIMMER: When Bucky hit the ball, I said, "That's an out." And usually you know when the ball hits the bat whether it's short, against the wall, in the net, or over the net. I see Yaz backing up, and when he's looking up, I still think he's going to catch it. When I see him turn around, then I know he's going to catch it off the Wall. Then the ball wound up in the net.

"I was so damn shocked," Torrez said. "I thought maybe it was going to be off the Wall. Damn, I did not think it was going to go out."

"When I hit the ball, I knew that I had hit it high enough to hit the Wall," remembered Bucky Dent. "But there were shadows on the net behind the Wall and I didn't see the ball land there. I was running from the plate because I thought I had a chance at a double. I didn't know it was a home run until the second-base umpire signaled it was a home run. It was an eerie feeling because the ballpark was dead silent."

STEVE RYDER: It was just a pop fly off Mike Torrez. It just made the netting. The crowd was just absolutely stunned, absolutely stunned.

Don Zimmer changed the Yankee shortstop's name to "Bucky F——g Dent." Red Sox fans were even more vulgar in their language.

Yaz had two hits in that game, including a homer off Ron Guidry, but he also made the last out.

DAN SHAUGHNESSY: I was covering for the *Baltimore Eagle Sun* in the second or third row. The old press box was down low. I was downstairs later in the stands when Gossage got Yaz to pop up because we were getting ready to go to the locker room and it looked like they were going down and that was interesting how Sox fans in those days had a sense of gloom, anticipating. Whatever happened, it wasn't going to end well.

DENNIS ECKERSLEY: Yaz was crying in the trainer's room. It was not as crushing for me because when you're 23 you think, well, we'll do it next year. We have such a good team. But if I knew what I know now, I would have been devastated. We never really got there again after that.

WALTER MEARS: Tip O'Neill went to Rome that fall and saw the pope. When he came back he was at some function with Yaz and told him the holy father had spoken of him. Yaz wanted to know what the pope had said.

"Tip," he said, "how the heck could Yastrzemski pop out in the last of the ninth with the tying run on third?"

After the game a Bucky Dent buddy called the Red Sox inquiring if the home-run ball was available. He was told that the net had been littered with balls from batting-practice home runs; the

"Bucky Dent ball" could not be identified amid all the others.

JOE MOONEY: I got blamed for taking the ball Bucky Dent hit for the home run. I never touched it. I never spoke to Bucky Dent, but later I found out that he was accusing me. I know who took that ball he hit. But I'd never say nothing. We'll leave that to history.

It was a disappointing finish for the Red Sox of Boston, but the season had been momentous. Very potent at home in 1978, winning 59 games against just 23 losses for a .720 percentage. Posting one of the franchise's best all-time home records, the team drew two million fans for the second straight season: 2,320,643, surpassing the 1977 mark of 2,074,549. Fans and franchise looked forward to the last year of the decade at Fenway Park.

For a time the lights on the Citgo sign were turned off in 1979 to save energy. Sox fans rallied, asking that the sign be declared a Boston landmark. It never was, but the city of Boston assumed financial responsibility for maintaining it.

Many in Red Sox Nation were ticked off that Don Zimmer, the butt of much criticism for the "Bucky Dent game" and the collapse in '78, was still skipper of the Red Sox. The word around Fenway was that he was afflicted by personal grudges and that this affected his managing. The word was that he overused his starting lineup, ran it into the ground. The one-time affable third-base coach, according to reports of the time, was an avid listener to talk shows and was very concerned about what was said about him on local TV and radio.

Ned Martin and Ken Harrelson handled local TV, while Ken Coleman and Rico Petrocelli did radio.

JOE CASTIGLIONE: The third game I ever saw at Fenway was the first big-league game I ever broadcast. It was the first for my partner, Fred McLeod, too. I was 32 and I think he was like 26—two rookies broadcasting for Cleveland. Dwight Evans hit the first home run I ever called. We were in the visiting TV booth. This was the fifth of April. Dennis Eckersley pitched seven innings, a 7–1 three-hitter.

Carl Yastrzemski gave fans much to cheer about at Fenway that 1979 season. On July 24, facing Mike Morgan of Oakland, he hammered his 400th career home run.

NED MARTIN (game call, WSBK-TV): *"Long drive, right field . . . way back . . . near the wall . . . and there it is! Home run number 400, Carl Yastrzemski! Now . . . listen and watch!"*

BRUCE TUCKER: We're finally at Fenway. Carl Yastrzemski is getting close to his 3,000th hit. We'd bought tickets hoping he didn't get that big hit before our game.

Every time we went down to the bathroom, someone would yell, "Yastrzemski's up!" The bathroom would clear because even if he wasn't really up, no one wanted to be the one that said, "I wasn't there, I was in the bathroom!"

NED MARTIN (game call, WSBK-TV, September 12, 1979): *"There goes a ground ball . . . base hit! Number 3,000 . . . Yastrzemski's got it! And all hell breaks loose at Fenway Park!"*

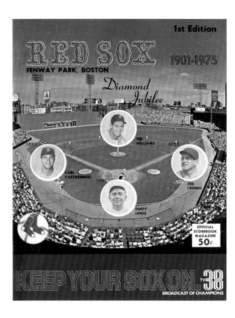

BRUCE TUCKER: In his third at-bat, he got a base hit up the middle. It almost looked like the guy just kinda let it go, like he didn't bend down quite far enough.

"I've been in pennant pressure, playoff pressure, and World Series pressure situations and wasn't bothered by any of them," Yaz said afterward. "I think it was the way the fans reacted the last three days. I wanted to get that base hit for the fans."

With 34,000-plus fans chanting his name, the Red Sox favorite stepped up to a microphone with his son and father beside him, extended a lot of "thank yous," and made special mention of his "two biggest boosters," his mother and Tom Yawkey.

For Yaz, 1979 was a dream season; for the Red Sox it was all right. Attendance was outstanding. They drew 2,353,114 into Fenway, a ballpark that seated 33,538. They were 57–32 at home, which was superb. But they finished in third place, with 91 wins and 69 losses. They would have to do better in the 1980s.

OPPOSITE: "Captain Carl" makes a terrific catch against the Yankees on September 9, 1978

–EIGHTIES–

MORGAN MAGIC

As the new decade got under way, the future looked bright. Long-time stars such as Yaz and Rice, Lynn and Evans, and others were still part of the scene. And although no one could have predicted it then, the 1980 season would be a time of transition. At season's end longtime fixtures would be gone: Don Zimmer, Fred Lynn, Carlton Fisk, Rick Burleson.

		YEAR	WON	LOST	PCT.	GB	ATTENDANCE
RED SOX YEAR BY YEAR	*1980 – 1989*	**1989**	83	79	.512	6.0	2,510,012
		1988	89	73	.549	—	2,464,851
		1987	78	84	.481	20.0	2,231,551
		1986	95	66	.590	—	2,147,641
		1985	81	81	.500	18.5	1,786,633
		1984	86	76	.531	18.0	1,661,618
		1983	78	84	.481	20.0	1,782,285
		1982	89	73	.549	6.0	1,950,124
		1981	59	49	.546	2.5	1,060,379
		1980	83	77	.519	19.0	1,956,092

Opening Day, April 14, 1980, turned out all right even though light rain fell at the start of play. The Red Sox defeated Detroit, 3–1. Dennis Eckersley hurled seven innings of three-hit ball, giving up just a run. Fred Lynn homered.

The Red Sox Opening Day lineup in 1980:

Jerry Remy	2B
Rick Burleson	SS
Fred Lynn	CF
Jim Rice	LF
Carl Yastrzemski	DH
Tony Perez	1B
Carlton Fisk	C
Jack Brohamer	3B
Dwight Evans	RF
Dennis Eckersley	P

JOE COSGRIFF: I'm a native New Yorker. My first games at Fenway Park were spent wondering, Where is the second deck? My first games were also spent enjoying the booming voice of Sherm Feller and Kiley's organ. I thought I was attending an organ concert.

Years later I was at a game where every song Kiley played in between innings was by Richard Rodgers. The Yankees and other teams were already playing far-too-contempo-

rary hits. Noisy stuff. It was old-time baseball listening that day to Kiley playing Rodgers.

My friend Paul Mirabella, Jersey boy made good, was slated to pitch for the Blue Jays this May day. I was in business school in Boston. I ran out of my second class to meet him at the Sheraton and found him with nine other Jays in a room watching a soap opera.

He gave me tickets in the front row between home plate and third. We heard everything, stuff you don't hear—Roy Howell walking back to the dugout after striking out against Renko and screaming, "He's throwing fucking balloons out there!"

Paul pitched great, making it into the seventh inning. Near the end of the game, with the Jays still ahead 4–3, Zimmer put Yaz in left field to replace Rice, probably to keep "Captain Carl" from leaving the game early. The word was that toll collectors would often spot Yaz hitting the Tobin Bridge on his way home before games had ended. We sensed something was going to come of Zim's odd move; something did. Fisk walked to start the ninth, and Yaz followed with a two-run homer to win the game. That was a great day for Sox fans.

The 20th of June 1980 was a memorable game under the lights for five-foot, four-inch Fred Patek. It wasn't as good for the Sox and their fans. The tiny Patek ripped three home runs—more than half his total of five for the season—and a double. California pulverized Boston, 20–2. Bobby Grich stroked 4 of the 26 hits the Angels managed.

ALAN CAMASSAR: On a beautiful June day, my wife and I were with our son at his first major league game. Two nuns in full black garb were behind us. It was a good game, but the Sox lost and my

son was visibly disappointed. One of the nuns just reached over, put her hand on his shoulder, and said, "Don't cry. It's just God's will."

Don Zimmer had survived the Bucky Dent home run and recorded a five-year tenure as skipper. He had survived Bill Lee's calling him a Gila monster and even less complimentary names. With five games left in the season, it was time for Zim to go. He was replaced as interim manager by Johnny Pesky, who had last managed in 1963. Boston drew 1,956,092 and finished in fourth place, 19 games out.

RALPH HOUK: Mr. Yawkey had been trying to bring me to the Sox for a long time. Whenever I was at Fenway with the Yankees, he would tell me, "If you ever need a job, come to our club."

I had been retired for two years in the autumn of 1980 when Don Zimmer was fired, and Haywood Sullivan hired me. It was great—they offered me such a good contract, our daughter lived in the Boston area, and I was treated real good by ownership and the writers. Of course, having Yaz on my side was a big help, too.

Fenway is always an exciting place to go because of the fence, and we managed differently because of it. We decided to pitch inside, which a lot of people didn't do.

Houk had Yaz, but not on Opening Day. Suffering from back spasms, Yastrzemski could not answer the bell. It was the only opener he ever missed.

PAGE 154: Like a jewel in the New England night, Fenway Park aglow from above
OPPOSITE: Sherm Feller, an original behind the mike; Jon Miller, one of the best baseball announcers ever, and now in the Hall of Fame

Carlton Fisk, longtime Boston stalwart and now brand-new member of the White Sox, homered, triggering a 5–3 Chicago win. The cheers that had greeted him at the start of the game turned to jeers.

Another longtime stalwart, Fred Lynn, came back to Fenway in 1980 wearing an Angels uniform.

FRED LYNN: If I made a good play, fans gave me a nice hand. So there was that. But one game I took a home run away from [Bill] Buckner diving into stands in the right-field corner. I came back out onto the field after hitting my head on the seats, bleeding from my forehead. The fans loved that. So there was that, too.

JON MILLER: In '81, there was a day game mid-April against Baltimore and a power outage.

BOB SULLIVAN: You could get a box of Cracker Jacks, you could get a candy bar. But you couldn't get any hot food. None of the coffee machines or hot dog machines worked. And it was really cold. There were all these hollow sounds coming from players taking batting practice.

Sherm Feller, the longtime PA man, leaned out of his window up on the rooftop with a megaphone and announced that there'd been a power outage but the game would be played anyway. You couldn't hear the lineup announcements; you couldn't hear anything. It was like people getting ready to play ball on a backyard field.

On his bullhorn, Feller began to sing "The Star-Spangled Banner," and everyone stood. A cappella, Fenway Park sang the national anthem along with him.

There was a complicated play in the sixth or seventh inning. A score was put up incorrectly, and it stayed up for an inning. Then a batboy

ran out across left field, opened the scoreboard door. A minute later a run came down and a zero went up.

Nowadays, they have generators that work. Quite possibly that was the last professional baseball game that was played that way. But it was magical. Sox, incidentally, won, 7–2.

GARY TITUS: Sherm Feller was proud of being the Red Sox announcer, and he was a real statesman for the Red Sox, too. He'd walk into the children's hospital with a box full of Red Sox paraphernalia that he probably just took from Fenway. Feller and Kiley—the one-two punch, the sound of Fenway Park.

JON MILLER: Organist John Kiley sat in the same area as Sherm Feller. They were old buddies. Kiley was big and had a very bassy voice. He was old school, polite, could have been cast in a movie as the lord of the manor in some castle in England.

I'd say, "John, how you doing?"

He'd say, "Ahh, Mr. Miller, good to see you. You know, I overheard you on the broadcast."

DANIEL MCGINLEY-SMITH: Kiley's organ interludes and our singing "Take Me Out to the Ball Game" accompanied by his organ playing had a unique place in the church of Fenway.

On September 3 and 4, the longest game at Fenway Park took place. Involving 46 players, the contest was stopped after nineteen innings, 7–7, at 1:16 A.M. because of the American League curfew rule mandating that no inning could start after 1:00 A.M. Later that day the game was

resumed, with the Sox eking out an 8–7 victory in 20 innings over the Seattle Mariners, on Joe Simpson's run-scoring triple. And Jerry Remy never got over talking about the six hits he had in that longest game.

FRED FROMMER: My first time at Fenway Park was September 6, 1981. I'd come along very early with my father, who was down on the field interviewing players during batting practice for a book he was writing. I was 14 years old and a huge baseball fan, and I had never been in a stadium that seated fewer than 50,000. Now I had this 34,000-seat ballpark virtually to myself; it felt like a backyard.

From the first row behind the short right-field wall by the foul pole, I could see balls careening all over the field like pinballs and my dad talking to Red Sox coach Johnny Pesky, who was hitting fungoes.

"That's my son out there, by the foul pole. Can you hit a ball to him?"

"No way," said Pesky. "What if it hits him in the head?"

"He'll catch it," my dad assured him. He was confident the endless evenings he had spent hitting me fly balls would pay off.

But Pesky shook his head. "Sorry, I can't do it."

A few minutes later, I heard a crack and a bunch of Red Sox players in right field yell, "Heads up!"

FENWAY PARK—BOSTON

RAIN CHECK

OPENING DAY

BOSTON RED SOX®

GAME 1 APR 13 1984
✻ DAY ✻
RESERVED $6.50

16 16 2
SEC. ROW SEAT

I looked up, and there in the blue New England sky was a perfect white sphere. I camped under it. With Pesky's incredible aim, I didn't have to move. The ball just landed in my mitt.

"Hey, nice catch," one of the Red Sox shouted up at me. "We could use you out here, the way we're playing."

Just before the game started, Pesky found my dad and told him to get the ball from me. He autographed it "To Freddy, Nice Catch. Best Wishes, Johnny Pesky."

I still have the ball.

Over the 1982–1983 off-season, roof boxes dating back to 1946 were replaced. Private suites were constructed on the grandstand roof along the foul lines atop the left- and right-field stands, reducing summer winds.

BRUCE HURST: My first full season with the Red Sox was 1982. Jimmy Rice then was probably the premier hitter in the American League. Opening Day they cheered him wildly his first two or three at-bats. And he had a hit or two. But he came up in the eighth inning and struck out with the bases loaded with two out; they booed him like crazy.

And I just remember looking around and thinking, "Oh, my gosh, if they boo him, what are they going to do to me?"

That was one of the times when I first started to realize what goes on inside Fenway; the passion was a little different than I was ready for.

CHRIS WERTZ: We used to sit by the dugout a lot when my brother had company seats. At night games my mother would bring a couple of paper bags and we'd be pulling out food. We'd use the Red Sox dugout top as a picnic table.

My nephew asked Dwight Evans for a baseball. He reached up over the dugout and rolled one to him. At eight years old, I didn't know you could ask for a ball. But seeing my nephew get one, I asked for a baseball, too. Only Evans ignored me.

Then Ed Jurak walked over and rolled me a baseball. I looked at him, wondering, "Who the hell are you?" I wanted a baseball from Dewey.

I still have that Jurak ball. I'm happier now to have it, since nowadays lesser-known Red Sox players seem to have more cachet among fandom.

JON MILLER: In the '80s a low backstop and then a screen covered up the fans in the lower deck behind the plate. That screen ran right up to the broadcast booth. Access for us to the press box and the broadcast booths was via the rooftop first. You literally walked into the press box from the rooftop. It was like being on a big naval ship walking down this little narrow stairway into a passageway where the broadcast booths were.

Red Sox announcers then did not go for flowery homerun calls. Curt Gowdy just said "home run." Ned Martin, Ken Coleman, they all just said "It's gone, home run."

Ken had a big, booming voice and loved poetry. He could recite famous poems from memory.

He told me about a little room with a fireplace and a bar that Yawkey used to go to oftentimes after games with the general manager, manager, and coaches. They'd sit and talk about the ball club and drink.

It was like a medieval castle. There was a secret panel, and you'd push a button and the thing would open up and you'd go through it and out into a passageway that could be used as an exit if they didn't want to be seen by fans.

Unfortunately, I never got to check out any of that.

CHRIS WERTZ: A chasm existed between the bleachers and the box seats. Forever, there has been a separate entrance to the bleachers. And forever there has been animosity between the two sections.

The guys up on the top row of the bleachers, which became the Dunkin' Donuts section now, were a bunch of big, fat, drunken beer guys that thought it was a terrific idea to just pull down their pants and flash the guys in the box seats.

Beer was cheap enough, and these guys would take turns going to the line and it seemed like by the third or fourth inning they'd have 25 beers under the bleachers because they just didn't want to be caught without beer by the time the cutoff came. There was no enforcement. Nobody around then really cared.

BRUCE HURST: I grew up with a picture of Yaz up over my bed, and then I became a teammate of his. He was a phenomenal player at the end of his career. If he had a rough day or two, once the game was over he would wait for the stadium to clear out and he'd still take extra batting practice. What a great worker he was, how much he loved to play the game.

On June 22, rookie Wade Boggs stroked his first major league home run, in the bottom of the eleventh inning, to give Boston a 5–4 win over Detroit.

OIL CAN BOYD: I was 22 years old when I got in my first big-league game, on September 13 against Cleveland. I mostly remember Toby Harrah hitting me good. He paid me a compliment after the game, though. He said, "From what I saw, Boyd will be around for a while."

Fenway Park is unbelievable when it comes to baseball. Passes down from generation to generation. It's the coolest.

─────────────────

BRUCE HURST: I loved Can. He was a little bit misunderstood, a pretty volatile personality. He would bounce around on the mound, and it seemed like he threw about 20 different pitches and invented stuff. But his eyes weren't really good. He had a hard time seeing the signals that catcher Geddy [Rich Gedman] put down.

─────────────────

RICH MARAZZI: On October 1, 1982, I covered a brief Old-Timers' Day game for a local newspaper in Ansonia, Connecticut. The great outfield of Ted Williams, Jimmy Piersall, and Jackie Jensen was reunited.

Afterward the regular game began, and I waited a few innings and took a shot. I walked into a deserted clubhouse. There was Ted all by himself with a towel wrapped around, ready to take a shower. I thought I had met Moses. We talked for several minutes. He was really cordial. At the time Ted was 64 years old. I asked him of all his achievements in baseball, which one was he the most proud of?

"The number of walks I received," Williams said. He had received 2,019 walks

PAGE 158–159: Wade Boggs gets three hits on October 6, 1985, clinching his second batting title in three years
RIGHT: Bruce Hurst elated after a victory over the Mets in fifth game of 1986 World Series

during his career. Only Babe Ruth had more walks at that time.

When you have press credentials, you're not supposed to ask for autographs. But I asked. He signed. Williams always had an impeccable autograph, too, like he was writing on a line. It was one of the nicest in baseball history.

———————————

On August 7, 1982, Jonathan Keane and his father and his brother Matthew were all at a game at Fenway against the White Sox. They sat in the second row of field box 29, just to the left of the Red Sox dugout.

In the fourth inning Jonathan's favorite player, second baseman Dave Stapleton, swinging late, smashed a foul ball into the stands to the right of home plate. It hit Jonathan.

ABOVE: Wade Boggs stroking it
OPPOSITE: Oil Can Boyd in full windup and ready, 1986

Jim Rice, standing with his left foot on the top stair of the dugout, heard a sickening crack and the sounds of the crowd.

"You try to raise up and see if it hits anyone," Rice said, "and then when it hits someone that's when you react, especially when blood is involved."

A father of two young children, Rice reacted by jumping out to pick up the bleeding child. Red Sox team doctor Arthur Pappas said, "There was blood on his face, his head, there was blood coming from his nose and his mouth."

Minutes later Jonathan was sped by ambulance to Children's Hospital, only a mile away. His skull was fractured and he had lost a lot of blood. Jonathan underwent delicate surgery and was released five days later.

On Opening Day, April 5, 1983, Jonathan Keane, five, of Greenland, New Hampshire, threw out the first pitch at Fenway to open the 1983 season. It was a moment that made Jim Rice and so many others very happy.

———————————

JOE CASTIGLIONE: I replaced Jon Miller in 1983 when he left for Baltimore. I worked seven years with Ken Coleman. He was a mentor without laying it on. My first game at home was with Toronto. We got wiped out, 7–1.

———————————

April 5, 1983, was the final Opening Day for Yaz, now a DH. He went nothing for three. There also was some posturing and bench clearing. Rance Mulliniks touched Dennis Eckersley for a home run in the second inning. Eck hit him with a pitch in the fourth. Jim Rice got nicked in his helmet and had to be restrained. Bullpens and dugouts emptied. As was often the case, no one threw a punch.

JOE CASTIGLIONE: I think we were off the next day. The following afternoon we won, my first win with the Red Sox, the last time the Red Sox drew a crowd under 10,000.

A real memory of my rookie season was Yaz's 44th birthday. On that day he lined a double into the right-field corner to give us a win. Even at 44, he could turn on anybody's heater.

———————————

LENNY MEGLIOLA: For Tom Yawkey, Yastrzemski was almost like an adopted son. And Yaz took advantage of that. He was, after all, the best player on the team. He had a director's chair in the Red Sox clubhouse with a glass holder on one side and ashtray on the other side and cigarettes. He sipped wine after the game and smoked.

He was king of the hill, and he exercised that status. But I always felt bad for him because he was uncomfortable with the camera on him. Basically all he ever wanted to do was play the game. He gave very few interviews and was extremely private even in the unprivacy of a baseball clubhouse.

When he was in the mood, he could be expansive, charming—even self-effacing. But if he went nothing for four, watch out.

There were a lot of people who didn't like Yastrzemski because of his personality and some begrudged him his body of work, his great accomplishments.

———————————

"Captain Carl" Yastrzemski hammered a homer off Baltimore's Jim Palmer on September 12 in the first inning at Fenway. However, the game was rained out in the third inning, so the homer did not count. His career total reverted to 452.

That October 2 Yaz played left field for the first time all season and went one for three. His last hit was number 3,419. In his last at-bat he popped out against Dan Spillner and was replaced in left field by Chico Walker. The Red Sox icon took one more "final lap" at the end of the game.

ART DAVIDSON: When I was still very new on the beat in the final years of Yaz's career, he would be one of the first out there in the trainer's room sitting in his long underwear with a cigarette in one hand and a beer in another. He didn't enjoy interplay with the media, but if you wanted an answer he would certainly provide you with one, although it may have been brief. By his last game at Fenway he at least knew my face if not my name.

HOWIE SINGER: There was Yaz bread, Yaz sausages. There was a song about Yaz.

I grew up as a Yaz guy. He started playing in 1961, when I was two. I had watched him from elementary school through my college years and then my first year in the workforce. I was at his last two games.

The day before his last game was Yaz Day. They gave posters out and the painter's Yaz Day hats.

DANIEL MCGINLEY-SMITH: I got a painter's cap that day that had "Thanks Yaz" on it and a button with his picture and his signature. I still have the newspaper headline "One Last Fenway Go-Around for Yaz" hanging on my office wall.

There were two go-arounds for Carl Yastrzemski. On October 2, 1983, he took a pair of final laps around Fenway during pregame ceremonies in his honor. The home team lost, 3–1, to the Indians that day.

TED SPENCER: October 2, 1983. I'm there for his 3,308th game. As an officer of the Hall of Fame, I had a season's pass, allowing me in the door with one guest. The pass just got you in the door. I had to stand up behind home plate, behind about 4,000 other people who were watching or trying to.

ART DAVIDSON: Yaz signed a few baseballs and gave them over to media members, sorta like a thank-you. He also spent about an hour signing baseballs outside Fenway.

BOB SANNICANDRO: During the game I had knocked on that clubhouse door. "You know I worked in '72. Any chance I could talk to Yaz after the game?"

"Come around the players' parking lot after the game," I was told.

Yaz came through the parking lot. He still had his uniform top on; it was unbuttoned.

I said, "Yaz, you probably don't remember me but I was a batboy in 1972 and you used to call me Blondie." I think he had a bottle of champagne in his hand. I got to talk to him a little bit.

Then he said, "I gotta run. I gotta go upstairs." We shook hands and off he went.

JOE COSGRIFF: Opening Day, April 13, 1984, I was about 25 minutes late. My reserved seat cost $6.50. And I heard the crowd noises. The Tigers were up. The ticket taker says to me, "Don't worry! They're still in the first inning."

It turned out it was 8–0 Detroit and Hurst was already out of the game. The Red Sox then got five in the bottom of the first. The Tigers held on for a 13–9 victory

And that was how the '84 season started at Fenway.

RALPH HOUK: Roger Clemens made his debut on May 15, 1984. He was only 21. He was a great pitcher even then. I used to warm him up in the bullpen. As a former catcher, warming up pitchers, especially at Fenway, was something I really liked to do.

———————

BRUCE HURST: From the first day Roger walked into the clubhouse, he was very respectful of the game, respectful of the guys who been in before him. He ran around Fenway getting wind sprints in. He also ran along Storrow Drive. He'd do his roadwork there. Part of his routine and preparation, a little solitude, running.

———————

The first two uniform numbers ever retired by the Red Sox were for Ted Williams (9) and Joe Cronin (4) during pregame ceremonies on May 29, 1984. Roger Clemens, whose number probably will not be retired, on August 21 fanned 15 Royals, pitching an 11–1 complete-game victory.

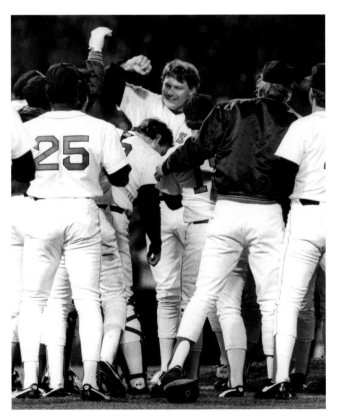

On September 14, the Yankees defeated the Red Sox, 7–1, dropping Boston 16½ games behind the first-place Tigers (with 16 remaining), eliminating them from contention.

Even with Clemens and the other stars, 1984 was another one of those disappointing seasons for Boston, finishing in fourth place. The Sox did finish 10 games over .500 (86–76), but surprisingly were better on the road, 45–36, than at Fenway, where they were 41–40.

———————

RALPH HOUK: The season over, I had managed the Red Sox since 1981. But my wife and I had decided that it was time to go. Sully [general manager Haywood Sullivan] had sent a contract to the manager's office with a note, "Is this the amount you want?" It was very generous. They didn't want me to retire.

Oil Can Boyd came into my office and cried. I liked him and he liked me. He said, "You're just like my grandfather; you can't leave."

———————

DICK BRESCIANI: 1985. We're opening the season against the Yankees. Terrible weather. Teams were going to work out the best they could. Joe Mooney, head groundskeeper, had covered the mound. Ron Guidry wanted to throw off it and removed the tarp. A bellowing voice screamed: "Get the hell off my mound!"

"I'm a Yankee pitcher," Guidry said.

"I don't care who the hell you are." Joe had a hose and he was spraying water. "If you don't get off there, you're going to get the full force," he said. Guidry left.

———————

That Opening Day Vinnie Orlando was in his 51st season as a clubhouse attendant. "I heard this loud knock," Orlando said. He opened the door

to the Red Sox clubhouse. "And here's this guy," Orlando continued," with pant cuffs out to here, shirt collars down to there, looking like Hollywood in his brown pinstripe suit. He says, 'My name's Joe DiMaggio and I want to go upstairs. Can you tell me how to go?'"

Forty-six-year-old Yankee pitcher Phil Niekro became the second-oldest pitcher to start an Opening Day game, but the knuckleballer lasted just four innings as the Red Sox ripped him and others in a 9–2 romp powered by home runs from Tony Armas, Jim Rice, and Dwight Evans. Oil Can Boyd got the win. And John McNamara, who had replaced Ralph Houk as manager, was off to a nice start.

———————

LARRY CANCRO: I first came to work at Fenway in '85. It was so different from today, more of an old-fashioned mom-and-pop baseball team organization. It was a comfortable place for people to work. Every single person at Fenway knew every person who preceded them at their job. Most of these people had worked under Mr. Yawkey initially.

Mrs. Yawkey was very much on the scene. To celebrate longevity, she had parties for employees who had 30, 40, 50, and 60 years' service. She wanted to see some changes in Fenway, some progress in things like how open we were to all people, how we treated people in the office with regard to gender and race. I was hired to bring more people to the ballpark on a consistent basis and also to try to diversify the fan base somewhat.

———————

JEFF IDELSON: I started as a vendor at Fenway in 1981. In the fall of 1985 I was hired as an intern in the public relations department. I didn't know the first thing about public relations. But I learned because I was given assignments that were meaningful. I wasn't just running the copy machine, although I did plenty of that.

Both clubhouses were tiny. Managers' offices were tiny. The walk down the runway to get to the home dugout was made of pieces of plyboard that weren't nailed down well. One of my jobs was to collect the lineup cards after they were exchanged at home plate from John McNamara. I got to know every dead spot that was on the runway.

———————

The '85 Bosox finished at 81–81, fifth in the American League East Division, drawing just 1,786,633 at Fenway.

With the Celtics battling the Hawks in the 1986 playoffs, only 13,414 showed up on the evening of April 29 to watch Roger Clemens pitching against the Seattle Mariners.

ART DAVIDSON: The Red Sox were second or third story at best that night.

———————

JOE CASTIGLIONE: I never saw a guy with such great velocity, with such awesome command and control.

———————

LOU GORMAN: I was up in the private box, but then I went down behind the stands and sat among three scouts. One of them had the radar gun; he was getting Clemens at about 94, 95 on the gun, 96 occasionally.

Toward the seventh inning he was approaching 15 to 17 strikeouts. Word got back to the Boston Garden, and most of the media rushed back to Fenway. In the ninth inning Roger struck out his twentieth batter.

———————

NED MARTIN (game call on NESN): *"A new record! Clemens has set a major league record for strikeouts in a game . . . 20!"*

———————

LOU GORMAN: We stopped the game and announced he struck out 20. The fans gave him a standing ovation.

———————

BRUCE HURST: I charted Clem's 20-strikeout game. It took on the mystique of a no-hitter. Nobody wanted to say anything. I think that one game made our pitching staff grow up and we all got better. It was always "They have the hitting but they don't have the pitching." And all of a sudden Roger does something that's never been done and he takes the weight of our pitching staff on his shoulders.

———————

LOU GORMAN: Game over, I picked up the game balls, five of them, and got him to sign four. I gave one to John Harrington and one to Haywood Sullivan. I kept one for myself, saved one for Roger, and we sent one to the Hall of Fame.

Clemens is probably the most dedicated athlete that I've ever been around. He ran four miles before every start. He would do hundreds of body crunches in the clubhouse. He would be on the stationary bike or running on the treadmill.

After every game his wife and four kids were waiting for him in the players' lounge. They'd get in the cab and drive away. Never failed, they were there.

Roger was a good teammate. He had a little arrogance about him, but all the great athletes do.

———————

ART DAVIDSON: He was hot and cold. The one thing about Roger was how hard he worked. I would pull up to the media lot on days when Roger wasn't pitching. He would be there in shorts and sweatshirt or T-shirt getting set to run the streets around Fenway.

———————

That May 16 at Fenway, the most horrific beaning of a player in the history of the Texas Rangers took place. Oil Can Boyd hit catcher Don Slaught on the left side of his face with a fastball, breaking his cheekbone in three places and his nose. The left side of Slaught's face was caved in. When the catcher returned on the Fourth of July, he wore a helmet with a face mask. He was never quite the same player.

———————————

LARRY CANCRO: In May 1986 I got all three DiMaggio brothers to agree to be at an old-timers' game. They had never appeared together in a major league ballpark before. At the very last minute I got a call from Vince in San Francisco. He said he wasn't feeling well, didn't think he should come. Dom, worried about his brother's health, said, "I want him to come because I want to take him to a doctor myself." Between the two of us, we convinced Vince to make the trip.

It ended up that Vince was in a very advanced stage of cancer. It was the last time the three of them were ever together, not just in a ballpark but anywhere. Vince died in October.

———————————

JOHN QUINN: On May 20 it was Roger Clemens against an in-his-prime Frank Viola and the Minnesota Twins. It turned out to be the shortest stint of Viola's career. He gave up six runs and did not get a batter out and he was yanked. The Red Sox won, 17–7.

Wade Boggs had five hits in his first five at-bats, hitting the ball all over the field. When he came up for the sixth time, the Fenway crowd was on its feet.

Boggs hit a ground ball to first base, and it went just right through Mickey Hatcher's legs. On the scoreboard they put up error. The whole stadium just booed.

———————————

BRUCE HURST: Wade Boggs and I signed together as 18-year-old kids in 1976. He made himself into an incredible hitter. He'd go through stretches where he'd put bat on ball square—consistently. I think he and we almost took it for granted that he would made good contact every at-bat. What didn't endear him to a lot of guys was that he was a little bit Jekyll/Hyde.

———————————

TOM CARON: My first job was in Plattsburgh, New York, as weekend anchor. I talked my way into doing a story on the Red Sox mainly because I wanted to go to Fenway and actually stand on the field. This was the first time I got to go on the hallowed ground.

It was a game against the Orioles. Tom Seaver blew me off for an interview, but Baltimore manager Earl Weaver did not.

———————————

BRUCE HURST: On July 10, after being told that he was not picked for the All-Star team (he was 11–6 at the break), Can Boyd threw a tantrum. The word was that as an All-Star he would get a $25,000 bonus. Roger [Clemens] and I were back behind the trainer's room and didn't go out and watch it. We could hear it. That got him suspended. He left Fenway in a huff, got into some trouble with local police, and was later checked into a local hospital for psychiatric testing. He was reinstated in August.

———————————

The "Can" went nine and fanned nine and cruised as the Sox pounded Toronto, 12–3, on September 28 to win the American League East title.

ABOVE: Dwight Evans makes an acrobatic grab of a ball hit by Oakland's Mike Davis, and robs him of a homer on May 3, 1986
OPPOSITE: Right fielder Dwight Evans briefly grasps a ball hit by Met Len Dykstra in the seventh inning of Game 4 of World Series at Fenway on October 22, 1986. The ball popped out of his glove for a two-run homer.

The Mets outscored the Red Sox, 32–27, in the World Series, but more importantly won the decisive seventh game set up after Mookie Wilson's grounder went through Sox first baseman Bill Buckner's legs in game six. It was quite a season for the Old Towne Team despite being runner-up for the world championship.

On Opening Day, April 10, 1987, longtime Boston politico Tip O'Neill, retiring that year as Speaker of the House of Representatives, was at Fenway Park to throw out the first ball.

"Oh, does this place bring back memories," O'Neill said. "I've been following these guys since I was a kid, back when we could get into the bleachers for 15 cents. I can still look out there in left and see it—Duffy's Cliff. Ira Flagstead played it better than all the guys we had."

The game took just two hours and four minutes to play. Bruce Hurst was on top of his form, spinning a two-hitter, fanning six.

CHRIS WERTZ: We wanted to rush the field so bad. We had seen videos for years of fans doing it. We were all crowding the baselines ready to jump onto the field. But they had put a moratorium on field rushing. All of a sudden many cops came out.

The Sox matched up against the Angels in the American League Championship Series. It went back and forth. In game seven, at Fenway Park, the ABC-TV game call of Al Michaels said it all:

"The Red Sox can go from last rites to the World Series . . . and they do!" Behind their horse Roger Clemens, who pitched a six-hitter, the Sox took care of the Angels, 6–1. The powerful Mets, who posted a 108–54 record in the regular season, were next.

ABOVE: The DiMaggio brothers in 1986 (L to R) Vince, Dom, and Joe. The final time they were together on a baseball field.
OPPOSITE: (top) Jean Yawkey; (bottom) Jim Rice gets into it in the 1986 World Series

JEFF IDELSON: I had gotten playoff and World Series tickets for Sherm Feller, but instead of giving me a check, he opened a small doctor's bag filled with cash and dumped it on my desk.

DICK BRESCIANI: We were in Yankee Stadium, and [longtime Stadium PA announcer] Bob Sheppard said, "You know, I've never been to Fenway. My wife and I are coming up to Maine in a few weeks, and I'd love to come in and see the game and meet Sherm and talk to Sherm Feller."

When I got back to Boston, I told Sherm. He said, "Great, I'll have him go on the air. Do a couple of hitters." It worked out. Bob Sheppard always talked about that. He had a terrific time.

Sherm had all the angles. He knew the best doctors, the top heart surgeons. He knew the bishop, the cardinal, all the rabbis. Sherm was such a likable, good-hearted person he could be friends with anyone on any level.

BRUCE HURST: Fenway was always a great ballpark to pitch in up to about the 1st of May, and then again from early September until the end of the season. But in between those times, it was tough. The wind blew the ball. The Wall giveth and the Wall taketh away. As a pitcher you have to learn how to use the Wall to your advantage. But there's a lot of places to keep the ball in the ballpark, a big area in right center and right field.

I listened to Mel Parnell a lot. He threw a lot harder than me and could bury guys on the inside. I always had to pitch in with a little more stealth. I couldn't just go hard, hard, in all the time. But I had enough of a fastball when mixed with the others that I could be effective with it.

GEORGE MITROVITCH: My first experience at Fenway was '87, Saturday afternoon game, 102 degrees. We were across the street in a souvenir store, and my wife fainted from the heat and humidity. Once we were inside the ballpark, however, all was quickly forgotten.

The Sox were playing the Mariners. Growing up as a San Diego kid, playing on the same University Heights ball field as Ted Williams, going to the same high school, dreaming of being a major league player, following the Red Sox from 3,000 miles away, never having been to Boston before, seeing the Green Monster and all the associations, made that day a moment unlike any other in my life.

――――――――――――

On the final day of the 1987 season, Roger Clemens had another of his great days at Fenway Park, notching his 20th win—a two-hit shutout against the Brewers. It was the workhorse Clemens's 18th complete game that season. He was one of the bright spots of a dismal season. Boston finished in fifth place.

A color video board with a black-and-white message board was installed in center field, and the playing area of Fenway Park was completely resod-ded over in 1987–1988. Stadium Club seats were constructed above the grandstand behind home plate, where the press box had been. Standing room, 1,300 more seats, additional concession stands and restrooms, widened concourses, and premium seating in a glassed enclosure behind home plate (known as the 600 Club) were all new for 1988.

Gone were Bill Buckner, Don Baylor, and other veterans of past campaigns. But despite the disappointing finish of 1987, John McNamara was still in the manager's chair as the 1988 season began. And he was ready for a fight: "The people who wrote our epitaph," he said, "may have to eat their words."

On May 13 the Sox and Mariners combined for nine homers, with Boston clawing out a 14–8 win. Oil Can Boyd was hit hard but earned credit for the win. Eight days later Bobby Doerr's number 1 was retired.

On June 13 Jim Rice slammed his 200th home run in a 12–6 loss to the Yankees and joined Ted Williams and Carl Yastrzemski in the Fenway Park 200-home-run club.

"The Green Monster cost me 10 home runs a year," Rice said, "maybe 20. Those are the number of line drives that I hit that went off the Wall and would have been home runs in other parks. I don't remember the Wall giving me any."

――――――――――――

JOE MORGAN: I was born just 17 miles away from Fenway Park, in Walpole, Massachusetts. I always had this memory of going with my dad and one of my brothers. The steel and concrete, the walk up the ramp, seeing Fenway Park for the first time. It looked so beautiful. I was in awe.

A half century later I was the bullpen coach for the Red Sox. It was Bastille Day, the 14th of July.

We had just come back to Fenway after the All-Star break when general manager Lou Gorman gave me the heads-up. "We're going to make a managerial change," he said. "And you'll be the interim manager."

――――――――――――

John McNamara, who had replaced Ralph Houk, would now be replaced by "Turnpike Joe." Ever since the 1986 World Series loss, "Mac" had been a man of dark moods. Mac said, "Some people pick you to finish first just to see you get [expletive] fired."

――――――――――――

BRUCE HURST: After our workouts Vinnie Orlando, our clubhouse guy, called us in for a meeting.

We were told that John McNamara had been fired and Joe Morgan had been named manager. It seemed Mrs. Yawkey made the decision; it was just that quick. She wanted Mac out of there.

JOE MORGAN: After all the years in the minors, the many, many bus rides, small hotels, meals in places you want to forget about, it was something special to move from coach to running the big-league team.

It rained the first days I was on the job. Then, when we finally played, [Roger] Clemens was on the mound, and we went off on a tear, winning the first 12 games. "Morgan Magic," they called it. They even had signs up at Fenway. We won 19 of the first 20 games I managed.

The win I remember best was against the Twins. Todd Benzinger smacked a walk-off homer around the Pesky Pole, capping a tenth-inning victory. That was our seventh straight win. Benzinger hit that home run and Mrs. Yawkey said, "Give Joe Morgan a contract for the rest of the year."

Beating the Tigers, 9–4, Boston won its 23rd consecutive game at Fenway on August 12. Two days later Detroit pounded the Sox, 18–6, ending Boston's home winning streak at 24.

Morgan Magic culminated with the Red Sox winning their second division title in three years. Unfortunately, the joy ended there. The Oakland A's swept Boston four straight in the American League Championship Series.

A curious coda to that sweep was that former Red Sox star starter Dennis Eckersley saved all four Oakland wins.

———————

BRUCE HURST: That 1988 season ended it for me as a Red Sox pitcher. Quite an experience, the players, managers, but especially the fans and the environment of Fenway Park. The head groundskeeper, Joe Mooney, had been there when I started, and he was still there when I ended. He's still there.

———————

JOE MOONEY: Once the sun came out in the morning I got up, and I got going. I arrived, six in the morning for day games, night games. If nobody was there at seven-thirty, when the real work started, then I closed the gate.

About 10 or 12 people worked with me, half of them regulars. They've called me all kinds of names. That don't bother me. I always had love and respect for Fenway Park.

———————

On August 6, 1989, when Carl Yastrzemski's number 8 was retired, the son of another legend was in the house.

HARRY BAULD: I was doing some stories for *Boston Magazine* when I tracked down John Henry Williams, the son of Ted Williams. He was agreeable to my doing a piece on him.

This was 1989. Ted was living in Florida. I went with John Henry to Fenway. He was in his early twenties, looked like Ted in the early pictures, really handsome, only skinnier.

Seeing him, every vendor, all the guards, the players lit up and waved. We sat in the Ted Williams seats. The visitors' dugout was to the left. John had brought along an old friend of the family, a New Hampshire state policeman, and his son.

John Henry Williams was really a nice kid. I got to write the piece but more important to see what it was like for the son of Ted Williams at Fenway Park.

———————

As the 1980s came to an end, Mrs. Jean Yawkey was still very much on the scene, attending every game at Fenway Park. Chairwoman of the board of directors of the JRY Corporation, the majority owner and general partner of the Red Sox, she worked with Haywood Sullivan making the major decisions.

The Red Sox finished 1989, their 77th season at Fenway Park, with an 83–79 record. It was good for third place in the American League East. Fenway's attendance was 2,510,012—the most in franchise history up to then.

The '90s beckoned.

ABOVE: Roger Clemens poses with baseball in a scene that would become ritual through the years
OPPOSITE: Celebration time! Sox rejoice in their winning of American League pennant in 1986
PAGE 172–173: Aerial view of jam-packed Fenway, 1983

—NINETIES—

"SAVE FENWAY PARK!"

On April 9, Opening Day, the first year of the last decade of the twentieth century, more than 35,000 were on hand at Fenway. They cheered loudly for Dwight Evans, who was DH-ing. His double into the triangle off Jack Morris cleared the bases and was the big hit for the Bosox. It was the 17th and last opener for the gritty outfielder at Fenway. Boston, behind Roger Clemens, defeated Detroit, 5–2.

RED SOX YEAR BY YEAR	1990 – 1999	YEAR	WON	LOST	PCT.	GB	ATTENDANCE
		1999	94	68	.580	4.0	2,445,590
		1998	92	70	.568	22.0	2,343,947
		1997	78	84	.481	20.0	2,226,136
		1996	85	77	.525	7.0	2,315,231
		1995	86	58	.597	—	2,164,410
		1994	54	61	.470	17.0	1,775,818
		1993	80	82	.494	15.0	2,422,021
		1992	73	89	.451	23.0	2,468,574
		1991	84	78	.519	7.0	2,562,435
		1990	88	74	.543	—	2,528,986

Dwight Evans was a household name throughout Boston and baseball. Not exactly a household name, William Joseph Robidoux, out of Ware, Massachusetts, was in the Opening Day starting lineup, too, playing in one of the 27 games he would get into for the Sox in his final big-league season.

The Red Sox lineup on Opening Day 1990 at Fenway:

Wade Boggs	3B
Marty Barrett	2B
Mike Greenwell	LF
Ellis Burks	CF
Dwight Evans	DH
Billy Jo Robidoux	1B
Tony Pena	C
Jody Reed	SS
Kevin Romine	RF
Roger Clemens	P

Seven days later the Brewers racked out 20 hits—no homers, though—and cruised over Boston, 18–0. Later that month, a gimpy Bill Buckner, playing his final season, struggled mightily to successfully run out an inside-the-park home run.

DAN WILSON: He was 40 years old. He didn't have very good legs to begin with. As he got older, he got slower. But this game, he hit one to the base of the right-field wall. The right fielder actually went over that low wall into the stands trying to make a catch.

The ball, however, just sat there at the base of the wall while Buckner loped around the bases. It took him so long, it was like cheering on a slow horse.

———————

On May 4, 1990, Tom Brunansky became a member of the Red Sox after being traded from the Cardinals for closer Lee Smith.

———————

TOM BRUNANSKY: My first home game, I came from the small locker room down those stairs through a dark, dank hallway. Out of nowhere, my first sight is the Wall.

Fenway was the taste of Boston Red Sox. I was a true fan, I would go inside the scoreboard. I actually wanted to go and climb up the Wall and walk it. They wouldn't let me do that. But I was inside the Wall, and I signed my name.

Sometimes I would get as close as I could to that Green Monster, look straight up to see the hundreds of dings in that wall, just dent after dent after dent.

That 1990 team had coaches Al Bumbry, Rac Slider, Richie Hebner. Bill Fisher handled the pitching. "Walpole Joe" Morgan was our manager. Some of his "magic" was still around.

Joe was an original. With the hitter in the on-deck circle, we'd be like two or three deep on the stairs of the dugout. Joe would turn around: "Let me ask you something?" he'd say. And we knew he had something up his sleeve. He would do it and it would work.

Another Joe—Joe Mooney—was a beauty. Head groundskeeper. You could tell whether rain was coming or not just by looking at his face. The sun could be shining, but if Joe had that scowl with his head tilted down, you knew that we were in for rain.

We'd hit in the batting cages out in center field during rain delays. You never, however, wanted to be the first group to hit because once you opened the door and flipped the lights on, all the rats would start running out. You always wanted to be that second or third hitting group. By then the rats would be gone.

During games, all of the grounds crew would start gathering in a section down in the right-field area. A couple of times balls would get smoked and a crew member would get hit. But it was nothing dangerous.

Playing the outfield in that small park, you'd hear the vendors for the Fenway Franks going up and down behind you. You would hear the fans voicing their displeasure or their excitement about something you did. Fenway was always full during my time. There was always tremendous fan support. It was a lot of fun.

———————

The Saturday NBC Game of the Week at Fenway September 1 was a lot of fun for Red Sox fans. Boston blasted the Yankees, 15–1. A blow that brought the crowd to its feet was Mike Greenwell's inside-the-park grand slam. It was the ninth straight victory for the Hub Team, pushing the seventh-place Yankees 19 games behind them.

That September Boston faced the Blue Jays. Both clubs were tied for the division lead. Leading by two runs in the ninth, Toronto had All-Star Tom Henke on the mound. Tying the score, the Sox had the bases loaded with one out.

Journeyman Jeff Stone, in his first at-bat of the season, pinch-hit and somehow managed to get the ball over the drawn-in outfielders. The Sox won the game and took the division lead that they never lost. "I'm numb," Stone said later. "I'm on cloud 10." It was more Morgan Magic.

DAN WILSON: Early that year I had bought tickets for the final game of the season at Fenway. We arrived about 45 minutes late, coming down from Maine. It had rained all morning, but nobody had stayed home.

═══════════════

TOM BRUNANSKY: It was October 3. We were playing the White Sox, and we had a one-game lead over the Blue Jays. A loss for us would have put us in a tie-breaker.

We had a 3–1 lead with two outs and two White Sox runners on. Top of the ninth. Jeff Reardon was pitching; Ozzie Guillen was hitting. Ellis Burks and Mike Greenwell were in the outfield with me. We backed each other up all the time, especially in Fenway, where you have to play not only your outfield position but your partners' as well and communicate with them.

We always played Ozzie around the other way. He was a left-handed line-drive hitter. But when he got ahead in the count, he liked to try to pull the ball. I knew that Greeny [Mike Greenwell] and Ellis were shifting the other way. I just went straight up, giving Ozzie the right-center gap.

The count went 2–0. Sure enough, Jeff threw the ball down, Ozzie's zone. He hit it hard, hooked it. I had a pretty good jump. Running, I knew either I was going to dive and make the catch and be a hero or I was going to miss, and the ball would probably be a triple, the game would be tied, and I would be the goat.

PAGE 174: Rooting, roaring, raving Red Sox fans
ABOVE: Crowded Fenway, April 1994
OPPOSITE: The grounds crew at work

There is no playing safe in Fenway. So I went for it full steam. Feeling dirt under my spikes, I knew I was about eight feet from the fence. I just dove and caught the ball, which landed short of the fence.

I knew I had to show the ball to the umpire who, by the angle of the fence, was trying to get around that little corner and had been taken out by a fan. The umpire was down. I jumped up and ran to show him the ball, jumping and hooting and hollering. He ruled it a catch.

In the celebration afterward, fully uniformed, glove and all, I got tossed into the Jacuzzi. But I didn't mind. I even turned the jets on and splashed water all around.

———

For the Red Sox, it was their second American League East Division championship in three years. But the A's swept them four straight in the ALCS.

Dennis Eckersley was still having a time of it, saving the second game in Fenway and the third contest in Oakland. Still, it had been a very successful year. Fans had clogged Fenway Park that 1990 season—2,528,986 of them—again setting an all-time best-season-attendance record to that point in time.

May 12, 1991, was the date of the 50th-anniversary celebration of Ted Williams hitting over .400, and the Boston legend was suitably honored at Fenway. Lansdowne Street, the road behind the left-field wall at Fenway Park, was renamed "Ted Williams Way."

———

LARRY CANCRO: As a major part of the anniversary, I had Joe DiMaggio and Ted Williams standing underneath the center-field gate. They were very nonchalant, like, "Hey, Joe," "Hey, Ted." I thought, this won't look good when they get out there.

They each got in a cart, and each cart went in the opposite direction, one toward right field and one toward left field. They met at home plate. Then, incredibly, the two icons got out and hugged each other like they hadn't seen each other in a hundred years.

Joe was so full of pride. It was always important to him to present the right image of what Joe DiMaggio means—like a kind of brand. Ted had his own persona—"I'm about the game and about kids," he'd say.

We had slotted all the players to be in one suite for the game, but Joe wanted to be by himself.

"Where would you like to sit?" we asked. He walked over to the left-field side of the booth. "I want to sit near my good friend the Wall," he said, pointing to the Green Monster. "That wall has been very good to me."

It was an inside joke. Joe DiMaggio had often said if he had been able to have had Fenway as his home field, if the Wall were part of his batting scene, he would have had like 800 home runs. Fenway seemed to be built for him, for the type of power he had.

We served him seafood—crab legs and lobster. "You sure know how to treat a fisherman's son," he said. Later on, he joined us for dinner.

———

Three days later, after the last man to hit .400 anniversary, the Red Sox defeated the White Sox, 9–6, in a night game that stretched on through 4 hours and 11 minutes—a new league record for a nine-inning night game, 9 minutes longer than the previous nocturnal marathon.

On October 1, Wade Boggs doubled twice, topping the mark of 40 in a season for the seventh straight year, tying Joe Medwick's major league career total.

———

ART DAVIDSON: Wade Boggs worked hard to make himself good. He had the reputation in the minor leagues of being a good hitter but not a good fielder. But every day, at the exact same time, long before the public was in the ballpark, he would come out and take hundreds of ground balls. I would be up working in the press box and knew that if I wanted to talk to him, I would have to get him before he started his fielding practice. He was on his strict time, honed in completely.

———

LARRY CANCRO: I went out into the ballpark every day to see Wade Boggs take ground balls as a five-minute afternoon break. It was often just him and Johnny Pesky or another coach. He ran every day before the game at 7:17 exactly.

ABOVE: Old warriors feeling it: Ted Williams and Joe DiMaggio in 1991
OPPOSITE: Commemorative baseball given to fans for 500th sellout at Fenway Park

There were times that he was totally accessible and times that were off-limits, like when he was going to run. Once you knew him and his habits, he was actually the easiest guy to deal with. He also was one of the hardest workers I have ever seen, like most star players.

————————————————

Apparently, however, there were not enough hard workers on the team. That may have been why the Sox finished a distant second place in 1991, seven games back of the first-place Blue Jays. Joe Morgan was canned on October 8, 1991, although he had one year remaining on his contract. "This team just isn't that good," Morgan warned.

Change was everywhere—on and off the field. On February 26, 1992, Jean Remington Yawkey died. She had sold the team after Tom Yawkey passed away to team executive Haywood Sullivan and former Red Sox trainer Buddy LeRoux. But the pairing did not work out, and at the suggestion—some would say prodding—of Major League Baseball, Mrs. Yawkey purchased the team back from them, becoming chairwoman of the board of directors of the JRY Corporation, as majority owner and general partner.

When Jean Yawkey died in 1992, John Harrington, head of the JRY Trust, orchestrated the buyout of general partner Haywood Sullivan's shares for an estimated $33 million.

————————————————

BUTCH HOBSON: I succeeded Joe Morgan in 1992. I felt it was quite an honor to come back and manage the Red Sox, the team I had played for.

————————————————

Despite his high hopes, the season was a disappointing one for Hobson, a former University of Alabama football star, and for Red Sox rooters. Boston wound up hitting but 84 home runs, their lowest full-season output. The Sox scored 599 runs

that season but allowed 669. There was no more Morgan Magic, and neither was there any Hobson Magic. The Sox logged a 73–89 record for a very disappointing last-place finish. Even with all that, fans still jammed their Back Bay ballyard: 2,468,574.

Players like Scott Fletcher, Billy Hatcher, Scott Cooper, Luis Rivera mixed and matched with the Greenwells and the Mo Vaughns as the decade of the '90s moved along.

On April 13, 1993, Opening Day at Fenway finally arrived. The Sox had played six games on the road. Field conditions were described as "soaked" as Frank Viola toughed it out and won his second game of the young season, trimming Cleveland, 6–2.

That season, poignancy and makeup merged. Almost 50 years after his "tryout" in April 1945, Sam Jethroe returned to Fenway that May as part of a tribute to Negro Leaguers. He took a final swing in the Red Sox batting cage.

Later that season, descendants of the 1918 world championship team members, who had never received their championship emblems, were presented with replicas.

Boston posted a winning record at home, 43–38. But on the road it was a different story. Butch Hobson, scuffling, struggling, could only manage his team to a fifth-place finish in 1993 and an 80–82 record.

The Red Sox Opening Day lineup on April 4, 1994, looked like this:

Otis Nixon	**CF**
Billy Hatcher	**RF**
Mike Greenwell	**LF**
Mo Vaughn	**1B**
Andre Dawson	**DH**
Scott Cooper	**3B**
John Valentin	**SS**
Dave Valle	**C**
Scott Fletcher	**2B**
Roger Clemens	**P**

Clemens was rocked in less than five innings against Detroit for eight runs. But Boston held on for a 9–8 win.

————————————————

GENE BRUNDAGE: I had retired from a career at Raytheon when I started working as an usher on Opening Day 1994. I'm still on the job. They put me in the bleachers but told me with time I'd move closer to home plate. I am now much closer to home plate.

There are maybe 50 or 60 of us. When there's an evening game, it starts at 7:05; the gates open at 5:05. Half an hour before, we have a roll call. Announcements are made; they'll warn us if there are any storms predicted.

I get there early and go to my locker to change clothes and put on the sneakers given to us by the Sox. My first year, they gave me a red jacket. Every year we get blue pants with red piping, but you have to bring your own white shirt and blue tie.

We dust off the seats (I bring my own towel). The average tip is about a dollar. Some people complain about the size of the seats. I tell them I didn't build them. We are constantly working even after people are seated. We'll direct traffic, keep people moving. The aisles are often clogged because they are so narrow.

JERRY TRUPIANO: The date is May 3, 1994. The Red Sox are ahead of the Mariners, 7–4, in the ninth. Seattle gets a runner on. Junior Griffey is due up. Righthander Greg Harris is lifted in favor of southpaw Tony Fossas, a pitcher who dominated Junior in the past. Fossas warms; Junior waits in the on-deck circle. A group of young fans start ragging Griffey about his failures against Fossas. There is a verbal exchange as Griffey moves to the rail. Security moves in.

Fossas delivers his first pitch. Junior hits it about nine miles into the right-center-field bleachers for a two-run home run. After crossing the plate he heads over to the fans, who are now doing a bowing salute. They had awakened a big dog, and he bit. The good thing about that game was the Sox eked out a 7–6 victory.

They say that every dog has his day. Griffey had his, and Texas's Jose Canseco had his a month later—a weekend, actually, the first one in June. Going 10 for 13, he scored 10 runs, drove in 10 runs, and clubbed 4 homers.

On July 8, John Valentin had his day of days, joining George Burns as the only player to turn an unassisted triple play at Fenway Park. Valentin also slugged a three-run homer, boosting Boston to a 4–3 win over Seattle.

The 1994 strike-shortened season was the only one in the '90s when Fenway Park drew fewer than 2 million fans: 1,775,818, to be exact.

Playing under .500 ball on the road and also at Fenway, the Red Sox went 54–61 for the season, finishing in fourth place in the American League East. That finish ended it for Butch Hobson—he was out as manager. Enter Kevin Curtis Kennedy, 41, as the 1995 season got under way.

The former Montreal Expos coach was let go after the '94 season as skipper of the Texas Rangers after posting a 52–62 record but a first–place finish, making him the only manager ever to win a division title with a sub-.500 record.

Kennedy took over the manager's office at Fenway. One can only wonder if he knew of the fate of some of the pilots who had preceded him: Don Zimmer, who scrupulously kept a clip file on those he decided had done him in or tried to; John McNamara, whose open mood had turned dark and sour; and Chick Stahl, who took his own life prior to the 1907 season.

The strike-shortened 1994 season had led to the cancellation of the World Series. The 1995 season got under way with a 144-game schedule for all teams.

The Sox finally opened rather late, April 26, against Minnesota. Aaron Sele hurled five shutout frames. Four other Boston hurlers went an inning each. Boston won the game, 9–0.

TOM CARON: New England Sports Network was in the ballpark from the time I got there in 1995 until 2006, when we outgrew our space. I would be at Fenway every day. When the team was on the road, we still would broadcast from Fenway.

They broadcast John Valentin's rapping out 5 hits, 3 of them home runs, for a total of 15 total bases in a 10-inning 6–5 win over the Mariners on June 2, 1995.

With Valentin and other Boston players enjoying their time at Fenway, the Sox went 42–30 at home, spent 137 days in first place, scored 791 runs, holding the competition to 698 runs—and won the American League East with an 86–58 record. In his third season with Boston, the staff ace that season, Tim Wakefield, posted a 16–8 record.

The Red Sox managed their first postseason appearance at Fenway since 1990. Unfortunately, Cleveland swept the Sox in the American League Division Series.

JOANNA RAPF: My dad, Maury Rapf—a highly successful screenwriter—was born and grew up in California. But after he moved to New Hampshire to teach film studies at Dartmouth, he became a diehard Red Sox fan. May 19, 1996, was his 80th birthday, and his friend Gene Lyons, a former Dartmouth professor, called

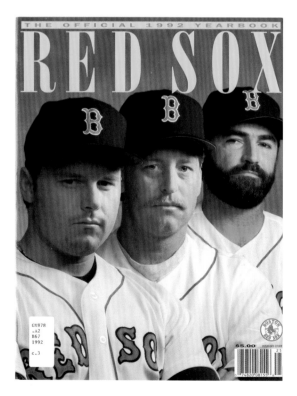

on his son Daniel, who handled Fenway special events, to do something special.

They set us up in a suite—my dad's friends, kids, and grandkids. Dartmouth alum and screenwriter Budd Schulberg, who had been my father's best friend when they were children, was there as well.

The message board flashed "HAPPY 80th BIRTHDAY, MAURICE." Some people from the Red Sox organization came by, and Danny gave him an authentic Red Sox cap and jacket, which he wore until he died.

———————

After Maurice Rapf's death in 2003, a memorial service was held for him at Dartmouth. A brief selection of comments and tributes appeared in the commemorative program. The last entry reads, "I hope the Red Sox win the World Series for Maurice this year . . . Daniel Lyons, friend."

On May 21, Seattle slugged Boston, 13–7. Ken Griffey Jr., 26, became the seventh-youngest player to collect 200 homers.

On June 6, 1996, John Valentin was showing off his offensive skills once again, hitting for the cycle. In that game the White Sox pulled off a triple play. It was the first time since the 1931 season that a game featured both of those rare baseball accomplishments.

———————

JOHN SHANNAHAN: Mid-1990s, the Sox had a family day for all employees following a Sunday afternoon game. Tables were placed along the track. A lot of the people there were interested in the food. But my brother and I and others who had brought our gloves along were interested in throwing balls off the Wall, turning and making the throw like Yastrzemski into second base.

It's late August, close to 7:30. The ballpark is all shadow when I finally get my chance to take a

few swings. I pull the ball and it's soaring in the sky. I'm at home plate and I'm thinking, "Holy cow, you did it. Not bad for a 40-year-old." The sky is still bright; the ball's perfectly silhouetted, and it's arching high, toward the Wall. The ball drops, landing at the edge of the warning track, 290 feet away—warning-track power. Oh, well.

———————

On September 28, 1996, in what would be his final appearance for Boston, Roger Clemens struck out 10 Yankees but lost to New York, 4–2, at Fenway Park.

The Sox finished third in '96, and Kevin Kennedy, who posted a record of 171 wins and 135 losses in two seasons as skipper, was replaced by Jimy Williams. The managerial musical chairs kept revolving.

On March 19, 1997, the Sox unveiled a 25-foot-high Coca-Cola contour bottle design on top of the left-field wall light tower. For each Red Sox home run over the wall or hitting the Coke bottle, contributions would be made to the Jimmy Fund.

That 1997 season Will Cordero hit one off the bottle on April 13, against Seattle. Then on May 11, Tim Naehring hit a Coke-bottle homer against Texas.

During the 1990s, discussions and at times angry debates about replacing Fenway Park raged. Plans were floated to build a virtual carbon copy of the original ballpark next door, replete with a new "Green Monster" in left field. A bigger second deck also was part of the scheme.

———————

DAN WILSON: In 1997 I was an attorney in Boston working with the Boston Preservation Alliance. There were rumors that the JRY Trust wanted to build a new stadium, and the "Save Fenway Park!" effort was just getting under way.

PAGE 180–181: Panorama of action on the field of play
ABOVE: Tom Brunansky watches as his homer heads over the Green Monster on June 21, 1991

BPA was looking for volunteers for "Save Fenway Park!" I said I could donate five hours a month. It became a running joke later, when we were donating 20 hours a week. I didn't get paid for this. I did it for myself. It was a combination of my interests in the Red Sox, in architecture, in history and ballparks. Our group positioned ourselves for renovation rather than being against a new stadium or demolition. We never tried to make villains out of the old ownership group, the Harrington regime, the JRY Trust.

While the fate of Fenway was being debated, 1997 was a year of outstanding individual accomplishment on the baseball field. On May 30, Mo Vaughn homered three times, going four for four, in Boston's 10–4 rout of New York.

On September 9 Boston rookie shortstop Nomar Garciaparra drove in his 87th run, setting a new majorleague record for leadoff men in an 8–6 Boston loss to the Yankees.

But perhaps the greatest accomplishment and the one spurred by the most motivation belonged to Roger Clemens. Returning to Boston in a Toronto uniform on July 12, he fanned 16, winning, 3–1. To many, it seemed that Clemens glared from the mound toward the general manager's suite at Dan Duquette, who let him move on and out of a Red Sox uniform.

Seventeen days after the Clemens highlighter, Seattle's Jay Buhner pulled off a gem, leaping over the four-foot wall in right field, landing in the bullpen, and robbing Boston's Scott Hatteberg of a home run.

"It was the kind of play outfielders always dream about," Buhner said.

Boston opened on the road again in 1998, a practice the team would often engage in because the weather in the spring in New England was so unpredictable.

The Sox returned home on April 10, having lost five of their last eight games. It was Good Friday and therefore no beer was for sale, something that hadn't happened since Prohibition. The competition was Seattle. The opposing pitcher was Randy Johnson—in his prime.

Fanning 15, allowing just 2 hits, the "Big Unit" over 8 innings was fabulous. After he had thrown 131 pitches, he was mercifully taken out of the game. Incredibly, off four relief pitchers, Boston rallied for seven runs, capped by Mo Vaughn's walk-off grand slammer. The Fenway control room operator threw a switch: "Dirty Water" by the Standells, a big hit in 1966, blared throughout the park. Red Sox Nation now had its anthem and victory song.

That "Dirty Water" moment in 1998 has become a permanent part of the Fenway scene, with every Bosox triumph triggering the PA system to blare the song. And if the win is a special one, fans will tarry in the old ballpark, singing, "I love that Dirty Water. . . . Oh, Boston, you're my home."

LOU MERLONI SR.: Everybody knew beforehand that my son Lou was coming back from a road trip to play his first game at Fenway on May 15, 1998. It was a special date, my wife's and my 33rd wedding anniversary. Relatives, friends, maybe two, three hundred of them had bought tickets to the game.

"Dad, if I ever make it to the big leagues," Lou had told me many times, "you guys are going to come and watch me play in style."

The white limo picked us up: my wife, daughters, son-in-law, three grandkids, mother-in-law, and me. We arrived at Fenway about three in the afternoon and because we were Lou's parents, they let my wife and me in through a side door. The others had to wait outside.

We sat in the family Section 21, behind home plate. Before the game, we went down to talk to our son. He was wearing number 50. "My God," I thought as we wished him luck, "this is my kid, going to play today at Fenway Park."

He came up to bat with a runner on third. I'm thinking, "Give us just a fly ball. You'll go 0–0, but you'll have a run batted in."

Louie had two strikes on him. I'm thinking, "Oh, my God, he's in the big leagues now. They're just going to eat him up."

And then he hit it. The thing never came down. It went into the net. I just couldn't believe it. My son's first at-bat at Fenway Park and he hits a home run.

LOU MERLONI: It was a fastball up. I didn't know if it was enough to get out. I come sprinting out. I think I was close to second base by the time the ball went out of the ballpark. I kept running and the crowd just went crazy: "Lou! Lou! Lou!"

Back in the dugout I got the silent treatment. Not even a high five. Then all of a sudden Mo Vaughn jumped up off the bench and just put his big paws on my head. And with that, all the guys surrounded me.

LOU MERLONI SR.: Lou went on to play in 423 games over 9 seasons. Not all of those were with the Red Sox, not all at Fenway. But whenever he played at Fenway I was there. I had waited all my life to do this. I watched them all.

RUSS COHEN: My first time at Fenway was for a day game on Saturday, June 6, 1998. The Big Dig was going on, so it took a long time to get to the stadium.

I was a Mets fan, and with interleague play, I had a perfect opportunity to see my team play at Fenway. There were a decent amount of Mets fans at the game. Probably a lot of college kids from New York.

Our seats were down the third-base line close to the left-field wall. I'm not that big a guy, like five-eight, and not that heavy. But my knees were almost touching the railing, and the seats were very narrow.

Still, being in that ballpark, the oldest one around, was incredible. I loved looking at the scoreboard, seeing how it was manually operated.

Tim Wakefield was on the mound for Boston. I watched him inning after inning. "How do guys not hit him?" I wondered.

In the top of the sixth inning, Brian McRae was dancing off third base. That got to

Wakefield. He balked, and the Mets—who had only gotten two hits that day—won on the basis of that balk. I was a winner all around. My team won. I experienced Fenway Park. And the game was most unusual.

CHARLIE PATTERSON: My friend Peter made a gift to the Jimmy Fund in my honor. August 1, I was invited to Fenway as part of the Jimmy Fund Fantasy Day. I would be allowed to swing at a dozen pitches.

Since I was almost 60 years old and hadn't played baseball in a while, I prepared for the experience by going to the batting cage on a

BELOW: Mo Vaughn: power personified
OPPOSITE: Flag unfurled

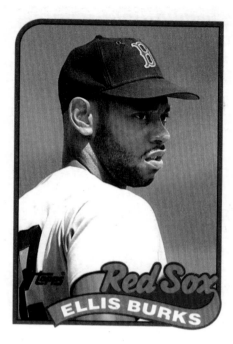
ELLIS BURKS

regular basis. My wife, Eleanor, would feed balls into the pitching machine, and I would take my cuts.

The big day arrived. Mike Andrews, former Red Sox second baseman and executive director of the Jimmy Fund, welcomed me. My name was announced over the PA system. I stepped into the batter's box, and my name appeared on the center-field JumboTron scoreboard. I looked down the short 312-foot left-field line. The Green Monster, which always had seemed so close, now looked like it was somewhere in Canada.

There were "players" at each position. I settled in to hit. Whiffing on only 3 of the 12 pitches, I made "contact" on the other 9 and had 4 clean singles. Thank goodness I did not have to run any of them out. It was only after the 12th pitch that I ran the bases. Going down to first base, I did the Carlton Fisk plea/wave, trying to keep the ball fair—even though it was a grounder. For an out-of-shape 60-year-old, running around the bases is like running uphill. I was stumbling at the end, but I made it to home plate.

Afterward I took my "shower of dreams" and thought of some others who had showered there, like Mantle, Feller, Musial, Kaline, Ruth, Gehrig, Frank and Brooks Robinson, Larry Doby, Ty Cobb, Christy Mathewson, Aaron, Shoeless Joe Jackson . . .

MIKE LOWELL: September of '98 was the first time I ever saw Fenway Park. I was a Yankee, on the bench, called up from the minors. I didn't play in the game.

It was as intense an environment as I'd ever seen in a baseball game. I asked veteran Luis Sojo, "Is this the way it is at Fenway every single game?"

"Yes," he said, "when it is Yankees–Red Sox."

I was traded afterward to the Marlins, and when we played the Red Sox in interleague play at Fenway, it wasn't as intense as that Yankees–Red Sox game.

Still, there was a lot of fan support and chants of "Nomar" and "Manny." It could intimidate opponents.

On September 9 the Yankees were not a bit intimidated as they trimmed Boston, 7–5, to clinch the American League East. Derek Jeter slammed a pair of home runs. Nevertheless, it had been a successful season for the Red Sox in their second year with Jimy Williams as manager, as they posted a 92–70 record, winning the wild card, finishing 22 games behind the American League East champion Yankees. The only "bummer" was that Cleveland eliminated the Sox in the American League Division Series.

ERICA TARLIN: I came out of Fenway the last game of the '98 season. Little card tables were set up on the street. A guy was sitting there with bumper stickers that said, "Save Fenway Park!" I was interested. And thinking, "Save it from what?"

December '98 I went to a rally outside the park in the snow. "Save Fenway Park!" was attracting attention. Practically every day there were newspaper stories that ownership had plans for a new stadium.

During the years of struggle it broke down to people walking by our table telling us to get a life or stopping to listen.

DAN WILSON: People came and left our movement to "Save Fenway Park!" as their lifestyle could permit. Some left, others stepped in. Against us was every power broker, every developer, every politician, every media outlet. Sports talk radio loved mocking us; the *Boston Globe* sports guys were not for us.

In the works was a $750 million project for a new ballpark. There was a lot of money to be made. The official word from the Red Sox was that it was impossible to renovate Fenway Park, absolutely impossible. Nobody made them prove what they were saying—it was just accepted.

But not by "Save Fenway Park!"

But not by the public.

We always had the public on our side. So many people didn't want a community bulldozed to make way for a gigantic new ballpark. The earliest polling showed 2–1 in favor of renovation and about 30 percent undecided. As the years went by, it was always 2–1 in favor of renovation. The undecided kept shrinking, getting smaller and smaller.

We were out there any chance we got to get our message out, rallies at ball games, media events. We were working the issue that it was wrong to use public money to build a stadium for private use and private gain.

ERICA TARLIN: We met with the old ownership, the John Harrington group, along with their architect in the visitors' clubhouse. They didn't look really happy with us. It was funny—they were giving us the time of day, but they didn't want to hear what we had to say.

Nobody did, aside from the people. The ballplayers, past and present, could not bite the hand that fed them. Bill Lee was an exception.

===

DAN WILSON: Bill was the one person in all of baseball that was 100 percent behind us. He was there for us from the beginning and a big help speaking at rallies.

One of the great heroes in the entire battle was architect Charles Hagenah. In 1999, he was teaching a class at Roger Williams University on Fenway Park. He tried to get some blueprints of the ballpark for his students, but the Red Sox were not sharing any information. The public records at the city of Boston were scrolled away somewhere and not being made public. He came to us to see if we had any blueprints he could share with his students, and over time he agreed to work with us, as if we were a client.

His renovation plan for Save Fenway Park! was ready for us in the spring of 1999. Some of his ideas are realities today, like the closing of Yawkey Way and Van Ness Street on game days. The use of the Jeano Building next to Fenway and contiguous with it, and the Laundry Building behind the bleachers, and the incorporation of them into the ballpark also came out of his plan. The Red Sox delayed and delayed in announcing their plan. It was critically important that we got our plan out there first.

We announced it at a public meeting on a Thursday evening in May of 1999. The Red Sox plan was announced the following Saturday. As we had expected, the estimated cost of theirs was $750 million, several hundred million dollars of which would be public money. We had always argued that every stadium that was ever built came in at a lowball price and left the government on the hook for any overruns.

The legislature told the Red Sox: "We're giving you $100 million, and that's it." The city of Boston said, "We'll give you $212 million, some of it in the form of a loan. If there are any overruns, the team will have to pay for it." Both the city and the state put the overruns on the team. Boston is the only city who's ever done that, and I think our campaign to save Fenway had something to do with that.

As things turned out, the Harrington group was lowballing it, hoping to stick the government and the people with the price tag for the overruns. Afterward, Harrington [the team owner] blamed the mayor for letting the new park proposal fall through by not giving him a blank check.

The Harrington group had allowed Fenway to deteriorate, but the essential ballpark was a very simple structure and was in good shape. We knew what had to be done. It was very clear: The team had to be sold to someone willing to renovate Fenway Park.

===

While the battle for the heart and soul and very life of Fenway Park was being waged, baseball as usual continued full force at the Boston ballpark as the century neared its end.

Jimy Williams was still skipper in 1999, and Dan Duquette was still in place as general manager. Mo Vaughn had left to play for the California Angels. Top reliever Tom Gordon would go down. Pedro Martinez would have a career year and at times be unhittable. Nomar Garciaparra would be every fan's favorite—bat .357 and win the first of two batting titles. Tim Wakefield, moved to the closer role, would save 15 games in 18 attempts. At Fenway Park

A lot of the National League stars got their first look at the manual scoreboard. Many came inside for a closer view; some signed the walls.

As the head of scoreboard operations since 1991, Chris Elias has had one of the best seats in the ballpark. Two others assist him.

CHRIS ELIAS: Our working space is pretty small, long but narrow. We're a little bit below the playing field. There's about six or seven slots that are there for us to view the game. We see everything perfectly except the center-field scoreboard. It's a unique and beautiful perspective, basically from a left-fielder's point of view.

One of the first things fans love to look at is the scoreboard when they come into Fenway for batting practice. So we like to have the "setup" for them just as they're arriving, who's playing who around baseball, with corresponding pitcher's number for those teams.

We watch the Red Sox game and constantly look at our laptop computers to update the American League games. We must go outside to post National League scores between innings. On the warning track and in full view of the crowd having only a minute and a half, we must put the correct numbers in the correct spots.

There's a few thousand signatures and messages, some messages in French, Spanish, Japanese. A lot of Hall of Famers have come in. Our oldest signing is from the 1950s — Red Sox outfielder Jimmy Piersall. We lost a few signa-

tures when they did the construction above us of the Green Monster seats.

Manny Ramirez used to come in all the time. We would talk about everything, especially cars. The crowd always cheered when Manny reemerged from the scoreboard.

We have no heating, no air-conditioning; we don't even have fans, because it's dusty. There's no bathroom. We typically don't bring food, only beverages, because we don't want to encourage any of our small friends to come around.

On September 27, Pedro Martinez was in the spotlight again, in the final home game of the twentieth century for Boston, against Baltimore.

The Red Sox lineup that day was:

Jose Offerman	2B
Damon Buford	CF
Jason Varitek	C
Mike Stanley	1B
Troy O'Leary	LF
Lou Merloni	SS
Brian Daubach	DH
Wilton Veras	3B
Trot Nixon	RF
Pedro Martinez	P

Boston won the game, 5–3, before 33,477. Pedro's won-and-lost record went to 23–4. Jimy Williams completed the third year of what would be a five-year stint as skipper of the Sox.

On October 10, racking up 24 hits, setting play-off records for most hits and runs scored in a game, the Bosox rolled, 23–7, over Cleveland in the ALDS. John Valentin led the charge — four hits, two of them home runs, and seven runs driven in. The Red Sox won the next day as well, 12–8, to take the series.

that season, Boston would be on its game big-time, winning 51 games, losing 30, outscoring teams 836–718, finishing second in the American League East, winning the American League wild card.

Nomar Garciaparra, in his prime of primes, strutted his stuff against Seattle on May 10, smashing 2 grand slams and a 2-run homer, becoming the first American League player with 10 RBIs in a game since 1975. The Red Sox won, 12–4. That was a special time at Fenway.

But one of the marker times, not only of that season, but of the entire decade, took place July 13, 1999, at the 70th All-Star Game. On hand were the candidates for the All-Century Team as well as the 1999 All-Stars. And since it was staged on Boston's home turf, the center of attraction was Theodore Samuel Williams.

Two days later the Red Sox and Yankees met for the first time in a playoff game since 1978, in a best-of-seven ALCS. The Yanks got up two games to none with wins at Yankee Stadium.

On the 16th of October the scene shifted to Fenway, where former Boston superstar stopper Roger Clemens took the mound for the Yankees against Martinez, who had led the league in wins, ERA, and strikeouts.

ED MARKEY: The ballpark was electric with anti-Yankee fever. Once again, we felt our redemption was at hand. The two greatest pitchers in baseball were matched up in our home ballpark. It was our best chance to break the curse, to break our historical inability to beat the Yankees. All of the hopes and all of the dreams of every Red Sox fan of all generations were at Fenway that night. And they were all fulfilled.

JOHN QUINN: My friend Gregg, a diehard Yankees fan, got tickets through a relationship with Willie Randolph for that October 16 game. We drove in from Manhattan. The seats were along the third-base line, about the second or the third row from the back. I noticed a Boston police officer standing not far from us. The game was progressing, and I noticed that he was still standing there.

"Yeah," Gregg explained, "the Yankees requested it."

It turns out, we were sitting in a section of all Yankees wives and families and girlfriends and stuff. People were wearing Yankees gear.

Everyone in the park booed as Roger Clemens came out to the mound, deep in shadows. Sunshine lit up the old grandstands. "Rog-er, Rog-er"—the place was filled with fans taunting him—but not in my section. I realized I'm the only person in the section standing and cheering. Everybody around me is like sitting on their hands.

Fans were getting more and more emotional. There was more and more verbal abuse. I didn't see anybody throwing any type of projectiles or anything like that, but the environment was pretty raw. It was the Clemens Massacre, the day for Red Sox revenge.

He had nothing.

In two innings, he gave up six hits and five runs. Joe Torre pulled him.

Massacre, the day for Red Sox revenge. A chant arose:

"Where is Roger? In the shower."

Really wild.

JOHN HARRELSON: I was one of 30,000-plus people booing him as he left the pitcher's mound and headed off the field. Roger's head was down. He did not make any eye contact with fans.

In came Hideki Irabu. He did worse than Clemens. In 4⅔ innings he was racked for 13 hits and 7 earned runs. Meanwhile, Pedro Martinez was knocking Yankees out like bowling pins, 7 innings, 2 hits, 12 strikeouts.

ED MARKEY: The Red Sox won, 13–1. Every Red Sox batter was perfect. The dream game of every Red Sox boy or girl had come to life for one shining moment, one shining night.

But like many Red Sox dreams back then, this one went unfulfilled. New York won the next two games, taking the series four games to one. "The Curse of the Bambino" persisted.

And so ended the tale of the Boston Red Sox's 87th season at Fenway Park as the twentieth century came to a close. The new century was just around the corner, when there would be many surprises, new heroes, and incredible feats and marker moments at the old Back Bay ballyard.

OPPOSITE: Yankee Roger Clemens pitches against the Red Sox in the first inning of Game 3 of the ALCS 1999

—21st CENTURY—

A NEW ERA
AT FENWAY PARK

The oldest remaining park in Major League Baseball began the first season of a new century on April 11, the continuum of its outer brick walls bearing the familiar banners with the names Babe Ruth, Cy Young, and Ted Williams.

   "Fenway Pahk," as locals call it, hosted the Minnesota Twins, and the Red Sox clobbered them, 13–4. Pedro Martinez's brother Ramon Martinez pitched five innings, yielding but one run.

RED SOX YEAR BY YEAR · **2000 – 2009**

YEAR	WON	LOST	PCT.	GB	ATTENDANCE
2009	95	67	.586	8	3,062,699
2008	95	67	.586	2.0	3,048,248
2007*	96	66	.593	—	2,971,025
2006	86	76	.531	11.0	2,930,588
2005	95	67	.586	—	2,847,888
2004*	98	64	.605	3.0	2,837,304
2003	95	67	.586	6.0	2,724,165
2002	93	69	.574	10.5	2,650,382
2001	82	79	.509	13.5	2,625,333
2000	85	77	.525	2.5	2,585,895

*WORLD CHAMPIONS

The Red sox lineup that day was:

Jose Offerman	2B
Trot Nixon	RF
Brian Daubach	DH
Nomar Garciaparra	SS
Troy O'Leary	LF
Carl Everett	CF
Mike Stanley	1B
Jason Varitek	C
Wilton Veras	3B
Ramon Martinez	P

TRACY NIEPORENT: I was at Fenway during the 2000 season for a series vs. the Mets. Outside the gates they were selling "Yankees SUCK" T-shirts. When I reminded the chowderheads that the Red Sox were playing the Mets, they disdainfully replied, "It's Noo Yawk, same thing."

Same thing for the "Sawks" in 2000—a third straight American League East second-place finish. But there was a lot to brag about. The winning of a second straight Cy Young Award by Pedro Martinez, the winning of a second straight batting title by Nomar Garciaparra, and the setting of a new Fenway park attendance record: 2,585,895.

JOHN SHANNAHAN: On a cold February morning in 2001, I met my brother, who was broadcast manager at Fenway, at the ballpark. It had snowed the day before, and I had my camera with me.

"Hey," I said, "can I get in and take some pictures of the ballpark with the snow on the field?"

I snapped a few. Then he asked if I wanted to see the clubhouse.

We went down through the Sox dugout, through a door, and up a set of stairs that led to the clubhouse, where the first thing I saw was a urinal on the wall. Next to it someone had written: "The official urinal of the 1999 All-Star Game." Equipment and trunks were all over the place, getting ready to be loaded onto the equipment truck that would head out to spring training in Florida. Johnny Pesky was sitting on a crate, bat in hand, surrounded by a bunch of clubhouse guys listening to him talk about hitting and his love of the game. It was a Norman Rockwell scene.

In a scene that underscored the long history of the Red Sox and Fenway Park, a 100th anniversary celebration was staged on May 27, 2001. A pregame ceremony featured 88-year-old "Broadway" Charlie Wagner, who pitched for the Sox in the late 1930s and the 1940s, tossing the first pitch to Carlton Fisk.

Less than a month later, on June 23, Manny being Manny Ramirez jerked two home runs, totaling 964 feet. The first one was reported as going 463 feet. The second one was measured at 501 feet, a foot short of Ted Williams's 502-foot homer, the Fenway record. Manny also came up twice with the bases loaded and left the bases loaded, prompting one disgruntled rooter to bellow, "You're no Ted Williams."

Mike Mussina of the Yankees was no Don Larsen, but on September 2, 2001, he did come within one pitch of perfection—a ninth-inning two-strike, two-out pitch to Carl Everett. The Sox pinch hitter managed a soft liner that fell in for a single. Mussina settled for a 1–0 victory and a one-hitter.

Drawing 2.6 million at Fenway, an average of 32,412 a game, the Red Sox finished the 2001 season in second place again, with an 82–79 record.

The new year of 2002 was one of rejoicing for Red Sox Nation. The old ownership group was out, and on January 17 Major League Baseball approved the new Red Sox consortium headed by principal owner John Henry. The executive chairman was Tom Werner, and Larry Lucchino was in as president and CEO.

Swift changes were implemented. Dan Duquette was removed as general manager. Mike Port, who had held that role for the Angels, replaced him. On November 25, 2002, Theo Epstein, who had grown up just a mile away from Fenway, replaced Port, becoming, at age 28, the youngest general manager in big-league history.

Grady Little came in as manager for the 2002 season, taking the place of Joe Kerrigan. Tony Cloninger was pitching coach, Mike Cubbage coached at third, and Dwight Evans was hitting coach. At first was Tommy Harper, in the bullpen Bob Kipper, and Mike Stanley held down the bench coach duties.

DAN WILSON: The new owners were outsiders, but they were very much able to see the beauty of Fenway Park. They were committed to its renovation.

BILL LEE: The difference between the old and new groups was the Henry group understood that the ballpark was integral to the neighborhood. The previous ownership couldn't have cared less about that. John Henry put his money where it was supposed to be, and he endeared himself to fans for eternity.

MICHAEL DUKAKIS: I can't say enough about how much I think of the way in which the new owners rethought the plan to tear down the place. Instead of a phony version of Fenway that would

PAGE 190: A picture is worth a thousand words for Red Sox Nation
OPPOSITE: Sox everywhere in this stunning view

have cost 850 million bucks, we have a gem, and it cost so much less than the other plan.

A position that had never existed before at Fenway was created for a young architect and urban planner from Mississippi.

JANET MARIE SMITH: I already had worked on Camden Yards in Baltimore, and that would be my model for Fenway. Our questions were: Could the park be made current in today's economic climate? Could we give our fans enough room? Could we have enough suites and club seats? Ultimately, could Fenway Park be saved? There was this sense that we were going to pull Fenway back from the brink of death.

By April 2002 there were two rows of "dugout" seats, a media interview room next to the Red Sox clubhouse, a players' lounge where the old family lounge had been, and a new family lounge.

Now a staple of the scene was Neil Diamond's 1969 hit "Sweet Caroline," which previously had been played from time to time but now was a permanent part.

Opening Day at Fenway in 2002 was a four-hour-plus marathon, a mess of a loss to Toronto, 12–11. Starter Pedro Martinez was not around at the end; Ugueth Urbina, however, was, and he gave up the losing run. But things would get much better.

NICK STEENSTRA: April 27, 2002: My wife, Cindy, and I were at Fenway, having driven up from New Jersey to see the Red Sox play Tampa Bay for my birthday. By the fourth inning, Cindy desperately needed a cigarette and wanted to pick up some gifts for our kids. We decided where we'd meet after the game.

But then I said, "Are you sure you want to leave now? Look at the line score. There's a no-hitter under way."

JOHN QUINN: In that game the Red Sox had scored early and often. After the fourth inning, I turned to my friend Mark: "Look up at the scoreboard. See how many hits the Devil Rays have? None."

"There's still a long way to go," Mark said.

By the time the sixth inning ended, we got serious and started counting down the outs.

I could see right into the Red Sox dugout, where Derek Lowe was sitting by himself in the far right-hand corner. Nobody was going near him.

The Red Sox scored three more times in the bottom of the eighth, beating up on the poor old Devil Rays. It was 7–0. Then it was 10–0.

After the final out, Lowe was surrounded by teammates. The sellout crowd of 32,837 cheered. Waving

his cap to the fans, Lowe walked to the dugout. Then he returned to the field with a microphone. He acknowledged the cheers and thanked the fans for hanging with him through the tough times.

Pedro Martinez, too, heard the cheers of the fans, on the 8th of May. He struck out the side on nine pitches in the first inning of a 4–1 Red Sox win over the Mariners. Martinez became the first hurler to win 20 games in a season while pitching fewer than 200 innings.

The date was July 6. The scoreboard message read, "At bat, number 9, batting .406."

Ted Williams, the last batter to bat over .400, hitting .406 in 1941, had died earlier that day. Members of the Red Sox and Tigers lined up along the baselines. Caps removed, heads bowed, they observed a moment of silence. Boston players wore black armbands with number 9 patches. Out in left field a trumpeter played "Taps." A Marine Corps honor guard carried the flag.

On July 22, no game was scheduled at Fenway Park. Instead, "Ted Williams: A Celebration of an American Hero" was staged. More than 10,000 fans that morning filed around the warning track.

TED SPENCER: We brought Ted Williams's plaque from the Hall of Fame, mounted it on the Green Monster, flanked it with American flags and a Marine honor guard. There was also an exhibit underneath the stands of Ted Williams artifacts.

A large "9" was mowed into left field and covered with flowers. Two billboards above the Wall read:

"Ted Williams: An American Hero 1918–2002."
"There Goes the Greatest Hitter Who Ever Lived."

On seat 21, row 37, Section 42, a single red rose marked the spot of Ted Williams's longest home run at Fenway, hit in 1946. The seat would be unoccupied all season long.

———————————

DICK FLAVIN: I can't believe that they let me on the field. I couldn't hit the ball out of the infield as a kid. I did my "Teddy at the Bat" through the old speaking system with that three-second feedback coming through the loudspeakers. It was tough to concentrate as I recited:

The outlook wasn't brilliant for the Red Sox nine that day
The score was 4–2 with but one inning left to play
So when Stephens died at first and Tebbetts did the same
A pallor wreathed the features of the patrons of the game.
Straggling few got up to go, leaving there the rest
With the hope that springs eternal within the human breast
They thought if only Teddy could get a whack at that—
They'd put even money now with Teddy at the bat.
But Dom preceded Teddy, and Pesky was on deck.
The first of them was in a slump. The other was a wreck.
So on that stricken multitude a deathlike silence sat,
For there seemed but little chance of Teddy's getting to the bat. . . . "

———————————

On August 28, Yankee hurler Mike Mussina blanked the Red Sox, 7–0. That was a day after

PAGE 194: Wonders never cease—Fenway embossed with signature B
PAGE 195: A jubilant and exultant Jonathan Papelbon. Another save!
RIGHT: A salute to all phases of Teddy Ballgame's life and times
OPPOSITE: Flag at half mast for the passing of Ted Williams

David Wells and Steve Karsay had combined on a 6–0 win over Boston. It was the first time since 1943 that the Yankees had pulled off back-to-back shutouts at Fenway.

Always known for their winning ways at Fenway, the Bosox were better than ever on the road in 2002, going 51–30, tying the Yankees for the best away-from-home record in baseball. Still the Sox finished in second place in the American League East, 10½ games back of the Yankees.

Green Monster Seats (or "Monstah" Seats) were the talk of the town as the 2003 season got under way. Located above the left-field wall, the three rows sat 310 feet from home plate, 37½ feet above left field, and featured 284 green barstool seats.

The ladder attached to the Green Monster, extending from near the upper-left portion of the scoreboard, had always been used by grounds crews to retrieve home-run balls from the netting. Although now obsolete, it remained.

A new manual out-of-town scoreboard and advertising panels were positioned on the left-field wall. There were two rows of additional seats and new camera pits on the outfield end of Red Sox and visitors' dugouts.

Opening Day may have been rainy and cold. But Ray Charles, singing "America the Beautiful," warmed the hearts of the assembled.

Public Address Announcer	Years
Sherm Feller	**1967–1993**
Leslie Sterling	**1994–1996**
Ed Brickley	**1997–2002**
Carl Beane	**2003–CURRENT**

LEFT: Pedro Martinez at the top of his hype—points up at special edition Wheaties box unfurled for him from the top of the Green monster
OPPOSITE: Historic and famous facade

CARL BEANE: Opening Day 2003 was my first day as public address announcer. I couldn't wait. The first thing I got to say was "Ladies and gentlemen, boys and girls, may I have your attention, please. If your car is parked on Lansdowne Street you have ten minutes to move it or it will be towed."

I got booed. When I told the crowd the game was postponed because of rain, I got booed even more.

I had always been a big fan of Sherm Feller. His style wasn't "big me." It was just do the information in a regular, sedate voice. He absolutely mentored me.

My opening announcement at Fenway begins: "Good afternoon, ladies and gentlemen, boys and girls. Welcome to Fenway Park." That is what Sherm always said. At the end of every announcement I'll add, "Thank you." Sherm did that, too. I sit in Sherm Feller's seat in more ways than I can say.

On August 9, 2003, the 10,000th home run in the ballpark's history was hit by Kevin Millar in a 6–4 Red Sox decision over the Orioles.

Then on August 31, Roger Clemens notched his 100th win at Fenway Park in his final regular-season start there, and the New York Yankees moved 5½ games ahead of Boston in the American League East with an 8–4 victory over the Red Sox.

"It was very special," he said. "It gave me the opportunity to say thank you."

Clemens allowed 4 runs on 6 hits in 6⅔ innings, and the capacity crowd gave him a standing ovation when he left. He came out for a curtain call, waved, and tipped his cap.

For the fourth consecutive season, the Bosox set a new home attendance record (2,724,165), a campaign when they were 53–28 at home, second best in the American League.

TOM CARON: In 2003, the Sox clinched the wild card, and a bunch of the players in full uniform and spikes grabbed some bottles of champagne and went over to the Baseball Tavern, the little pub down at the corner. Kevin Millar, Gabe Kapler, Derek Lowe, Lou Merloni, Tim Wakefield poured beers for the celebrating fans.

ART DAVIDSON: Pedro Martinez was a diva, a prima donna. He was also funny and street smart. He could be an annoyance. But on his good days, Pedro was fun to talk to. And boy, could he pitch.

Pedro was especially on when he faced the New York Yankees—sometimes too much so. On October 11, 2003, in the top of the fourth inning, game three of the American League Championship Series, he popped Yankee outfielder Karim Garcia in the back of the shoulder with a pitch. Garcia slid hard into Todd Walker at second base moments later, and Martinez made menacing gestures to the Yankee bench.

Bottom of the fourth, Manny Ramirez batted against Roger Clemens. A pitch sailed high but not that close, and the excitable Manny screamed a few profanities at Clemens while holding his bat menacingly. Clemens repeated the choice of language to Manny. Dugouts emptied. Snarling, out of control, Ramirez was restrained by teammates.

Yankee bench coach and senior citizen Don Zimmer was somehow not noticed as he moved slowly around the crowd of pushing and milling players. He lunged at Pedro Martinez, threw a left hook in the hurler's general direction. Pedro grabbed Zimmer around the neck and threw the 72-year-old to the ground, where he tumbled over and over.

Boston police and Yankees gathered around their feisty coach to make sure he was all right. The umpires huddled during a 15-minute break. No one was tossed from the game, but beer sales were suspended.

Later Martinez expressed regret over the Zimmer incident. He did not, however, apologize. "I would never raise my hand against him. I was just trying to dodge him and push him away."

Although the Martinez-Zimmer encounter was the big attention-grabber that day, there was more excitement in the ninth inning in the Yankee bullpen. Boston grounds crew member Paul Williams, 24, got into it with Yankee reliever Jeff Nelson. Then Karim Garcia, already agitated from what had transpired earlier, hopped over the short right-field wall and joined the fracas. Williams, reportedly with cleatmarks on his back and arms, was transported to a hospital.

Major League Baseball fined Martinez $50,000, Ramirez $25,000, Garcia $10,000, and Zimmer $5,000.

ABOVE: Ray Charles sings "America the Beautiful" in the rain prior to the 2003 Fenway home opener that was rained out
OPPOSITE: (top left) Josh Beckett pitches against Colorado in Game 1 of the World Series, October 24, 2007; (top right) Yankees coach Don Zimmer thrown down by Pedro Martinez during bench-clearing brawl in the third game of ALCS 2003; (bottom left) Red Sox vs. Yankees: Jeter vs. Youkilis; (bottom right) The majestic swing of "Big Papi"

New York City tabloids had a field day reporting on the confrontations as well as the 4–3 win eked out by the Yanks, who went on to win the series in seven games.

As 2004 began there was new seating for 200 on the right-field roof and a new statue of Ted Williams outside Gate B. Most important, Grady Little was out as manager and Terry Francona was in.

The sword that Little fell on was a decision in game seven of the 2003 ALCS. With a 5–2 lead in the eighth inning, the Sox needed five more outs to reach the World Series. Pedro Martinez gave up three straight hits. Little visited the mound but kept his ace in the game. A few batters later, a two-run double by Jorge Posada tied the game, and the Yanks won it in the eleventh. It seemed the "Curse of the Bambino" would linger forever.

On April 16, 2004, the Yankees and Red Sox met in the first game of a four-game series. Six months had passed since the dramatic come-back win of the Yanks in the ALCS. The Fenway crowd was more than up for it. New Yankee Alex Rodriguez went 1 for 17 and was booed constantly throughout the series.

It was again Red Sox vs. Yankees at Fenway on July 24. Boston starter Bronson Arroyo popped Alex Rodriguez in the arm with a pitch in the third inning. On his way to first A-Rod gave Arroyo the dirtiest of looks and uttered the nastiest of words. Sox catcher Jason Varitek moved in front of A-Rod. More words. Varitek slugged A-Rod. Bedlam followed. Varitek and Rodriguez were ejected. Finally, after 3 hours and 54 minutes, a Bill Mueller walk-off home run off Mariano Rivera gave the Sox an emotional, hard-earned 11–10 triumph. Boston, however, was still 8½ games behind the Yanks in the American League East standings.

OPPOSITE: Curt Schilling putting all he has into a pitch

But the Sox made up ground as the season moved along and nearly caught the Yanks. "Nearly" didn't count. Boston finished in second place, becoming the first team in big-league history to finish second in seven straight years.

On October 8, the Sox swept the American League Division Series over the Angels. David Ortiz's two-run, tenth-inning homer put an exclamation point on the runaway victory in the ALDS.

On October 16, in a marathon game-three ALCS contest that lasted more than four hours, the Red Sox were gouged, 19–8 by the Yankees who went up 3–0 in the series.

———————

DAN SHAUGHNESSY: My son, a high school student then, gave up his ticket for game four. He didn't want to see the Yankees win in Fenway.

After the 19–8 game I went down to get some quotes from Larry Lucchino about just how bad this was. We had hammered the Sox pretty good in the paper on Sunday. My lead was that they were not going to win again, for the 86th year. It was just gloomy getting to the park the next day.

———————

LARRY CANCRO: That next morning Lucchino says, "We are all going to have to think of something that's going to get us back in this thing and win it."

Most of us were looking at him like he was completely insane.

"Hey, you know Mike Eruzione, from the 1980 Miracle Olympic hockey team," he says to me. "Call and see if he can come here and be part of the first-pitch ceremony. He was part of a miracle; let's see if he can inspire us."

Mike and I had been at Boston University together. I left the meeting, hit speed dial for Mike. He answered.

"Where are you?"

"Storrow Drive," he says.

"Any chance you'd like to come to the game tonight? We want you to be part of the pregame ceremony and maybe meet some of the players."

Mike came in that night; the players were excited to meet him, and he participated in our pregame ceremony. Late in the game Dave Roberts stole a base to match Eruzione's goal in 1980.

The movie *Miracle* had just come out, although many of the players had not seen it. For game five, Mike came in with blue hats and the word "Miracle" emblazoned on them.

———————

GEORGE MITROVICH: In the bottom half of the seventh inning, the Sox were losing 4–2 to the Yankees. In the private box of Red Sox president Larry Lucchino, with John Henry and Tom Werner sitting there along with Mr. Lucchino, the mood was one of frustration and anger. To be confined in a small area with men who spent $650 million to buy a baseball team that was about to be swept was hardly pleasant.

The night before, I had made the mistake of saying to Mr. Henry, "It will be okay."

"No, it won't," he pointedly responded.

And an angry Larry Lucchino slammed the palms of his hands against the wall. I had never seen that kind of emotion from him.

Now, Dr. Charles Steinberg, the Red Sox vice president for public affairs who had been with Larry Lucchino for 25 years, asked if I would write a congratulatory statement to the Yankees. He hoped I might bring an outsider's perspective to the unfolding denouement, one that would provide Mr. Lucchino with a gracious concession statement that would congratulate the Yankees while letting the heartbroken Red Sox fans know this isn't the end.

I sat down at the computer and tried writing what I thought Dr. Steinberg wanted me to say, seemingly oblivious to the fact that the Sox had pulled within a run of the Yankees.

———————————————

TERRY GUINEY: I was at that game with my son. It seemed more like a wake than a baseball competition. Then the rally started. It was absolutely electrifying. Mariano Rivera was "Mr. Automatic" at that point, the greatest stopper in baseball. Millar walked. Dave Roberts, God love him, came in as a pinch runner. Everybody on the planet who knew anything about baseball could tell Roberts was going to steal.

I can't remember how many throws over to first Rivera made. Everybody was standing. Then Roberts goes. He makes it. Then Billy Mueller hits one up the middle, and the game is tied!

What a scene! People hugging people they didn't know; everybody high-fiving.

———————————————

TERRY FRANCONA: Roberts' steal was the most thrilling event I've been associated with. I doubt we could have done all that we did without that happening.

———————————————

GEORGE MITROVICH: After tying game four 4–4 in the bottom of the ninth inning, the Sox won it in the twelfth on a towering home run off the bat of David Ortiz.

———————————————

TOM CARON: We were doing the postgame in the studios at NESN in Fenway Park. They estimated that by the end of the night there were

over a million people in and around Fenway. We had a camera pointing out from the roof showing the celebrating throng at Kenmore Square. The police actually came in and asked us not to show that camera shot anymore because they thought it was causing more people to come into town to celebrate and would lead to problematic crowd control conditions.

———————————————

On October 18 the fifth game of the ALCS started at 5:10 P.M., just 16 hours after game four had ended early that morning. It was Mike Mussina vs. Pedro Martinez.

———————————————

HOWIE SINGER: Game five had so many strange things: Tony Clark's ball that thankfully went into the seats, the ground-rule double, the game that seemed as if it would never end.

———————————————

JOE CASTIGLIONE: If Tony Clark hadn't hit a ball that literally climbed the wall and went in for a ground-rule double, the Yankees would have scored the go-ahead run in extra innings and won the game. But it bounced in and we got out of that jam. We had so many things break our way.

———————————————

After nearly six hours, in the bottom of the fourteenth inning, Johnny Damon and Manny Ramirez drew walks. Two outs. David Ortiz comes up. A single to center on the tenth pitch thrown to him. Red Sox win, 5–4.

Red Sox fans chanted "Who's your Papi?" to Ortiz, refering to the "Who's your daddy?" chant directed at Pedro by Yankee fans.

LARRY CANCRO: Game six, we go to New York. We win that. Now I'm starting to feel, "Hey, we're going to win, this is cool."

Game seven, I decide to go out to the ballpark early and watch batting practice. Our team doesn't show up. They've voted to watch the movie *Miracle* in the clubhouse. They come out and clobber the Yankees.

———————————————

LENNY MEGLIOLA: For a lot of people, beating the Yankees four straight in that playoff was their World Series.

———————————————

JARED MAX: My media access had gotten me a full Fenway Park tour that included going inside the Monster. I don't want to be sacrilegious, but it was like there's a wailing wall of baseball inside of Fenway Park. The old, etched cement, the writing on the wall. I took some photos inside and through the little slit shot out to the field. Then I asked the Green Monster attendant if he would take my photo.

He said, "Why don't you take a number here?" He was referring to numbers used for the scoreboard hanging on flat metal boards.

Being a Yankees fan, and I guess feeling a little cocky, I said, "Why don't you give me that number 3? Babe Ruth's number."

He took my photo. There I am holding number 3.

The Yankees never won again that series. The curse was reversed. Maybe I had a part in all that posing with the Babe's number 3. Who knows?

———————————————

DAN SHAUGHNESSY: Two thousand four in my view is still the greatest sports story ever told. The idea that you would have the Red Sox win their first World Series in 86 years, to do it at

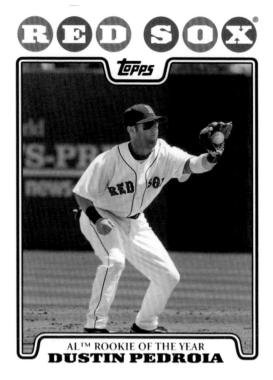

RED SOX

topps

AL™ ROOKIE OF THE YEAR
DUSTIN PEDROIA

the expense of the Yankees, and to do it in something that hadn't been done in 140 years in a seven-game series in baseball. The World Series was clearly anticlimactic.

The Sox swept the Cards four straight. The curse was broken.

JOE CASTIGLIONE (game call, station WEEI): *"Foulke to the set, the 1–0 pitch, here it is. Swing and a ground ball, stabbed by Foulke. He has it. He underhands to first. And the Boston Red Sox are the world champions. For the first time in 86 years, the Red Sox have won baseball's world championship. Can you believe it?"*

"I don't believe in curses," said Manny Ramirez. "I believe you make your own destination."

In 2005, ads for Granite City Electric, Red Sox Foundation, and F. W. Webb were added to the Green Monster. Changes to Fenway Park that season included Gate E, now transformed into a grand

entrance, with a new restaurant in the adjacent Jeano Building, Lansdowne Street remodeled with cherry trees and historic streetlamps, and a roomier concourse behind Section 16 on the first-base side.

Completely dug up, the old field was replaced with a $2 million version containing modern drainage and heating systems. The old infield crown, once needed for drainage, was flattened. The clubhouse now had a new weight room, batting cage, interview area, and physical training and therapy areas.

The Red Sox lineup on Opening Day, April 11, 2005:

Johnny Damon	CF
Trot Nixon	RF
Manny Ramirez	LF
David Ortiz	DH
Kevin Millar	1B
Edgar Renteria	SS
Bill Mueller	3B
Doug Mirabella	C
Tony Womack	2B
Tim Wakefield	P

On Opening Day 2005, Johnny Pesky was given the honor of raising the World Series banner over Fenway Park.

JOHNNY PESKY: I thought about the guys we had played with. Ted Williams and Bobby Doerr and Dom DiMaggio. There were a lot of tears.

That day the Red Sox received their World Series rings before a game with the Yankees, who applauded their longtime rivals. During the lineup announcements, many in the crowd of 33,702 gave Yankee closer Mariano Rivera a loud standing ovation. It was a perfect day at Fenway—the Sox won 8–1.

A week later, Sox fans had more to cheer. Manny Ramirez homered over the Monster Seats. The ball reportedly bounced off the parking garage across Lansdowne Street and finally stopped on the train tracks next to the Massachusetts Turnpike.

JEAN RHODES: Going to games at Fenway I had heard that Manny Ramirez's mentor was often there. As a mentoring expert, I thought I would write about his relationship with his mentor.

I became a Manny Ramirez fan sitting in left field, watching him and the way people responded to him. In writing "Becoming Manny," I became kind of an extended Ramirez family member.

Once I sat with Manny's mom at Fenway Park in the family seats behind home plate. There's a very strong hierarchy, where the very best players get the very best seats for their families. We were surrounded by Ortiz's wife (and kids), and the wives of Wakefield, Pedroia, and Lowell—all younger than me, much more attractive and stylish.

Manny gets up to bat, and he's looking for his mom. He sees her and gives this big smile. He notices me, and it looks like he's wondering who I am because even though I had interviewed him a few times, he never quite remembered who I was.

PEARL HOUGHTELING: I started at Fenway in 2005 as a hawker going all around the park, selling stuff, wearing bright yellow T-shirts and blue shorts, a blue apron, and a yellow hat. And always sneakers.

I work on commission; sometimes I get tips. Many vendors have been here for 20-plus years. So what you sell is based entirely on seniority. The most senior members take the beer and popcorn and peanuts. If it's a day game in July some of the most senior members might choose to sell water because it will go very well.

I get to the park about an hour and a half before game time. My trick is that I can balance pretty much anything on my head—ice cream or a case of soda or water, clam chowder. It's much easier to have two hands free. I keep all the money in my hands. The bulk of the vendors do the same, turning in money periodically. But there's a kind of trust with the fans because you have to send stuff and wait for money to come back.

One day this guy with books and magazines motioned what he wanted to buy. I was only about five feet away, but I insisted he put all of his stuff down so I could throw. And he's kind of like, "Oh, whatever." He caught my very soft toss to him.

"That was Stephen King," I was told. So that was my big celebrity sighting. I've seen John Kerry, too, and I think that's about it.

Not being able to watch the game is something I've become accustomed to, unfortunately. Early on, I hardly sold anything because I was so excited watching the game. Now when there's an exciting moment the whole crowd gets into it and it's impossible to even try to sell something. So I get to stand up and watch.

On June 13, 2005, the Cincinnati Reds appeared at Fenway Park for their first visit since the 1975 World Series. The Red Sox honored Carlton Fisk for the twelfth-inning home run that won game six, naming the left-field foul pole "Fisk Pole."

Down the summer months of the 2005 season the Sox surged and fell back a bit and surged some more. In his second season as skipper, Terry Francona kept the Red Sox rhythm going.

TERRY FRANCONA: Not too up and not too down. It is a very long season, and the best a manager can do is keep everyone ready and on an even keel.

From September 3 to October 2 the Yankees came into Fenway for a three-game series. At stake was the American League East championship. Hype and hullabaloo preceded and pervaded the games. It was like a World Series atmosphere, even better.

Tickets for the three games ran in the four-figure range. And the "A list" crowd, some of whom were actually baseball fans, was out in force. There was a bearded Ben Affleck, there was Jennifer Garner, and Renée Zellweger, who made her way to her choice seat though the Bosox executive offices. Stephen King was present and accounted for. He spent time reading a paperback of Lee Child's *Tripwire.*

Other "A listers" included Theo Epstein's dad, BU writing professor Leslie Epstein; David Halberstam; and Lorraine Bracco. A very casually dressed Robert Redford sat very close to Giant Glass's Dennis Drinkwater, a regular who sits in the same seat directly behind home plate for every home game. Others taking in the action included James Taylor, Patriot owner Bob Kraft, designer Joseph Abboud, Tim Russert, and Jim Lonborg.

Breaking the hearts of the Fenway Park faithful, the Yankees swept the series. And although both Boston and New York finished the season with identical 95–67 records, the Yanks had the edge in the season series between the teams, enabling them to clinch their eighth consecutive American League East crown. The good news was that the Bosox won the wild card and a berth in the post-season. The bad news was that the Chicago White Sox swept them in three.

Off-season changes were part of the scene as Fenway Park prepared to open for the 2006 season.

The glass bubble that had separated the 406 Club from the ballpark was no longer there. In its place was a more user-friendly facility. Many were elated that the sterile, glassed-in structure—with its piped-in music and air-conditioning—was no more.

The State Street Pavilion was now in place. What had been a tiny top level was transformed into a true upper deck, with 1,300 new seats and improved sight lines. There was standing room as well, additional concession stands and restrooms, an overall seating capacity exceeding 38,000, and wider concourses that made for easier movement throughout the park.

Fenway had been renovated within its historical footprint but not without a nod to 21st-century economic realities in the form of new luxury seating areas sporting corporate names, upscale restaurants and bars, and, inevitably, higher ticket prices.

In-depth explanations of Fenway's past and present were part of an expanded and enhanced tour program starting in 2006.

LARRY CANCRO: I had initiated the tour programs in the early nineties. In the old ownership, we only did about four to five hours a day, Monday through Friday, because the philosophy was to not inconvenience anybody working at the ballpark. Now as many people as possible are accommodated—weekends, too.

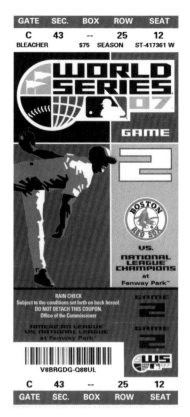

ED CARPENTER: Tours last about an hour. We walk around, go to the right-field roof deck, the State Street Pavilion, and sit in the Green Monster seats. The last stop is the grandstand, which has the oldest seats in the ballpark. We talk about the red seat, where Ted Williams hit the home run. We talk about the Pesky Pole.

During the season, we cap attendance at 125. In the off-season, the numbers are much lower. Once we gave a tour with a group of one. I've had a guy propose to his girlfriend. There are people who cry.

No one was crying on Opening Day, April 11, 2006, when, before 35,491, the Red Sox, behind Josh Beckett, nipped Toronto 5–3. Six days later, Seattle took the lead in the ninth. The Sox response came in a two-out, two-run homer by Mark Loretta to give Boston a 7–6 win. David Ortiz hit a pair of homers in the game, and the Red Sox tied an obscure record by winning their 18th straight one-run game at Fenway.

MIKE LOWELL: In 2006 I was a new guy coming in from another organization. I fell into the seats and caught a foul ball for the second out of an inning. Walking back to third base, I got a standing ovation.

To me, that was incredible. I could understand it if I had hit a big home run. But this was for a defensive play.

My job at third base is actually made easier by the foul territory not being that large. I can run less. At first, I found it a little tricky because of the nuances of the carom back past

third base. You have to pay closer attention. It's an old-style infield. But the grounds crew has done a really good job of maintenance.

Left field behind me can also be tricky. A lot of times you really have to get out there quick for the cutoff. Since they play shallower, you know balls to the left fielder are quick.

On June 28 former Red Sox ace Pedro Martinez came to Fenway in a Mets uniform and heard boos instead of cheers as he was thumped for eight runs, seven hits, and two walks in three innings.

On August 18 and 19 the Yankees and Red Sox slogged through 520 minutes in a day-night doubleheader, part of a five-game series. The Yanks bombed the Sox, 12–4, in the first game and won the nightcap, 14–11. New York outscored Boston, 49–26, in the series, giving grief to Sox supporters.

On Johnny Pesky's 87th birthday, September 27, the Red Sox dedicated the right-field foul pole as Pesky's Pole, placing a commemorative plaque at its base.

JOHNNY PESKY: The term "Pesky Pole" came from Mel Parnell when he was broadcasting a game with Ken Coleman and Ned Martin. Someone hit a home run down the line and right around the pole. And Mel started talking about the time I hit a homer to win a game. But I had only 17 home runs in my career. I was nothing like Ted Williams.

TINA CERVASIO: Pesky used to tell me how Williams, just by picking up a bat, could tell its exact length and weight. He thought Ted had magical hands. He was always talking to me about his old friend Ted.

Johnny Pesky's new friend David Ortiz, on September 21, 2006, rapped out three hits including a pair of homers, to set the Boston Red Sox single season record for homers with 52.

A record for home attendance was set for the seventh straight season: 2,930,588. The Bosox had become the only big-league team to increase attendance in each of its last eight seasons.

Boston ended the 2006 season with 307 consecutive regular season sell outs, the second longest streak in major league history. Late season injuries to players, however, was disappointing as the team finished the year an unremarkable 86-76.

TINA CERVASIO: Early December 2006 will be remembered as the time of the coming of Daisuke Matsuzaka to the Red Sox. The day he arrived, it was bitterly cold. Nevertheless, the ballpark was packed. The Red Sox had spent $103 million on this Japanese pitcher who may have been a rock star in Japan but was virtually unknown in the United States. People all over Yawkey Way were buying Dice-K's jersey even before he arrived.

At an elaborate press conference in a jam-packed EMC Club, Theo Epstein explained in great detail how Matsuzaka and his agent Scott Boras came to a contract agreement.

Then Theo, the ownership, and Matsuzaka (accompanied by his translator) came down to the Red Sox clubhouse where a NESN camera was waiting. Daisuke shook hands with the varied owners. In addition to John Henry, Larry Lucchino, and Tom Werner, many other partners were there.

Terry Francona popped out of his office. "Daisuke, great to meet you. Welcome. I'll talk to you later. Have a great day." Daisuke didn't know whether to shake Francona's outstretched hand or bow.

Daisuke had a great smile. He was very focused. There were a lot of "Hello"s and "Thank you"s. They had hung his jersey up. He touched his jersey and he posed with it.

JONAH KERI: On April 11, 2007, I was a journalist masquerading as a fan, there for Dice-K in his first Fenway Park start. Fans wore rising-sun Japanese headbands and red paper "Diceheads," paper cones over their heads. T-shirt shops were selling shirts with "Red Sox" written in Japanese characters. It was the first time I saw every single seat full at a baseball game before the first pitch. The attendance was 36,630.

CARL BEANE: The game was live in Japan both on radio and on TV and there was a national Japanese media contingent at the ballpark, 170 members. I announced him in Japanese: "Now welcome to Boston, number 18, Daisuke Matsuzaka."

He looked up. I could tell that he was very happy.

The Red Sox lineup on Opening Day, April 11, 2007:

Julio Lugo	SS
Kevin Youkilis	1B
David Ortiz	DH
Manny Ramirez	LF
J. D. Drew	RF
Mike Lowell	3B
Jason Varitek	C
Coco Crisp	CF
Dustin Pedroia	2B
Daisuke Matsuzaka	P

JONAH KERI: The leadoff hitter for the Mariners was Ichiro Suzuki. Matsuzaka wound up to pitch, and the entire stadium erupted in flashbulbs.

MIKE LOWELL: I didn't want Ichiro to hit the ball to me because so many flashbulbs were going off. I hoped for a ground ball because I thought if he hits a line drive right at me, I'm seeing stars.

JONAH KERI: Matsuzaka ended up getting Ichiro out and the crowd just went nuts. But then the Mariners started getting to Dice-K and took a 3-0 lead.

The Sox were no-hit until the bottom of the eighth, and then J. D. Drew singled, sending a ground ball between short and second. Fans cheered—it was not only we broke up the no-hitter, it was let's go win this frickin' game. But that turned out to be the only hit for Boston.

On April 22, there was no shortage of offense by the Sox in the third inning when four consecutive home runs were hit, a first in Fenway Park history. The dingers all came off Yankees rookie Chase Wright, making just his second major league start.

MIKE LOWELL: Manny hits the first home run. We're on the board. Then J. D. hits one. I'm not really thinking home run. Still I hit one to tie the game. I go into the dugout, and Coco Crisp says: "You've got to sit next to me. Everyone who sits next to me, the next batter hits a home run."

I sat next to him. Sure enough, Jason Varitek hits a homerun. We were going crazy. It was probably a lot sweeter because the four homers came against the Yankees and off a total of ten pitches.

MIKE NARRACCI: Fenway, the first of September. As the TV director of the games, I see everything and look at nothing. The sixth inning ends. I look at the scoreboard: "Oh, my goodness. [Clay] Buchholz's got a no-hitter going."

A no-hitter in progress changes the style, the approach to televising the game. You don't want to say the word "no-hitter." And you don't want to keep showing the scoreboard, the zero under the hits. You certainly don't want to miss a pitch, you don't want to miss a hit that may break it up.

By the eighth inning, all of Fenway Park was locked into the no-hitter in progress. Every pitch by Buchholz, every swing by a Baltimore batter, every challenge for the Sox defenses—tension.

TERRY FRANCONA: I think that was about as nervous and excited as a lot of us have been in a long time.

By the ninth inning, Buchholz's teammates were lined up at the dugout railing. The entire crowd was standing, cheering every pitch, taking pictures. Brian Roberts fanned on a 93-mph fastball.

Corey Patterson hit a line drive to center. The crowd groaned, but Coco Crisp easily caught the ball.

MIKE NARRACCI: As you approach the final out you need to formulate a plan. You calmly tell the camerapeople, "If this situation ends up like it's going to end up, camera 1 you're going to do this, camera 2 you're going to do that." You want to avoid a free-for-all of cameras.

OPPOSITE: Dice K in the groove set to deliver

Orioles designated hitter and former Boston player Kevin Millar said, "I nicked a ball tonight. This guy threw a great game. He had his stuff, man. He had a great changeup, and his fastball was in some nice locations. It was just one of those nights. We got no-hit. You tip your hat to Clay Buchholz."

JOHN HARRELSON: A beautiful night—September 30. I went with my brother to the game. If the Sox won, it would be the first time we clinched the division in 12 years. The Yankees were playing the Orioles. The Red Sox were playing the Twins. They had to win, and the Yankees had to lose for Boston to clinch the division. Behind Dice-K in one of the fastest games of the year, the Red Sox won. The Yankee game was still going on.

TOM CARON: The team was waiting inside the locker room, with the door closed. Eckersley and I were on air with the postgame show for about 45 minutes. Those at home were watching Dennis Eckersley and watching the Yankees game. We kept showing the closed locker room door and the stands.

MIKE NARRACCI: People had lingered in the park; they put the YES broadcast up into the JumboTron. Fans were coming into the park and we're showing people milling, watching the Yankee game on the JumboTron. There were thousands and thousands who ultimately came in.

JOHN HARRELSON: We stayed to watch the Yankee game. By the time it was 11, 11:30 there were probably 5,000 people in the ballpark. We moved from right field to right behind the Red

---

Buchholz gets ahead on Nick Markakis, 1–2. Fenway rocks with noise. Flashbulbs are popping. It's maddening. Buchholz delivers his 115th pitch— a 77-mph curveball. Markakis watches it go by.

Plate umpire Joe West hesitates. Catcher Jason Varitek does not. Springing up and out of his crouch, he runs to the mound. The Red Sox win, 10–0, and record their 17th no-hitter in franchise history.

It seems that West signaling Markakis was out was not even noticed. Sox players charge the mound. Big David Ortiz smothers the rookie hurler in a bear hug. "He's somebody you don't want to see running at you full speed," Buchholz later said.

MIKE NARRACCI: I had our Red Sox dugout camera isolated on Clay Buchholz, the rookie. So the final out's a strikeout. I cut to that camera. We're just isolated on him. But the dugout empties out, and he gets lost in the crowd.

The cheering continued until Buchholz appeared on the scoreboard for a television interview. There were "hushes" as the fans tried to hear him through the din. And when "Clay Buchholz, No-hitter" appeared on the message board, the rocking and rolling began all over again.

Sox dugout. It felt like you were sitting in your living room watching a big-screen TV.

And then—the Orioles won on a bunt!

There was huge applause. Sox players came out of the locker room. Everybody came out onto the field, spraying champagne on the fans. Jonathan Papelbon, the closer, came out in his underwear. With a Bud Light box on his head, he does an Irish jig in the infield.

They played "The Impossible Dream." Some of the players went up to the press box and put on "Sweet Caroline."

Pitching and power had personified the Sox throughout the 2007 season. They scored 867 runs, allowing the opposition 657 runs. Never giving up the top spot that they held since April 18, the Bosox won the American League East with a 96–66 record and racked up another astounding Fenway Park attendance performance: 2.97 million.

Sweeping the Angels in the ALDS, outlasting Cleveland four games to three in the ALCS, the highly confident Red Sox swept the Rockies four straight. Another world championship!

After 18 days on the road and opening ceremonies in three different countries—Opening Day was in Tokyo on March 25—the Red Sox returned to Boston on April 8 to begin the 2008 season and the quest for another world championship before a very noisy crowd of 36,567. It was Fenway's 97th Opening Day, and an occasion for celebration. There was music, courtesy of the Boston Pops Orchestra; championship banners were unfurled on the Green Monster, and flags from 62 nations, rep-

resenting the myriad homelands of members of Red Sox Nation, fluttered in the breeze as team personnel received their 2007 World Series rings. Hall of Famers from every sport with a New England connection were on the scene. And a new video of Neil Diamond singing "Sweet Caroline" was broadcast for everyone's pleasure. Behind Daisuke Matsuzaka, the Bosox blanked the Detroit Tigers, 5–0. And everyone rooting for the Red Sox went home happy.

The Red Sox lineup that day:

Dustin Pedroia	2B
Kevin Youkilis	1B
David Ortiz	DH
Manny Ramirez	LF
Mike Lowell	3B
J. D. Drew	RF
Jason Varitek	C
Coco Crisp	CF
Julio Lugo	SS
Daisuke Matsuzaka	P

The 19th of May was a windy Monday night. A sellout crowd of 37,746 was in the house, and Jon Lester was on the mound. It was his night of nights right from the start.

In 2007, the 24-year-old had beaten non-Hodgkin's lymphoma. On this night he beat all the odds, pitching a no-hitter against the Kansas City Royals.

"It seemed like he got stronger as the game went on," pitching coach John Farrell said. "He had all four pitches working. His fastball command, his power, for all of us it was something special to witness."

A sinking liner by Jose Guillen to right center with two out in the fourth was the only near-hit. Racing for it, Jacoby Ellsbury, at the last instant, dove and snared the ball inches off the grass.

By the seventh inning most everyone was standing, cheering Lester on in his bid for a no-hitter. Owners John Henry and Tom Werner moved from their upstairs suite to the box seats to get a closer view.

A cold, wailing, and whipping wind added to the atmosphere. Many in the crowd were wearing winter coats.

RIGHT: Having fun: Pedro Martinez (with pail on head) and "Big Papi" celebrate the Red Sox winning of the AL Division Series on October 8, 2004; David Ortiz showing off his World Series championship rings. The ring on his right hand is for 2004, and the ring on his left hand is for 2007.
OPPOSITE: Celebrating victory on a walk-off hit by "Big Papi" in 2004

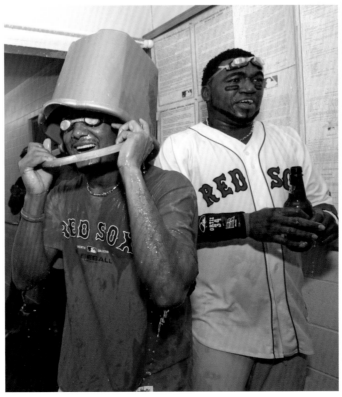

AAA Auto Insurance

SPORTS AUTHORITY | UNDER ARMOUR

WORLD SERIES 20
WORLD SERIES 20

VOLVO
RED SOX
COOL BASE
THE FUTURE
07 CHAMPIONS
04 CHAMPIONS

Lester walked Esteban German to start the ninth. Tony Pena Jr. grounded out. David DeJesus grounded out. Alberto Callaspo was next.

Fans roared. Cameras clicked. Red Sox players were honed in at the front of their dugout. Those playing defense stood at the ready—for anything.

The count on Callaspo was 0–2. He took a ball, fouled a pitch off. Lester unleashed a 96-mph fastball that came in high and outside. Swing and a miss!

Lester thrust both fists forward, and then was lifted in the air by Varitek. Manager Terry Francona embraced his kid pitcher. Sox players charged out of the dugout to congratulate the rookie. Fenway speakers blared "Tessie," the victory anthem the team had adopted through their two world championships in four seasons.

"I've been through a lot the last couple of years," Lester told the media afterward. "I'm sure it will hit me in the morning. How many people get to say they've won the World Series? And a no-hitter is a no-hitter."

Nine Red Sox pitchers have pitched no-hitters at Fenway Park:

George Foster, June 21, 1916
Dutch Leonard, August 30, 1916
Ernie Shore, June 23, 1917
Mel Parnell, July 14, 1956
Earl Wilson, June 26, 1962
Dave Morehead, September 16, 1965
Derek Lowe, April 27, 2002
Clay Buchholz, September 1, 2007
Jon Lester, May 19, 2008

Trying to win back-to-back world championships, the Red Sox came up a bit short in 2008. They finished two games behind the Tampa Bay Rays in the battle for the American League East. Out of their wild card slot they got past Cleveland in the ALDS. That road led to a matchup against the Rays for the right to go to the World Series.

DAVE STANLEY: I was a lifelong Red Sox fan who had never been to Fenway Park. Then, out of the blue, a subcontractor I was working with gave me a couple of tickets to the October 16 Tampa Bay–Boston, game five of the 2008 ALCS.

I called my friend Nathan Wright in Randolph, Vermont, the night before. We made plans to drive from my home in Bethel, Vermont, to Fenway.

I was so excited, I only got three hours of sleep the night before. The next morning, I went to work, but I left at 1:00 P.M. When I got back home, I threw on a pair of jeans and a sweatshirt and my Boston Red Sox cap. At three o'clock, Nate picked me up, and we set out in his old Honda Accord.

With the traffic and all, it was about six when we got into Boston. We parked at a T stop outside the city limits. That was Nate's idea. He knew his way around Boston. We got off the T, walked probably 100 yards, and Nate said, "There you are." And it was like "Wow!"

I showed the usher my ticket. He said, "Right this way, sir." And he marched us right down to field box A, Section 22, box 47, row G, seat 6, basically nine rows up from home plate. I told him this was my first time at Fenway, and he goes, "You guys enjoy the game."

It was a full house and a really warm and friendly environment. All the people around us were terrific. I looked out on the field and saw Dice-K and all those guys. It was fantastic seeing them in person. I took pictures of every Red Sox player.

I didn't want to see the Red Sox lose my first time at Fenway. Daisuke Matsuzaka was pitching, and he's one of my favorites. But as the game progressed, I was getting pretty nervous. They didn't start coming back until the seventh and right up to that time, it was 7–0.

People around us began to leave. I looked at Nate and I said, "Win or lose, we're here to the end." For a guy who always dreamed about sitting in these wonderful seats, seeing these people get up and leave because their team wasn't winning was like blasphemy.

As the Red Sox started coming back, I felt energy like I had never felt before in my life. Justin Masterson came out and pitched. Then we had the last at-bat. Youk got on, and J. D. Drew came up and hit that line drive over the right fielder's head, and Youk scored.

The place erupted; it completely blew up.

———

Boston scored eight times in the final three innings to pull out an 8–7 victory over a stunned Tampa team, extending the ALCS.

———

DAVE STANLEY: The game ended. Drew came out for the curtain call. We listened to him being interviewed over the loudspeakers. The groundskeepers came out, and they began dressing the field, closing it down.

There it was, right in front of my eyes, my first game, my first experience. And it was a history-making game. It had been something like 79 years since the Red Sox had come back from that kind of deficit in a playoff game.

We took the T, got to the old Honda, and drove back. On the way, we stopped off at a McDonald's in Concord, New Hampshire, and had a hamburger and soda before continuing our way up 89, both of us trying to keep each other awake by talking. By the time Nate dropped me off, it was 6:00 A.M. The whole adventure had taken almost three quarters of a day.

I still have the ticket stub. The price on it is $175. I've been told I could have scalped that ticket for up to $1,500. But it didn't matter. There was no way I was going to scalp them.

It had taken a long time for me to get to Fenway. But it won't take so long for me to go back again. And the next time, I'll take my son Noah along. I don't want him to have to wait as long as I did to see the Red Sox play.

———————

For Dave Stanley and so many other Sox fans, game five of that ALCS was truly a high Fenway Park moment in 2008, but Boston was eliminated in seven games by the Rays, who moved on to the World Series, losing it to the Phillies.

The Boston Red Sox began their 108th season in franchise history on April 7, 2009. Opening at home for the first time in seven years. Tampa Bay was the opposition.

Key departures characterized Opening Day

activities, a makeup of the rainout of the day before. The game began at 4:06 P.M., a tip of the cap to Ted Williams's batting average in 1941. Players came out of the stands, high-fiving fans on their way to the field. And the Boston Pops played the national anthem.

Jim Rice, the newest Bosox Hall of Fame inductee, traveled out in a golf cart with Senator Ted Kennedy, recently diagnosed with brain cancer. Aided by a cane and Terry Francona, Kennedy came to the mound to throw out the first ball. His first toss was short, but he reached a beaming Rice on the fly with his second try.

"I wasn't born when my grandfather Mayor Honey Fitz threw out Fenway Park's first-ever pitch," Senator Kennedy said, "but I know how proud he was to be a loyal member of the famous 'Royal Rooters' and to be a part of Red Sox history that day."

The Red Sox Opening Day lineup, April 7, 2009:

Jacoby Ellsbury	**CF**
Dustin Pedroia	**2B**
David Ortiz	**DH**
Kevin Youkilis	**1B**
J. D. Drew	**RF**
Jason Bay	**LF**
Mike Lowell	**3B**
Jed Lowrie	**SS**
Jason Varitek	**C**
Josh Beckett	**P**

On April 25, a day before his 100th birthday, Arthur Giddon was in the house, mingling with players and executives and operating as a ceremonial batboy. The retired Connecticut attorney had been a real batboy for the Boston Braves in the 1920s.

ARTHUR GIDDON: I was treated royally. I got an autographed bat from Big Papi and an autographed ball from the 2007 World Series team. I wore a jersey with the number 100 and the name "Big Pappy." And maybe best of all, I saw the Red Sox win the game, 16–11, their biggest comeback against the Yankees since 1968.

———————

The honoring of deserving personages, marker moments, and ceremony all were part of the 2009 Fenway season. A festive atmosphere was in the air on June 17, when Brad Penny won his 100th career game as the Sox trimmed the Marlins, 6–1.

Head groundskeeper Dave Mellor, on the scene for nine years, added a special touch to Fenway that day.

———————

DAVID MELLOR: We had a giant "500" mowed into the field, marking the longest sellout streak in major league history—one that began on May 15, 2003.

Depending on the time, what is happening on the baseball field, the history—we have done a lot with the field and the grass to memorialize and to tell a story.

I get goose bumps every day I walk onto the field. I get there early, and I leave late. Fenway, with all its idiosyncrasies and the weather of New England, certainly poses a challenge. You kind of have three microclimates on the field, and every grass blade there has a story to tell.

———————

On July 12 the Red Sox honored Dom DiMaggio, who had passed away on May 8 at age 92, by raising a banner bearing his name on the center-field flagpole.

On July 28 eight-time All-Star Jim Rice saw his number 14 retired and unveiled on the facade of the right-field roof. Johnny Pesky raised the number. Rice affirmed that he wouldn't have become the first African-American Red Sox player with a retired number if it weren't for Pesky. "He would work with me every day," Rice said. "He was a father figure, a mentor to me."

Red Sox retired numbers:

1	**Bobby Doerr**
4	**Joe Cronin**
6	**Johnny Pesky**
8	**Carl Yastrzemski**
9	**Ted Williams**
14	**Jim Rice**
27	**Carlton Fisk**
42	**Jackie Robinson** (retired by Major League Baseball)

9-4-1-8: Until the late 1990s, Red Sox retired numbers hung on the right-field facade in the order in which they were retired: 9-4-1-8. The numbers, when read as a date (9/4/18), marked the eve of the first game of the 1918 World Series, the last championship series that the Red Sox won before 2004. After the facade in right field was repainted, the numbers were rearranged in numerical order.

On August 21 celebrated crooner John Pizzarelli, a loyal member of the BLOHARDS (Benevolent and Loyal Order of Honorable and Ancient Red Sox Diehard Sufferers of New York) was conscripted to sing the national anthem at Fenway.

JOHN PIZZARELLI: My daughter Maddy and I left for Boston from the East Village in Manhattan at 9:30 A.M. on a Professor Thom's bus trip, which we'd booked well in advance of the invitation. Chris Wertz, chatty New York governor of Red Sox Nation and owner of Thom's Red Sox Bar, hosted a program of Sox films, trivia, and Yankees "Match Game" that had us on the Mass Pike in what felt like nine minutes.

A friendly Sox ambassador met me at Gate E in left field and led me through a maze of unmarked doors and narrow hallways (in one of them A-Rod was throwing a rubber ball against a wall) to an area behind home plate. I was given a hard start time of 4:00.

Much as I tried to blend in with the guys, dressed as I was in an authentic number 8 jersey from 1967 (it was Yaz's 70th birthday, after all), not one player even considered having a catch with me. It could have been the jeans that tipped them off.

At 3:59 Carl Beane checked in on the PA. And then . . . "To sing our national anthem today . . ."

I opened my mouth, and, fortunately, musical sounds came out. Facing Section 20 of the grandstand and the Fenway Park sign above the press box, I quickly noted that the audio system was pristine and the spectators behind the plate were looking everywhere but at me. The song passed in a blur. By the time I hit "And the rockets' red glare," I was finally able to savor the moment. Here I was in the greatest ballpark of them all, my 11-year-old daughter standing on the field with her favorite team, and the archrival Yankees dressed in their road grays, just 50 feet to my right.

Fans cheered the final words of the national anthem. I didn't want this extraordinary 70-second experience to end. But since a game cannot start with a guy standing 10 feet behind the catcher, I was quickly led back through the Red Sox dugout to my assigned seat.

Four days after Pizz's singing stint, Jacoby Ellsbury set a new team record for stolen bases in a season, racking up his 55th and passing Tommy Harper, who stole 54 for the Red Sox in 1973.

On August 26, a day after Senator Edward M. Kennedy passed away, a lone air force bugler played "Taps" as both teams lined up on the baselines; the Red Sox paid tribute to his life and career with a moment of silence and a video tribute. The American flag flew at half staff at Fenway Park.

On the 28th of September, in a steady drizzle, Johnny Pesky was honored before the first game of a day-night doubleheader against the Yankees. It was a day after the 90th birthday of the former star

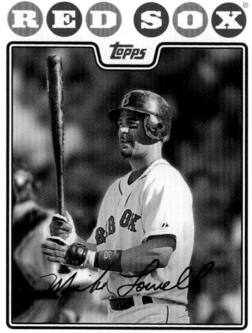

MIKE LOWELL

"The season doesn't wind down," Red Sox manager Terry Francona said. "It just comes to a crashing halt. You go into the top of the inning excited because you think you're going to keep playing. Half an inning later, you're going home."

The old ballpark beginning its 98th year did not have some of the massive changes of recent seasons, but some of the changes were interesting.

"We finally had to spend a little bit of money on the visitors' clubhouse," said Larry Lucchino," Red Sox president and CEO, "as hard as it was to do that."

Seats had more cup holders. The park's 12,000 blue seats, the last remaining wooden seats in Major League Baseball, were equipped with new springs that enabled them to pop up when the fan stood up. Veggie burgers were readily available.

Enhanced seating capacity for 2010 was now 36,945 for day games and 37,373 for night games. That number was on hand and more (37.440/101.3% full) for the Major League Baseball opener staged at Fenway Park—the first night game opener in the ballpark's history.

The game was an upper for Sox fans. Former Red Sox ace Pedro Martinez threw out the ceremonial first pitch; Neil Diamond sang his "Sweet Caroline"—in person. Kevin Youkilis stroked three extra-base hits, and Dustin Pedroia hammered a two-run homer. Boston rallied to nip the defending champion and hated Yankees, 9–7.

"It's just one game," Kevin Youkilis said.

Those words proved prophetic. Despite the signings of a trio of players with standout abilities—outfielder Mike Cameron, third baseman Adrian Beltre, and shortstop Marco Scutaro—as the season

moved along, more and more Red Sox players wound up on the disabled list with assorted injuries minimizing Boston's win potential while easing the team's pathway to losses even at Fenway. One such moment took place in early May when Yankee Mark Teixeira slugged three homers as the Yankees pounded the injury-ridden Sox, 14–3.

There were thrilling moments at the old park. Young Daniel Nava hit the first pitch he saw as a big leaguer for a grand slam—only the second player to accomplish that feat.

The oldest Boston player of them all—44-year-old Tim Wakefield—like old man river kept rolling along. In May, he fanned Toronto's Vernon Wells recording his 2,000th career strikeout. In September, the Fenway faithful cheered as the knuckleballer, despite a very sub-par season, at age 44 years and 37 days, became the oldest hurler in franchise history to win a game—his 179th in a Red Sox uniform.

Despite the fact that the team was lodged in the American League East's tough division with the Yankees and Rays, despite the fact that injuries beat up almost half the Opening Day roster, Red Sox Nation kept coming out in record numbers to Fenway.

And the 109th season of the franchise ended as it began at Fenway Park with a series at home against the Yankees. It lacked some of the fire and fury of past confrontations especially since there would be no play-off appearance for Boston for the first time since 2006.

Nevertheless, while it was a disappointing season for the team—the Red Sox failed to finish in first or second place in the American League East (only the second time in 13 seasons)—for Fenway Park it was another banner year. The home of Red Sox Nation drew more than 200,000 tourists from around the world and 3,046,445 fans into its unique confines—an average of 37,410 a game. At season's end, the consecutive-games-sold-out streak moved to 631.

2011: The 99th year of fabled Fenway Park was next.

---

infielder, coach, manager, front-office official, television and radio announcer, and good-luck charm for the Red Sox. His number 6 was retired; it was the seventh number the franchise retired.

The long 2009 season of the Red Sox that had begun in the chill of April would end in the chill of October, with the team winning its last four games, a series sweep over Cleveland, making for a final record of 95–67, eight games behind the Yanks.

It had been a season of ups and downs—ups at home especially, where the Sox posted a 56–25 mark, although down on the road, where they went 39–42.

The Los Angeles Angels of Anaheim were the competition in the ALDS. Down two games to none, having lost two games to the Angels on their turf, the wild-card Bosox faced elimination on October 11 in a game that began a little after noon.

Confidence was the mood of the Sox and Red Sox Nation. And why not? The team had the second-best home record in the American League in 2009. But scoring twice in the eighth and three times in the ninth, the Angels upended the Sox and their fabled closer, Jonathan Papelbon, 7–6, ending the Old Towne Team's season.

MUSINGS

LEIGH MONTVILLE: A couple of years ago I was at Opening Day, and the thought crossed my mind that I might be the only guy here who was here Opening Day 1967. So much in life disappears. Sometimes I get a little sadness just thinking of the people that I knew, those old baseball writer guys. They're all gone.

BILL NOWLIN: I always liked these guys who smoked cigars; a lot of them sat out near right field. I think there were some Italians that congregated out in the right-field grandstand. There was a lot of gambling. In the latter days of the old regime, the time of John Harrington and John Buckley, it was like an Irish mafia from Jamaica Plain.

It used to be just men, and white men. In the late '50s, actually up until the time Pumpsie Green came, you didn't see too many African-Americans at the ballpark. It wasn't until the late '90s, when Pedro came up, that a lot of Dominicans began showing.

JOE CASTIGLIONE: Pedro is my favorite all-time pitcher, the best pitcher I've ever seen. When Pedro pitched, it was an event, with Dominican flags flying and all the excitement in the ballpark.

DON PEASE: I believe the first time I saw David Ortiz play was one of his very first games. He had a couple of hits. They weren't homers, but just to see that was important.

Manny was there already, but Ortiz is the figure who gave a changed image to the team. There was something about him that was not as volatile, not as edgy as Manny. They called him Big Papi. He was a leader and a slugger. He represented a force, an authority who consolidated the other Latino or Chicano players. I liked his persona, I liked the way that he authorized and at the same time gave a kind of ease to the change on the team.

Seeing the Red Sox go through that change in the demographics of their team, overcoming the reputation of the team as a racist organization and the city of Boston as a racist city, was so moving for me.

MIKE ANDREWS: The first time I saw Fenway Park was in September 1966, when I came up from Toronto Triple A. The only sign in the ballpark then was a billboard above right field that said "Jimmy Fund." That meant nothing to me. But I soon learned it was Tom Yawkey's favorite charity and that it raised money for cancer research and care, with a special emphasis on children's cancer. It had been founded in 1948 with the help of the Boston Braves, and when the Braves moved to Milwaukee in 1953, the Red Sox took it on as their official team charity. It's an affiliation that has existed ever since.

I've been told the Red Sox–Jimmy Fund connection is the longest and most extensive team-

charity relationship in all of professional sports, and it seems to me that through the years, each team has had some special feeling for it. I can remember when we got together in the clubhouse to vote our shares for the 1967 World Series, Carl Yastrzemski got up and said, "In honor of Mr. and Mrs. Yawkey I'd like to suggest that we give a full share of our World Series to the Jimmy Fund." And we did.

Through the decades, there have been many Red Sox players who were big supporters of the fund. But I believe it was Ted Williams who demonstrated the greatest commitment. He publicized Dr. Sidney Farber's research and his efforts to help cancer patients, especially children, at the Children's Cancer Research Foundation (today the Dana-Farber Cancer Institute), which the Jimmy Fund is part of; he was personally responsible for raising millions of dollars in the fight against cancer and other related diseases.

Ted just loved kids. He'd visit them at the clinic. One time he was holding a little kid's hand and the kid didn't want to let go. So Ted had them pull up a cot, and he spent the night at the clinic, sleeping next to the little boy. Now, Ted was a guy who was very hard to get to know. And yet, when it came to the Jimmy Fund he was very, very available.

During my rookie season in 1967, I met Bill Koster, the longtime executive director of the fund. He used to bring cancer patients to Fenway. Sometimes in the winter, he'd have us go to different places, VFWs or whatever, make a pitch, pick up checks. It was very, very grass roots then.

Once, before a game in '67, Bill asked me to spend a few minutes with a 12-year-old boy. It turned out the kid had been an All-Star in Little League when he was 11. He was missing this season because of his cancer, he told me, but he hoped he'd be back again next year. Evidently he'd been a pretty good ballplayer. We talked for a while. Then I shook his hand, wished him good luck, and hurried off to my warm-ups.

As we were walking down the runway Bill said, "I really appreciate you doing this because we're sending that boy home. There's nothing more we can do for him." I stopped in my tracks. "Oh, my God," I said. "My little 0–4, 0–5 doesn't mean a damn thing compared to what that family and what that boy are going through." That was my wake-up call, my realization of the impact you, as a ballplayer, can have and how important that is.

In 1976, I had retired from baseball and was working for Massachusetts Mutual Life Insurance Company when Ken Coleman asked if I'd be willing to help him out at the Jimmy Fund. Ken had been a Red Sox broadcaster and one of the fund's top fund-raisers, and after Bill Koster died (ironically from cancer), he became its executive director. Now he wanted me to come on board because he wanted to grow the Jimmy Fund. What started out as part-time volunteer work soon became full-time, and when Ken was rehired as Red Sox broadcaster, I took over his job as executive director.

When I look at where Dana-Farber was when I started, in terms of recovery rates and treatment methods, and where we are now, it's a great motivator. We still have a long way to go; we still lose too many people. But we've made tremendous strides.

I had 13 wonderful years of professional baseball. I got to play in an All-Star game, I was part of the Impossible Dream year, I played on a world championship team with Oakland. But in terms of satisfaction, those 13 years don't even come close

ABOVE: The famous red seat for Ted Williams
OPPOSITE: Bobby Doerr in dugout, pointing out something to a youngster

to the more than 30 years I had as chairman of the Jimmy Fund. What I did there was the best thing I'd done in my life. It also is one of the things that made me so proud to have been a Red Sox.

BISHOP JOHN D'ARCY: Going to Fenway is like going back to your youth. When you sit there for three hours it's a squeeze. But to me it's a cathedral, a baseball cathedral.

FRED LYNN: I am very happy they kept the ballpark. We walk on the same field that Babe Ruth, Ted Williams, and Mickey Mantle and all the other greats walked on. It may be a tight quarter for a big guy because the seats are still pretty old. But no one cares. Being at Fenway is like being on sacred land.

JON MILLER: Fenway has always reminded me of a place you'd find in an old European city where there is the blending of the old and the new, where you'll find an ancient little passageway lined with old buildings and then come upon a new office tower.

The old-time basic shell of the ballpark has remained. If you look back at pictures of Fenway taken in 1912, you'll recognize the place. The brick, the shape of the main seating bowl is very similar. But rows of seating have been added on the rooftop over the years, and they don't always blend together. One row of seating goes across the luxury suites. Another drops down about 10 or 12 feet. The rooftop doesn't have a single smooth line.

No other ballpark looks like Fenway. All the new ballparks are sleek. Everything fits together in the

single vision of an architect. But in Fenway there are seven or eight visions that coexist because changes were made in increments, at various times, by different architects, with the input of different people.

LARRY CANCRO: I think there's 20-some-odd ballparks now that have imitated Fenway Park. They're close; they're good. But they're not quite Fenway Park. I've had great architects come to Fenway Park and ask me, "What makes it great?" And I show them. Then they build a ballpark that's almost as great, but it doesn't quite match up. And I think, and I'm kind of paraphrasing Larry Lucchino, why would we try for something else when we have the best one right here?

TOM CARON: When the new owners first proposed getting this team, they were the only group talking about saving Fenway. Everyone else had plans for a new ballpark. They saved Fenway but they changed things you don't see. The locker rooms are totally renovated; there are new interview rooms, assembly rooms, function rooms.

The old owners did a great job; they were the standard-bearers of a proud franchise. But the new owners came in with a vision of taking Fenway into the modern age, not only with the team but with the ballpark as well. Still it's the grand old lady my father brought me to when I was a kid.

LARRY CANCRO: Fenway is a second home to New Englanders. For generations people have thought of this as part of the rite of passage for families. It's almost like going home at Thanksgiving. There's hardly a New Englander that doesn't have some story about their time with their family at Fenway.

JOE CASTIGLIONE: In 2010, I completed 27 years with the Red Sox. I've done 4,000 games behind the microphone on Red Sox radio from the best seat in the house, and every day I think I'm blessed.

Broadcasting at Fenway, I think of the "eccentric angularities," as Bart Giamatti called them. I remember the advice Ken Coleman gave me: "Wait on fly balls to left, don't call them home runs before they are. And don't call them outs—they might hit the Wall; they might be a paint-scraper."

My memories include Sherm Feller, who seemed to know every surgeon and every Mafia figure in Boston. He did the balls and strikes using the bulbs on the scoreboard. If he had a conversation going, and usually he had three or four at once, those bulbs were not always correct. He had some long stories. If he got ahold of you, you'd better have the time to spare.

My memories include Joe Mooney, the general. Lots of times there would be no early hitting if he didn't think the field was ready. He looked out for that playing field like it was his own lawn.

My memories include Big Papi with his walkoffs, the magnetism of his personality, that smile; a 10-pitch at-bat by Brian Daubach and his hitting a ball off the Wall to win a game against Oakland.

I remember Boggs hitting balls off the Wall. He'd hit balls almost out of the catcher's mitt. Then they built the high structure behind home plate and it became harder to hit the Wall than it used to be.

I remember the longest shot ever. It was hit by Mark McGwire, one of three hits in one game off of Zane Smith. Probably all of them were hit off 78-mile-per-hour fastballs. We sent our intern to find the third one. It was on the railroad tracks by the Mass Pike. McGwire said he didn't want the ball. I think the intern still has it.

I remember when we used to come back from a trip at three or four in the morning. The bus would leave us off at the stadium, and we'd have to wait around for the truck that carried our luggage. Sometimes we'd just sit in the stands and look out on the field. Sometimes we'd hang out in the clubhouse. The place was silent, with just a few lights and the clock on. Now I get picked up at the airport

in a limo and go directly home. Of course it's more convenient. But there was something cool about the way we did it before.

TERRY FRANCONA: Nineteen eighty-eight would have been my first year in the American League. The cab dropped me off in front of Fenway. I walked in through right field and thought, "Wow, what a wonderful place to play."

I still think it's wonderful. There hasn't been a game here since I arrived that hasn't been a sellout. That's a pretty amazing statistic. If you're a player it's got to be one of the greatest places to play because the fans show up every day, and every day there's a play-off-game atmosphere, an edge. Come about the seventh inning, if the fans have one iota of a thought that we can win the game, the place starts shaking. There's electricity in the stands.

MICHAEL DUKAKIS: It's interesting that the largely non-Bostonian new ownership and management have transformed this club into an extraordinary civic institution. Like most cities, we've lost our major corporate citizens who were committed to the community. Bank Boston, John Hancock, Gillette—they are no longer; they've all been acquired. The Red Sox have emerged as that kind of corporate citizen.

DAN SHAUGHNESSY: I hold Fenway very dear. A lot of my memories of it are very personal. The last time I saw my father alive was at Fenway in September of 1979. I was traveling with the Orioles and went down to say hello and good-bye in the stands on my way to the locker room. He died a month later.

I was with my sister at the sixth game of the '75 World Series, sitting in Section 27, left-field grandstand, when Fisk hit the home run off the pole. I was working for the Associated Press as a stringer that summer, and that enabled me to buy tickets. What a thrill it was to be around Fenway in a kind of professional capacity.

My daughter threw out the first pitch at Fenway in 1994. She was nine years old, and she had leukemia. It was Children's Opening Day, and we have a lot of photographs of her on the mound, Roger Clemens giving her tips. Thankfully, she's recovered nicely and she's a high school teacher now.

I have a son who played college baseball in the Atlantic Coast Conference. They have a tournament at Fenway, and he got to play left field in the stadium last year. I have pictures of him standing in front of the Green Monster wearing his uniform and manning his position like Ted Williams did.

I love sitting in the ballpark when it's empty early before a game. There's a great quiet to it. I love sitting in the ballpark in September, when the weather is the best we get during the daytime.

There will always be some inconvenient things that don't work, those seats in right field that face the bullpen, not much room for your knees, the parking, and the poles. But the new owners have done a tremendous job of refurbishing while holding on to the old.

BRUCE TUCKER: Going to Fenway has become, at least during the years since the new ownership took over, a much more social experience. It's not just about baseball. Back in the day, they didn't block off Yawkey Way before the game, there weren't guys walking around on stilts. Today you can go to a game two hours early and still find plenty to do. Recently I went to a game with one of my sons and we stood behind the television guys at RemDawg's during the pregame show. Later, my wife said she saw us on TV. Luis Tiant is always hanging around,

and a couple seasons ago I saw Dennis Eckersley walk right in front of me while we were waiting for the gates to open.

LARRY CANCRO: The truth is people like coming here. They like knowing that this is the place that their families have been coming to for generations, that Babe Ruth played here and Tris Speaker played here and Jimmie Foxx played here and Jim Rice and Yaz.

LEIGH MONTVILLE: The Red Sox used to have two things going for them: Fenway Park and the fact that they hadn't won in 86 years. Now they've got one thing going: Fenway Park. Fenway, Fenway, Fenway . . .

OPPOSITE: Bobby Doerr, Ted Williams, and Dom DiMaggio showing off their reaches
BELOW: Cheering fans in silhouette on Opening Day, April 9, 2004

BROADCASTS – TELEVISION

YEAR	CHANNEL	PLAY-BY-PLAY	COLOR COMMENTATOR(S)	FIELD-LEVEL REPORTERS	STUDIO HOST	STUDIO ANALYSTS
2009	NESN	Don Orsillo	Jerry Remy or guest analysts	Heidi Watney	Tom Caron	Jim Rice, Dennis Eckersley, or guest analyst
2008	NESN	Don Orsillo	Jerry Remy	Heidi Watney	Tom Caron	Jim Rice, Dennis Eckersley, Dave McCarty, Lou Merloni, or Ken Macha
2007	NESN	Don Orsillo	Jerry Remy	Tina Cervasio	Tom Caron	Jim Rice, Dennis Eckersley, Dave McCarty, Ken Rhan, or Ken Macha
2006	NESN	Don Orsillo	Jerry Remy	Tina Cervasio	Tom Caron	Jim Rice, Dennis Eckersley, or Dave McCarty
2005	NESN	Don Orsillo	Jerry Remy	Eric Frede	Tom Caron	Jim Rice, Dennis Eckersley, Sam Horn, Gary DiSarcina, or Bob Tewksbury
	WSBK (Friday night games; Boston area only, NESN throughout New England) and WBZ-TV (Fourth of July)	Don Orsillo	Jerry Remy	Dan Roche	Bob Lobel	Jim Corsi, Steve Buckley, or Tony Massarotti
2004	NESN	Don Orsillo	Jerry Remy	Eric Frede	Tom Caron	Jim Rice, Dennis Eckersley, Sam Horn, Gary DiSarcina, or Bob Tewksbury
	WSBK (Friday night games; Boston area only, NESN throughout New England) and WBZ-TV (Fourth of July)	Sean McDonough	Jerry Remy	Dan Roche	Bob Lobel	Jim Corsi, Steve Buckley, or Tony Massarotti
2003	NESN	Don Orsillo	Jerry Remy	Tom Caron	Bob Rodgers	Jim Corsi, Jim Rice, or Dennis Eckersley
	WSBK (Friday night games; Boston area only, NESN throughout New England) and WBZ-TV (Fourth of July)	Sean McDonough	Jerry Remy	Dan Roche	Bob Lobel	Jim Corsi, Steve Buckley, or Tony Massarotti
2002	NESN	Don Orsillo	Jerry Remy	Tom Caron	Bob Rodgers	Jim Corsi, Jim Rice, or Dennis Eckersley
	WFXT	Sean McDonough	Jerry Remy		Butch Stearns	Rico Petrocelli
2001	NESN	Don Orsillo	Jerry Remy	Debbi Wrobleski	Bob Rodgers	Rico Petrocelli
	WFXT	Sean McDonough	Jerry Remy		Butch Stearns	
2000	NESN	Bob Kurtz or Bob Rodgers	Jerry Remy	Debbi Wrobleski	Bob Rodgers or Tom Caron	Rico Petrocelli
	WFXT	Sean McDonough	Jerry Remy		Butch Stearns	
1999	NESN	Bob Kurtz	Jerry Remy	Debbi Wrobleski	Bob Rodgers	
	WLVI	Sean McDonough	Jerry Remy			
1998	NESN	Bob Kurtz	Jerry Remy	Debbi Wrobleski	Bob Rodgers	
	WABU	Sean McDonough	Jerry Remy	John Holt	Doug Brown or Butch Stearns	
1997	NESN	Bob Kurtz	Jerry Remy	Debbi Wrobleski	Bob Rodgers	
	WABU	Sean McDonough	Jerry Remy	John Holt	Doug Brown or Butch Stearns	Dick Radatz
1996	NESN	Bob Kurtz	Jerry Remy	Debbi Wrobleski	Bob Rodgers	
	WABU	Sean McDonough	Jerry Remy	Butch Stearns	Doug Brown	Rico Petrocelli or Dick Radatz
1995	NESN	Bob Kurtz	Jerry Remy	Kim Walden	Tom Larson	
	WSBK-TV	Sean McDonough	Bob Montgomery			
1994	NESN	Bob Kurtz	Jerry Remy	Amy Stone	Steve Burton	
	WSBK-TV	Sean McDonough	Bob Montgomery			
1993	NESN	Bob Kurtz	Jerry Remy	Amy Stone	Steve Burton	
	WSBK-TV	Sean McDonough	Bob Montgomery			
1992	NESN	Ned Martin	Jerry Remy		Bob Kurtz	
	WSBK-TV	Sean McDonough	Bob Montgomery			
1991	NESN	Ned Martin	Jerry Remy		Bob Kurtz	
	WSBK-TV	Sean McDonough	Bob Montgomery			
1990	NESN	Ned Martin	Jerry Remy		Bob Kurtz	
	WSBK-TV	Sean McDonough	Bob Montgomery			
1989	NESN	Ned Martin	Jerry Remy		Bob Kurtz	
	WSBK-TV	Sean McDonough	Bob Montgomery			
1988	NESN	Ned Martin	Jerry Remy		Eric Reid	
	WSBK-TV	Sean McDonough	Bob Montgomery			
1987	WSBK-TV and NESN	Ned Martin	Bob Montgomery		Sean McDonough	
1986	WSBK-TV and NESN	Ned Martin	Bob Montgomery		Sean McDonough	

BROADCASTS – TELEVISION

YEAR	CHANNEL	PLAY-BY-PLAY	COLOR COMMENTATOR(S)	STUDIO HOST
1985	WSBK-TV and NESN	**Ned Martin**	Bob Montgomery	Sean McDonough
1984	WSBK-TV	**Ned Martin**	Bob Montgomery	Tom Larson
	NESN	**Kent Derdivanis**	Mike Andrews	
1983	WSBK-TV	**Ned Martin**	Bob Montgomery	Tom Larson
1982	WSBK-TV	**Ned Martin**	Bob Montgomery	Tom Larson
1981	WSBK-TV	**Ned Martin**	Ken Harrelson	Tom Larson
1980	WSBK-TV	**Ned Martin**	Ken Harrelson	Tom Larson
1979	WSBK-TV	**Ned Martin**	Ken Harrelson	Tom Larson
1978	WSBK-TV	**Dick Stockton**	Ken Harrelson	Tom Larson
1977	WSBK-TV	**Dick Stockton**	Ken Harrelson	Tom Larson
1976	WSBK-TV	**Dick Stockton**	Ken Harrelson	Tom Larson
1975	WSBK-TV	**Dick Stockton**	Ken Harrelson	Tom Larson
1974	WBZ-TV	**Ken Coleman**	Johnny Pesky	
1973	WBZ-TV	**Ken Coleman**	Johnny Pesky	
1972	WBZ-TV	**Ken Coleman**	Johnny Pesky	
1971	WHDH-TV	**Ken Coleman and Ned Martin**	Johnny Pesky	
1970	WHDH-TV	**Ken Coleman and Ned Martin**	Johnny Pesky	
1969	WHDH-TV	**Ken Coleman and Ned Martin**	Johnny Pesky	
1968	WHDH-TV	**Ken Coleman and Ned Martin**	Mel Parnell	
1967	WHDH-TV	**Ken Coleman and Ned Martin**	Mel Parnell	
1966	WHDH-TV	**Ken Coleman and Ned Martin**	Mel Parnell	
1965	WHDH-TV	**Curt Gowdy and Ned Martin**	Mel Parnell	
1964	WHDH-TV	**Curt Gowdy, Art Gleeson, and Ned Martin**		
1963	WHDH-TV	**Curt Gowdy, Art Gleeson, and Ned Martin**		
1962	WHDH-TV	**Curt Gowdy, Art Gleeson, and Ned Martin**		
1961	WHDH-TV	**Curt Gowdy, Art Gleeson, and Ned Martin**		
1960	WHDH-TV	**Curt Gowdy, Art Gleeson, and Bill Crowley**		
1959	WHDH-TV	**Curt Gowdy, Bob Murphy, and Bill Crowley**		
1958	WHDH-TV	**Curt Gowdy, Bob Murphy, and Bill Crowley**		
1957	WHDH-TV	**Curt Gowdy or Don Gillis, Bob Murphy, and Bill Crowley**		
1956	WBZ-TV or WNAC-TV	**Curt Gowdy and Bob Murphy**		
1955	WBZ-TV or WNAC-TV	**Curt Gowdy and Bob Murphy**		
1954	WBZ-TV or WNAC-TV	**Curt Gowdy, Tom Hussey, and Bob Murphy**		
1953	WBZ-TV or WNAC-TV	**Curt Gowdy, Tom Hussey, and Bob DeLaney**		
1952	WBZ-TV or WNAC-TV	**Curt Gowdy, Tom Hussey, and Bob DeLaney**		
1951	WBZ-TV or WNAC-TV	**Curt Gowdy, Tom Hussey, and Bob DeLaney**		
1950	WBZ-TV	**Jim Britt and Tom Hussey**	Bump Hadley	
	WNAC-TV	**Jim Britt and Tom Hussey**	Les Smith	
1949	WBZ-TV	**Jim Britt and Tom Hussey**	Bump Hadley	
	WNAC-TV	**Jim Britt and Tom Hussey**	Les Smith	
1948	WBZ-TV	**Jim Britt and Tom Hussey**	Bump Hadley	
	WNAC-TV	**Jim Britt and Tom Hussey**	Les Smith	

LONGEST

ON MAY 15, 1991, THE RED SOX DEFEATED THE WHITE SOX, 9–6, IN A NIGHT GAME AT FENWAY PARK THAT TOOK 4 HOURS AND 11 MINUTES TO COMPLETE, 9 MINUTES LONGER THAN THE PREVIOUS LONGEST NIGHT GAME, SETTING A NEW AMERICAN LEAGUE RECORD.

THE PREVIOUS GAME BEGAN ON SEPTEMBER 3, 1981, AND WAS SUSPENDED AT 1:16 A.M. ON SEPTEMBER 4, 1981, AT THE END OF 19 INNINGS, SINCE THE OLD CURFEW RULE HELD AN INNING COULDN'T BEGIN AFTER 1:00 A.M. THE GAME RESUMED LATER THAT DAY, WITH BOSTON LOSING TO SEATTLE, 8–7, IN 20 INNINGS. JERRY REMY HAD 6 HITS, TYING THE AMERICAN LEAGUE RECORD.

OLDEST

FENWAY PARK IS THE OLDEST EXISTING SITE TO HAVE HOSTED THE WORLD SERIES. THE RED SOX WON THE WORLD SERIES ON ITS HOME FIELD IN ITS FIRST YEAR OF EXISTENCE, 1912, AND THREE MORE TIMES BY 1918.

FIRSTS

FIRST GAME: APRIL 20, 1912, BOSTON DEFEATS NEW YORK, 7–6, IN 11 INNINGS

FIRST HOME RUN: APRIL 26, 1912, HUGH BRADLEY, OVER LEFT-FIELD WALL

FIRST NO-HITTER: JUNE 21, 1916, RUBE FOSTER VS. NEW YORK, 2–0

FIRST SUNDAY GAME: JULY 3, 1932, NEW YORK DEFEATS BOSTON, 13–2

FIRST ALL-STAR GAME: JULY 9, 1946, AMERICAN LEAGUE DEFEATS NATIONAL LEAGUE, 12–0

FIRST NIGHT GAME: JUNE 13, 1947, BOSTON DEFEATS CHICAGO, 5–3

FIRST PLAY-OFF GAME: OCTOBER 4, 1948, CLEVELAND DEFEATS BOSTON, 8–3

THE FIRST 1-MILLION SEASON WAS IN 1946, WHEN 1,416,944 FANS ATTENDED GAMES AT FENWAY PARK.

THE FIRST 2-MILLION SEASON WAS IN 1977, WHEN 2,074,549 FANS ATTENDED GAMES AT FENWAY.

THE FIRST 3-MILLION SEASON WAS IN 2008, WHEN 3,048,248 FANS ATTENDED.

THE SCREEN BEHIND HOME PLATE AT FENWAY, DESIGNED TO PROTECT FANS AND ALLOW FOUL BALLS TO ROLL BACK DOWN ONTO THE FIELD OF PLAY, WAS THE FIRST OF ITS KIND IN THE MAJORS.

YEAR	FLAGSHIP STATION	PLAY-BY-PLAY	PLAY-BY-PLAY NO. 2	COLOR COMMENTATOR(S)
2009	WRKO or WEEI	**Joe Castiglione**	Dave O'Brien or Jon Rish	
2008	WRKO or WEEI	**Joe Castiglione**	Dave O'Brien or Dale Arnold or Jon Rish	
2007	WRKO or WEEI	**Joe Castiglione**	Dave O'Brien or Glenn Geffner	
2006	WEEI	**Joe Castiglione**	Jerry Trupiano	
2005	WEEI	**Joe Castiglione**	Jerry Trupiano	
2004	WEEI	**Joe Castiglione**	Jerry Trupiano	
2003	WEEI	**Joe Castiglione**	Jerry Trupiano	
2002	WEEI	**Joe Castiglione**	Jerry Trupiano	
2001	WEEI	**Joe Castiglione**	Jerry Trupiano	
2000	WEEI	**Joe Castiglione**	Jerry Trupiano	
1999	WEEI	**Joe Castiglione**	Jerry Trupiano	
1998	WEEI	**Joe Castiglione**	Jerry Trupiano	
1997	WEEI	**Joe Castiglione**	Jerry Trupiano	
1996	WEEI	**Joe Castiglione**	Jerry Trupiano	
1995	WEEI	**Joe Castiglione**	Jerry Trupiano	
1994	WRKO	**Joe Castiglione**	Jerry Trupiano	
1993	WRKO	**Joe Castiglione**	Jerry Trupiano	
1992	WRKO	**Bob Starr**	Joe Castiglione	
1991	WRKO	**Bob Starr**	Joe Castiglione	
1990	WRKO	**Bob Starr**	Joe Castiglione	
1989	WPLM or WRKO	**Ken Coleman**	Joe Castiglione	
1988	WPLM or WRKO	**Ken Coleman**	Joe Castiglione	
1987	WPLM or WRKO	**Ken Coleman**	Joe Castiglione	
1986	WPLM or WRKO	**Ken Coleman**	Joe Castiglione	
1985	WPLM or WRKO	**Ken Coleman**	Joe Castiglione	
1984	WPLM or WRKO	**Ken Coleman**	Joe Castiglione	
1983	WPLM or WRKO	**Ken Coleman**	Joe Castiglione	
1982	WITS	**Ken Coleman**	Jon Miller	
1981	WITS	**Ken Coleman**	Jon Miller	
1980	WITS	**Ken Coleman**	Jon Miller	
1979	WITS	**Ken Coleman**		Rico Petrocelli
1978	WITS	**Ned Martin**	Jim Woods	
1977	WMEX	**Ned Martin**	Jim Woods	
1976	WMEX	**Ned Martin**	Jim Woods	
1975	WHDH	**Ned Martin**	Jim Woods	
1974	WHDH	**Ned Martin**	Jim Woods	
1973	WHDH	**Ned Martin**	Dave Martin	
1972	WHDH	**Ned Martin**	John MacLean or Dave Martin	
1971	WHDH	**Ned Martin**	Ken Coleman	Johnny Pesky
1970	WHDH	**Ned Martin**	Ken Coleman	Johnny Pesky
1969	WHDH	**Ned Martin**	Ken Coleman	Johnny Pesky
1968	WHDH	**Ned Martin**	Ken Coleman	Mel Parnell
1967	WHDH	**Ned Martin**	Ken Coleman	Mel Parnell
1966	WHDH	**Ned Martin**	Ken Coleman	Mel Parnell
1965	WHDH	**Curt Gowdy**	Ned Martin	Mel Parnell
1964	WHDH	**Curt Gowdy**	Ned Martin and Art Gleeson	
1963	WHDH	**Curt Gowdy**	Ned Martin and Art Gleeson	
1962	WHDH	**Curt Gowdy**	Ned Martin and Art Gleeson	
1961	WHDH	**Curt Gowdy**	Ned Martin and Art Gleeson	
1960	WHDH	**Curt Gowdy**	Bill Crowley and Art Gleeson	
1959	WHDH	**Curt Gowdy**	Bob Murphy and Bill Crowley	
1958	WHDH	**Curt Gowdy**	Bob Murphy and Bill Crowley	
1957	WHDH	**Curt Gowdy or Don Gillis**	Bob Murphy and Bill Crowley	
1956	WHDH	**Curt Gowdy**	Bob Murphy	
1955	WHDH	**Curt Gowdy**	Tom Hussey and Bob Murphy	
1954	WHDH	**Curt Gowdy**	Tom Hussey and Bob DeLaney	
1953	WHDH	**Curt Gowdy**	Tom Hussey and Bob DeLaney	
1952	WHDH	**Curt Gowdy**	Tom Hussey and Bob DeLaney	
1951	WHDH	**Curt Gowdy**	Tom Hussey and Bob DeLaney	
1950	WHDH	**Jim Britt**	Tom Hussey and Leo Egan	
1949	WHDH	**Jim Britt**	Tom Hussey and Leo Egan	
1948	WHDH	**Jim Britt**	Tom Hussey and Leo Egan	
1947	WHDH	**Jim Britt**	Tom Hussey	
1946	WNAC	**Jim Britt**	Tom Hussey	
1945	WNAC	**Jim Britt**	Tom Hussey and George Hartrick	
1944	WNAC	**Jim Britt**	Tom Hussey and George Hartrick	
1943	WNAC	**Jim Britt**	Tom Hussey and George Hartrick	
1942	WNAC or WAAB	**Jim Britt**	Tom Hussey	
1941	WAAB	**Jim Britt**	Tom Hussey	
1940	WAAB	**Jim Britt**	Tom Hussey	
1939	WAAB	**Tom Hussey**		Frankie Frisch
1938	WNAC	**Fred Hoey**		
1937	WNAC	**Fred Hoey**		
1936	WNAC	**Fred Hoey**		
1935	WNAC	**Fred Hoey**		
1934	WNAC	**Fred Hoey**		
1933	WNAC	**Fred Hoey**		
1932	WNAC	**Fred Hoey**		
1931	WNAC	**Fred Hoey**		
1930	WNAC	**John Shepard III**		
1929	WNAC	**Fred Hoey**		
1928	WNAC	**Fred Hoey**		
1927	WNAC	**Fred Hoey**	Gerry Harrison	
1926	WNAC	**Gus Rooney**		

GROUND RULES AT FENWAY PARK (A SAMPLING)

FOUL POLES AND SCREEN POLES ARE OUTSIDE THE PLAYING FIELD.

A BALL GOING THROUGH THE SCOREBOARD, EITHER ON THE BOUNCE OR ON THE FLY, IS TWO BASES.

A FLY BALL STRIKING THE LEFT-CENTER-FIELD WALL TO THE RIGHT OF THE LINE BEHIND THE FLAGPOLE IS A HOME RUN.

A FLY BALL STRIKING THE WALL OR THE FLAGPOLE AND BOUNCING INTO THE BLEACHERS IS A HOME RUN.

A FLY BALL STRIKING THE LINE OR RIGHT OF SAME ON THE WALL IN CENTER IS A HOME RUN.

A FLY BALL STRIKING THE WALL LEFT OF THE LINE AND BOUNCING INTO THE BULLPEN IS A HOME RUN.

A BALL STICKING IN THE BULLPEN SCREEN OR BOUNCING INTO THE BULLPEN IS TWO BASES.

A BATTED OR THROWN BALL REMAINING BEHIND OR UNDER THE CANVAS OR IN THE TARP CYLINDER IS TWO BASES.

CINEMA

FENWAY PARK APPEARED IN THE MOVIE *FIELD OF DREAMS* (1989), STARRING KEVIN COSTNER, JAMES EARL JONES, AND RAY LIOTTA.

THE 2005 MOVIE *FEVER PITCH* INCLUDED SCENES SHOT ON LOCATION DURING THE 2004 AMERICAN LEAGUE CHAMPIONSHIP SERIES GAMES, AND SCENES FROM BUSCH STADIUM WERE FILMED AFTER GAME FOUR OF THE 2004 WORLD SERIES.

SOME SCENES FROM *BLOWN AWAY* (1994) AND *LITTLE BIG LEAGUE* (ALSO 1994) WERE FILMED AT FENWAY PARK.

ALL-TIME STANDINGS AND ATTENDANCE

SEASON	TEAM	LEAGUE	W	L	PCT	GB	ATTENDANCE
2009	Boston Red Sox	American League	95	67	.586	8.0	3,062,699
2008	Boston Red Sox	American League	95	67	.586	2.0	3,048,248
2007	Boston Red Sox	American League	96	66	.593	—	2,971,025
2006	Boston Red Sox	American League	86	76	.531	11.0	2,930,588
2005	Boston Red Sox	American League	95	67	.586	—	2,847,888
2004	Boston Red Sox	American League	98	64	.605	3.0	2,837,304
2003	Boston Red Sox	American League	95	67	.586	6.0	2,724,165
2002	Boston Red Sox	American League	93	69	.574	10.5	2,650,382
2001	Boston Red Sox	American League	82	79	.509	13.5	2,625,333
2000	Boston Red Sox	American League	85	77	.525	2.5	2,585,895
1999	Boston Red Sox	American League	94	68	.580	4.0	2,445,590
1998	Boston Red Sox	American League	92	70	.568	22.0	2,343,947
1997	Boston Red Sox	American League	78	84	.481	20.0	2,226,136
1996	Boston Red Sox	American League	85	77	.525	7.0	2,315,231
1995	Boston Red Sox	American League	86	58	.597	—	2,164,410
1994	Boston Red Sox	American League	54	61	.470	17.0	1,775,818
1993	Boston Red Sox	American League	80	82	.494	15.0	2,422,021
1992	Boston Red Sox	American League	73	89	.451	23.0	2,468,574
1991	Boston Red Sox	American League	84	78	.519	7.0	2,562,435
1990	Boston Red Sox	American League	88	74	.543	—	2,528,986
1989	Boston Red Sox	American League	83	79	.512	6.0	2,510,012
1988	Boston Red Sox	American League	89	73	.549	—	2,464,851
1987	Boston Red Sox	American League	78	84	.481	20.0	2,231,551
1986	Boston Red Sox	American League	95	66	.590	—	2,147,641
1985	Boston Red Sox	American League	81	81	.500	18.5	1,786,633
1984	Boston Red Sox	American League	86	76	.531	18.0	1,661,618
1983	Boston Red Sox	American League	78	84	.481	20.0	1,782,285
1982	Boston Red Sox	American League	89	73	.549	6.0	1,950,124
1981	Boston Red Sox	American League	59	49	.546	2.5	1,060,379
1980	Boston Red Sox	American League	83	77	.519	19.0	1,956,092
1979	Boston Red Sox	American League	91	69	.569	11.5	2,353,114
1978	Boston Red Sox	American League	99	64	.607	1.0	2,320,643
1977	Boston Red Sox	American League	97	64	.602	2.5	2,074,549
1976	Boston Red Sox	American League	83	79	.512	15.5	1,895,846
1975	Boston Red Sox	American League	95	65	.594	—	1,748,587
1974	Boston Red Sox	American League	84	78	.519	7.0	1,556,411
1973	Boston Red Sox	American League	89	73	.549	8.0	1,481,002
1972	Boston Red Sox	American League	85	70	.548	0.5	1,441,718
1971	Boston Red Sox	American League	85	77	.525	18.0	1,678,732
1970	Boston Red Sox	American League	87	75	.537	21.0	1,595,278
1969	Boston Red Sox	American League	87	75	.537	22.0	1,833,246
1968	Boston Red Sox	American League	86	76	.531	17.0	1,940,788
1967	Boston Red Sox	American League	92	70	.568	—	1,727,832
1966	Boston Red Sox	American League	72	90	.444	26.0	811,172
1965	Boston Red Sox	American League	62	100	.383	40.0	652,201
1964	Boston Red Sox	American League	72	90	.444	27.0	883,276
1963	Boston Red Sox	American League	76	85	.472	28.0	942,642
1962	Boston Red Sox	American League	76	84	.475	19.0	733,080
1961	Boston Red Sox	American League	76	86	.469	33.0	850,589
1960	Boston Red Sox	American League	65	89	.422	32.0	1,129,866
1959	Boston Red Sox	American League	75	79	.487	19.0	984,102
1958	Boston Red Sox	American League	79	75	.513	13.0	1,077,047
1957	Boston Red Sox	American League	82	72	.532	16.0	1,181,087
1956	Boston Red Sox	American League	84	70	.545	13.0	1,137,158
1955	Boston Red Sox	American League	84	70	.545	12.0	1,203,200
1954	Boston Red Sox	American League	69	85	.448	42.0	931,127
1953	Boston Red Sox	American League	84	69	.549	16.0	1,026,133
1952	Boston Red Sox	American League	76	78	.494	19.0	1,115,750
1951	Boston Red Sox	American League	87	67	.565	11.0	1,312,282
1950	Boston Red Sox	American League	94	60	.610	4.0	1,344,080
1949	Boston Red Sox	American League	96	58	.623	1.0	1,596,650
1948	Boston Red Sox	American League	96	59	.619	1.0	1,558,798
1947	Boston Red Sox	American League	83	71	.539	14.0	1,427,315
1946	Boston Red Sox	American League	104	50	.675	—	1,416,944
1945	Boston Red Sox	American League	71	83	.461	17.5	603,794
1944	Boston Red Sox	American League	77	77	.500	12.0	506,975
1943	Boston Red Sox	American League	68	84	.447	29.0	358,275
1942	Boston Red Sox	American League	93	59	.612	9.0	730,340
1941	Boston Red Sox	American League	84	70	.545	17.0	718,497
1940	Boston Red Sox	American League	82	72	.532	8.0	716,234
1939	Boston Red Sox	American League	89	62	.589	17.0	573,070
1938	Boston Red Sox	American League	88	61	.591	9.5	646,459
1937	Boston Red Sox	American League	80	72	.526	21.0	559,659
1936	Boston Red Sox	American League	74	80	.481	28.5	626,895
1935	Boston Red Sox	American League	78	75	.510	16.0	558,568
1934	Boston Red Sox	American League	76	76	.500	24.0	610,640
1933	Boston Red Sox	American League	63	86	.423	34.5	268,715
1932	Boston Red Sox	American League	43	111	.279	64.0	182,150
1931	Boston Red Sox	American League	62	90	.408	45.0	350,975
1930	Boston Red Sox	American League	52	102	.338	50.0	444,045
1929	Boston Red Sox	American League	58	96	.377	48.0	394,620
1928	Boston Red Sox	American League	57	96	.373	43.5	396,920
1927	Boston Red Sox	American League	51	103	.331	59.0	305,275
1926	Boston Red Sox	American League	46	107	.301	44.5	285,155
1925	Boston Red Sox	American League	47	105	.309	49.5	267,782
1924	Boston Red Sox	American League	67	87	.435	25.0	448,556
1923	Boston Red Sox	American League	61	91	.401	37.0	229,688
1922	Boston Red Sox	American League	61	93	.396	33.0	259,184
1921	Boston Red Sox	American League	75	79	.487	23.5	279,273
1920	Boston Red Sox	American League	72	81	.471	25.5	402,445
1919	Boston Red Sox	American League	66	71	.482	20.5	417,291
1918	Boston Red Sox	American League	75	51	.595	—	249,513
1917	Boston Red Sox	American League	90	62	.592	9.0	387,856
1916	Boston Red Sox	American League	91	63	.591	—	496,397
1915	Boston Red Sox	American League	101	50	.669	—	539,885
1914	Boston Red Sox	American League	91	62	.595	8.5	481,359
1913	Boston Red Sox	American League	79	71	.527	15.5	437,194
1912	Boston Red Sox	American League	105	47	.691	—	597,096

BY THE NUMBERS

0

No player has ever hit a home run over the right-field roof at Fenway Park.

1

Dutch Leonard's 1.00 ERA in 1914 remains the all-time major league record.

Bobby Doerr's retired number.

2

Bobby Doerr, alone among Red Sox players, hit twice for the cycle.

The scoreboard numbers used for errors, innings, and pitchers' numbers weigh two pounds. (They measure 12 by 16 inches.)

Tom Yawkey and Jean Yawkey's initials—TAY and JRY—appear in Morse code in two vertical stripes on the scoreboard.

John Valentin (July 8, 1994) and George Burns (September 14, 1923) remain the only players to turn an unassisted triple play at Fenway Park.

Mo Vaughn is the only Red Sox player to have two career three-homer games at Fenway Park.

Fenway Park is two miles away from the bar in the TV program *Cheers* whose main character, Sam Malone, pitched for the Sox in the 1970s and remains baseball's only switch-hitting pitcher.

3

The Red Sox have played at home on Patriots' Day each year since 1960, except for off days in 1965 and 1967 and the players' strike in 1995.

The weight in pounds of each scoreboard number used to indicate runs and hits. (They measure 16 inches by 16 inches.)

4

With their four hits each, Ted Williams in 1946 and Carl Yastrzemski in 1970 share the major-league record for the most hits in an All-Star Game.

A major-league record set by Ted Williams on July 22, 1960, as the only player to steal bases in four consecutive decades.

The cost ($3.80 plus 20 cents tax = $4.00) for a foot-long dog with fixings such as onions, peppers, diced tomatoes, and giardiniera at the 1999 All-Star Game.

George Mogridge (April 24, 1917), Walter Johnson (July 1, 1920), Ted Lyons (August 21, 1926), and Jim Bunning (July 20, 1958) are the only opposing pitchers to have hurled no-hitters at Fenway.

Joe Cronin's retired number.

Justin Masterson is the first pitcher in Red Sox history to go undefeated in his first four starts at Fenway Park, in 2008.

6

Johnny Pesky's retired number.

7

Pedro Martinez's consecutive games with at least 10 strikeouts (1999).

8

Tris Speaker's inside-the-park home runs (1912).

Carl Yastrzemski's retired number (worn by Ed Sadowski in 1960).

9

Number of runs scored by the Red Sox in the entire 1918 World Series, a record for the least runs by the winning team in the history of the fall classic.

Ted Williams's retired number.

10

Record number of RBIs in one game: Nomar Garciaparra in 1999, Fred Lynn in 1975, Norm Zauchin in 1955, Rudy York in 1946.

13

Number of consecutive postseason games lost by the Red Sox, 1986–95—a major league record.

The ladder once allowing a groundskeeper to remove batting-practice home-run balls from the netting above the wall, starts near the upper-left corner of the scoreboard, 13 feet aboveground. It rises to the top of the Green Monster. With Monster Seats added in 2003, the ladder has remained. Any batted ball hitting it makes for the only ground-rule triple in baseball.

14

Most home runs in a month: Jackie Jensen, June 1958; David Ortiz, July 2006.

Jim Rice's retired number.

17

Former Sox manager Joe Morgan was born 17 miles from Fenway, in Walpole, Massachusetts.

18

Number of turnstiles at Fenway when it first opened—the most in the majors.

20

Record number of strikeouts in one game—Roger Clemens, April 29, 1986.

Number of feet above sea level of Fenway Park.

21

Number worn by Roger Clemens.

23

Record number of game-winning RBIs set by Mike Greenwell in 1988.

25

Most losses by a Red Sox pitcher in a season—Red Ruffing in 1928.

26

Number of homers hit by Carlton Fisk in 1973 and again in 1977, tops for a Red Sox catcher in a season.

27

Number of consecutive batters retired by Ernie Shore on June 13, 1917. The first batter was walked by Babe Ruth, who was ejected for arguing with the umpire. Shore replaced Ruth. The runner was caught stealing, and the next 26 batters were retired in a row.

Carlton Fisk's retired number, reversed to 72 when Fisk moved on to play for the White Sox.

28

Number of bases stolen by Mo Vaughn while with the Red Sox, including home in 1996.

29

Runs scored against St. Louis on June 8, 1950. The Sox won, 29–4.

34

Games won by Smokey Joe Wood in 1912, a Red Sox record.

34, 35

Bleacher sections at Fenway that are covered with tarps for day games because their glare affects the batters' eyes.

Number of sections in Fenway Park.

37

Number worn by Bill Lee and Jimmy Piersall.

40

Number of pigeons Ted Williams and Tom Yawkey reputedly shot before a game. After reporters told the Humane Society, Williams vowed not to repeat the action.

44

Number of years Tom Yawkey was sole owner of the Red Sox.

47

Number of games the Sox lost in 1912. They won 105 for a franchise-best .691 winning percentage.

48

Number of words in the song "Tessie," sung by the Royal Rooters.

Number of inside-the-park home runs hit at Fenway by Red Sox players, the most recent by Kevin Youkilis, May 28, 2007.

49

Total home runs Babe Ruth hit as a Red Sox player.

52

The height (in meters) of the center-field wall.

53

The record number of homers hit by the Sox in one month (July 1964).

55

The number of different players used by the Red Sox in 1996, a team record.

Jacoby Ellsbury's record-breaking steal on August 26, 2009, broke Tommy Harper's franchise record of 54.

60

The vertical dimension (in feet) of the Citgo sign that sits atop a building near Fenway. It's been there since 1940.

66

Number worn by Joe Cascarella, 1935.

67

Number worn by coach Eddie Riley, 2001, and Anastacio Martinez, 2004.

68

Number worn by Devern Hansack, 2006.

71

Number of career triples by Ted Williams.

82

Highest uniform number worn by a Red Sox player (Johnny Lazor, 1943).

84

Earl Webb's extra-base hits in 1931; 67 of them were doubles, a record.

89

Number of games Babe Ruth won pitching for the Sox.

93

Number of errors committed by the 1988 Red Sox, the fewest errors in a 162-game schedule in franchise history.

94

Number of times the 1942 Red Sox grounded into a double play, the fewest ever in franchise history.

100

The 100th World Series took place at Fenway in 2004.

104.1%

With the sale of standing-room tickets, Fenway Park's attendance becomes 104.1 percent of its official seating capacity.

260

Number of relief appearances recorded by Sparky Lyle, 1967–1971, the most by a lefthander.

300

The win number recorded by Lefty Grove (July 25, 1941).

302

Although the distance has never been posted on the wall, the right-field stands are only 302 feet from home plate at the foul pole.

409

The lowest attendance at a Fenway Park game (September 29, 1965, against the California Angels). Just 409 watched Boston lose its 100th game of the season.

501

Number of feet of Manny Ramirez's homer over the Green Monster (June 23, 2001).

502

Number of feet of Ted William's homer, the longest ever hit at Fenway (June 5, 1946).

521

Career number of home runs hit by Ted Williams, making him the team's all-time leader in home runs (followed by Carl Yastrzemski's 452).

.606

Joe McCarthy's winning percentage, the highest of all Red Sox managers (223 wins and 145 losses, 1949–1950).

.760

Pedro Martinez's career winning percentage, a record 117–37, the best in Red Sox history.

1,000

Manny Ramirez's solo homer for Boston, his 1,000th hit in a Red Sox uniform in his 1,388th at-bat with the Sox, making him the fastest player in team history to reach that plateau.

1,042

One thousand and forty two miles from Fenway, the 2004 Red Sox win the 100th World Series, completing a four-game sweep of the St. Louis Cardinals with a 3–0 victory.

2,007

The number of games managed by Joe Cronin, more than any other manager in Red Sox history.

3,000

On September 12, 1979, at Fenway Park, Carl Yastrzemski recorded his 3,000th hit.

9-4-1-8

Until the late 1990s, Red Sox retired numbers hung on the right-field facade in the order in which they had been retired: 9-4-1-8. Read as a date, they become 9/4/18, the eve of the first game of the 1918 World Series, the last championship series the Red Sox would win before 2004. After the facade in right field was repainted, the numbers were rearranged in numerical order.

10,000

The 10,000th home run in Fenway history, a two-run shot in the eighth inning by Kevin Millar on August 9, 2003. Boston bested Baltimore, 6–4.

16,098

From 1912 to 2009, the Red Sox played 16,098 games, won 7,879, lost 7,379, and had 59 tie games.

39,968

Red Sox expectations for Fenway Park seating capacity by 2012, the year that would mark the 100th anniversary of the ballpark.

46,766

The third-largest crowd at Fenway, a Yankee doubleheader, August 12, 1934.

46,995

The second-largest crowd at Fenway, a Detroit Tigers doubleheader, August 19, 1934.

47,627

The largest crowd at Fenway, a Yankee doubleheader, September 22, 1935.

350,000

In dollars, the original cost of building Fenway Park.

2,000,000

The number of fans at Fenway by September 28, 1977, the first time the ballpark drew its two-millionth fan.

BIBLIOGRAPHY

Berry, Henry. *Boston Red Sox.* New York: Macmillan, 1975.

Bryant, Howard. *Shut Out: Race and Baseball in Boston.* New York: Routledge, 2002.

Frommer, Harvey. *Remembering Yankee Stadium.* New York: Stewart, Tabori & Chang, 2008.

Frommer, Harvey, and Frederic J. Frommer. *Red Sox vs. Yankees: The Great Rivalry.* Champaign, Ill.: Sports Publishing, 2005, 2006.

Frommer, Frederic J. *1859 to Today: The Story of Baseball in the Nation's Capital.* Dallas: Taylor, 2006.

Gershman, Michael. *Diamonds: The Evolution of the Ballpark.* Boston: Houghton Mifflin, 1995.

Golenbock, Peter. *Fenway: An Unexpurgated History of the Boston Red Sox.* New York: G. P. Putnam's Sons, 1992.

Halberstam, David. *Summer of '49.* New York: William Morrow, 1989.

Lee, Bill, and Richard Lally. *The Wrong Stuff.* New York: Three Rivers Press, 2007.

Lowry, Philip J. *Green Cathedrals: The Ultimate Celebrations of All 273 Major League and Negro League Ballparks Past and Present.* Reading, Mass.: Addison-Wesley, 1992.

Montville Leigh. *Ted Williams: An American Hero.* New York: Random House, 2004.

Nowlin, Bill, and Jim Prime. *Tales from the Red Sox Dugout.* Champaign, Ill.: Sports Publishing, 2002.

Shaughnessy, Dan. *The Curse of the Bambino.* New York: Penguin Books, 1991.

Shaughnessy, Dan, and Stan Grossfeld. *Fenway: A Biography in Words and Pictures.* Boston: Houghton Mifflin, 1999.

Smith, Ron. *The Ballpark Book: A Journey Through the Fields of Baseball Magic, rev. ed.* St. Louis: Sporting News, 2003.

2009 Boston Red Sox Media Guide
http://www.baseball-reference.com/.

WorldSeries.com (MLB.com).

ACKNOWLEDGMENTS

Researching, interviewing, organizing, and writing *Remembering Fenway Park* has been one of the most positive experiences in my long writing career.

Authors usually write that their work could never have been possible without the assistance of others. In my case, that is especially true.

The task at hand had been done before: *Remembering Yankee Stadium* (2008) was an oral and narrative history, a book with many visuals. In fact, that work and this one are looked upon as twins.

I had a lot of support from all kinds of people for the Yankee book—but nothing like the encouragement, aid, interest, and pleasantness I experienced in doing this exciting project.

Myrna Katz Frommer, my caring and constant wife, is always at the very top of the list. She read every word of the manuscript, sometimes twice, sometimes three times. Her cuts, queries, organizational tweaks, and more are all over the book—and the book is all the better for it.

My son Fred Frommer, Associated Press journalist extraordinaire, was there for me, as he has been for so many projects of late. A critic, a catcher of proofing flaws and factual mistakes, he took time away from his hectic schedule to help his dad—just the way I trained him.

My son Ian Frommer, technological whiz, put hundreds of images in an organized manner onto DVDs—a task I could never have accomplished on my own.

The team on the bench—Jennifer and Jeff, Michele, and Laura—I thank them for rooting.

Nate Berger, editorial assistant, researcher, enthusiastic constant. How lucky I was to have this highly competent and intelligent young man always at the ready.

The 133 oral history "Voices"—the famous and the not-so-famous, the busy and not-so-busy, the strangers and the guys I know, the ones who had a lot to say and those who had just a few lines—all gave of their time, priceless memories, and insights. They helped make this book a true remembering of Fenway Park in the way oral history does so well.

Steve Ryder and Kevin Ramos-Glew for leading me to so many of the "voices."

At Dartmouth College: Susan Bibeau, Wole Ojurongbe, Mike Beahan, Helmut Baer, Arthur Hanchett, and the Dartmouth Library and Jones Media center staff.

Al Zuckerman: If a Hall of Fame existed for literary agents, he would certainly be enshrined there.

The team at Stewart, Tabori & Chang: Jennifer Levesque, Leslie Stoker, and the rest.

For images: Pat Kelly, photo archivist at the National Baseball Hall of Fame; Matt Lutsky and Yvette Reyes, Associated Press/Wide World; Seth Swirsky, David R. Mellor, and Robert Lifson of Robert Edward Auctions; Bob Brady and John Shannahan; Aaron Schmidt of the Boston Public Library; and especially the Boston Red Sox.

William Staley, Red Sox fan without equal, and super guru without equal, for all things Harvey Frommer and Myrna Frommer on the Internet.

Charles Ragan, who always keeps all of my equipment running; Sean Holtz of *Baseball Almanac*; Erica Tarlin and Dan Wilson of "Save Fenway Park!".

And the Boston Red Sox, most especially:
Debbie Matson, director of publications
Dick Bresciani, Red Sox vice president/ historian
Larry Cancro, senior vice president, Fenway Affairs
Michael Ivins, manager of photography
Pam Ganley, director of media relations

Their assistance, their kindness, their unfailingly instant responses to my many questions and requests enriched the experience of writing this book and my immersion into the narrative of this fabled franchise. The result is the transformation of a lifelong New York Yankee rooter into a proud new member of Red Sox Nation!

PHOTO CREDITS

Every effort has been made to trace copyright holders. If any unintentional omissions have been made, Stewart, Tabori & Chang would be pleased to add appropriate acknowledgments in future editions.

© Associated Press: pages 2, 4, 11, 12 (chapter 5), 13 (chapters 7 and 10), 67, 70–71, 75, 77, 79, 81 (Ted Williams), 85, 88, 96 (Mel Parnell in snow), 101, 105, 112, 116, 117, 118, 120, 123, 125, 127, 130, 134, 135, 140–141, 144, 145, 147 (John Kiley, organist), 149 (Don Zimmer), 150, 151 (Jackson and Dent), 158–159, 161, 166, 167, 170, 171, 177, 180–181, 183, 184, 187, 188, 190, 196, 197, 198, 200, 201 (Beckett pitching), 201 (Zimmer thrown down), 213 (Ortiz and rings), 213 (Martinez and "Big Papi"), 214–215, 225

Courtesy of Bob Brady Collection: pages 53, 72, 81 (Bobby Doerr card), 91, 92, 93, 95 (Pesky card), 96 (Charity Field Day ticket), 104 (Monboquette card), 111, 119, 124, 128 (Casale card), 132, 137, 138, 143 (Ekersley card), 143 (rain check), 147 (World Series ticket), 148, 149 (rain check), 153, 160, 176, 186, 189, 206, 207, 218, 223

Courtesy of Boston Red Sox: pages 1, 13 (chapter 9), 14, 113, 133, 139, 142, 146, 157, 162, 165, 168, 169, 172–173, 174, 178, 179 (ball), 194–195, 199, 201 (Jeter vs. Youkilis), 201 (Big Papi), 202, 205, 209, 210, 212, 216, 217

Courtesy of the Boston Public Library: pages 8–9, 12 (chapters 2, 3, and 4), 13 (chapter 6), 16, 26 (fans dressed up), 30 (ticket) 32 (1912 champions), 32 (teens team), 35, 37 (John I. Taylor), 39 (Jerry McCarthy), 39 (Boston Globe), 40, 42, 43, 44, 45, 50, 52, 54, 56–57, 59, 60, 61, 62, 63, 64, 69, 76, 80, 86, 87, 90, 94, 95 (Williams signing contract), 97, 98–99, 106 (Wilson and "Pumpsie"), 108, 119, 126, 129, 222, 224

Courtesy of Christian Elias: page 219

© Getty Images: pages 5, 12 (chapter 1), 13 (chapter 8), 22, 47, 83, 114, 121, 154

Courtesy of John Miller Archives: page 193

Courtesy of John Shannahan Collection: page 152

Courtesy of the National Baseball Hall of Fame Library: pages 24 (all), 25, 26 (construction), 28–29, 30 (ticket), 32 (1912 team), 32 (1912 team), 33, 34, 37 (field), 38 (1912 World Series crowd), 38 (1912 World Series crowd), 46, 48, 55, 62 (scorecards), 73, 74, 78 (1946 team), 82, 102, 103, 104 (Mel Parnell), 106 (program), 107, 136, 163, 164, 169, 182, 185

Courtesy of Robert Edward Auctions LLC: pages 25 (ball), 27, 30 (balls), 31, 36, 110, 115

Courtesy of Seth Swirsky Collection, seth.com: 114 (bat), 128 (1967 World Series ticket), 151 (balls), 156 (hat)

INDEX

Page numbers in *italic* refer to illustrations

INDEX

ALSO BY HARVEY FROMMER

Remembering Yankee Stadium
Five O'Clock Lightning
Beyond a Yanke Century
Old Time Baseball
Where Have All Our Red Sox Gone?
The Sports Junkie's Book of Trivia, Terms, Lingo
Red Sox vs. Yankees: The Great Rivalry (with Frederic J. Frommer)
A Yankee Century
Shoeless Joe and Ragtime Baseball
Rickey and Robinson: The Men Who Broke Baseball's Color Line
New York City Baseball: The Last Golden Age, 1947–1957

It Happened in the Catskills (with Myrna Katz Frommer)
It Happened in Brooklyn (with Myrna Katz Frommer)
It Happened on Broadway (with Myrna Katz Frommer)
It Happened in Manhattan (with Myrna Katz Frommer)
Growing Up Jewish in America (with Myrna Katz Frommer)

BOSTON RED SOX

FENWAY PARK

1946 WORLD SERIES

AMERICAN LEAGUE VS. NATIONAL LEAGUE

BOX SEAT $7.20

Est. Price $6.00 - Tax $1.20 - TOTAL

★ ★

GAME 3

Right hereby reserved to refund said price and revoke license granted by this ticket.

Thomas Al. Yawkey
PRES.

1967
WORLD SERIES

AMERICAN LEAGUE vs.
NATIONAL LEAGUE

FENWAY PARK

BOX SEAT
$12.00

DO NOT
DETACH
THIS
COUPON
FROM
RAIN
CHECK

GAME
7

1967 WO?
BOSTON
FENWA
AMERICAN LEAGUE
ADMIT
SUBJECT TO THE C
SET FORTH ON BA
PLAYED UNDER THE SL
WILLIAM D. ECKERT, Comm